A SIXERS ODYSSEY

A SIXERS ODYSSEY

Exploring the Forgotten Players of

76ers Yesteryear

Dave Rueter

Paperback ISBN: 978-1-7356370-0-6

Ebook ISBN: 978-1-7356370-1-3

First paperback edition: November 2020.

Cover art by Ernon Wright

Contact author: SixersOdyssey@gmail.com

Table of Contents

Prologue

The idea for *A Sixers Odyssey* came from another book. My best friend growing up had this giant coffee table book in their living room. It took up half the table and eventually served as an oversized coaster. The book ranked the Top-100 greatest basketball players of all time. It was an older book, probably published in the early 1990's. Michael Jordan wasn't even ranked in the top-10 to give you an idea. Between commercials of *Saved by the Bell* and *Hangin' with Mr. Cooper* or listening to my friend try to correctly pronounce Alaa Abdelnaby's name - I'd leaf through the pages. Read up on Elgin Baylor or Pete Maravich or Nancy Lieberman or Dave Cowens. Over the years, I read the book cover to cover countless times. Each player profile was accompanied by a photo, and with each passing reading, my attention focused to the other players – the guys in the background while Bill Russell grabbed a rebound, or the defender tasked with covering Jerry West. There are Twitter handles dedicated to posting pictures of NBA superstars from the 1990s. I look past the Jordans and the Barkleys. Instinctively, I'm like, "Is that Vincent Askew ready to check in?" or "Joe Kleine was on the Nets?" Each photo is like a *Where's Waldo* Book. I spy with my two eyes, a journeyman who averaged 4 and 5.

Fast forward years later when the Phillies were in the midst of their late-2000s dynasty. I started a sports blog that no longer exists on a platform that vanished eons ago. The blog idea wasn't an original one, considering *everyone* had a Philly sports blog back then. In fact, someone even compiled and created a 64-blog bracket (March Madness style) devoted solely to sites covering the Phillies. I hadn't yet found a voice. I wrote 'previews' for the Phillies postseason games, which told the two or three family members who read the site where to watch the game. As if there was someone frantically trying to find out which station was airing Game 5 of the 2008 World Series.

"You can watch tonight's game on Fox."

Thanks, random blog. What would I have done without you?

The half-assed coverage of the current Philly sports scene mixed in with information easily accessible through the TV Guide wasn't a sustainable business model. So I pivoted. One day, I wrote about former Sixers center, Charles Shackleford (the OG), who hadn't played in Philly in over fifteen years. No one may care, I figured, but no one else was writing about Charles Shackleford in 2009 either. A handful of people I didn't know actually read that post. One even commented like, "I remember him."

What a ringing endorsement. I was over the moon. "I remember him too!" I commented back. Tell your friends. Maybe I'm on to something, I thought. When everybody zigged, I zagged. While the current Phillies blogging world was writing about the best era in franchise history, I wrote about Ricky Otero and Calvin Maduro and his 7.23 ERA in 1997. Was it Dallas Week for the Birds? Maybe, but in the interim, here's 600 words on Eric Leckner. That became my niche. I wrote about the forgotten. I don't remember specific details from an Allen Iverson 34-point effort against the Wizards. Iverson did that all the time. His heroic efforts get lost in the wash. But the James Anderson Game? Manute Bol's six threes against Phoenix? A random 1993 preseason game in Pittsburgh? That's an entirely different story. Those nights, those games stand out because of their unexpected heroes.

The Sixers site, Liberty Ballers, plucked me from obscurity and asked me to write for them. The site provided a great forum to feed my obsession of random Sixers while also writing recaps of meaningless Sixers/Hawks games. And I got stuck with a lot of Sixers/Hawks games. I think the other writers were hazing me. As I wrote more and more, someone asked me if I had a plan for these mini essays. I joked, "Yeah, I'm gonna create a coffee table book."

So here we are ten years later: *A Sixers Odyssey*. Since a global pandemic shut down the entire country, I suddenly had a lot more free time on my hands. It's amazing what you can accomplish when you're not hamstrung by the Phillies 162 days a year. I kept my ass at home. After putting our son to bed, I would write and write. The project stayed under wraps at first, when the end goal seemed so far away. I finally told my dog while we were out for a walk one night. I took his silence as his blessing. Thanks for believing in me, Rupert.

Inside you will find essays on Sixers you loved, or loathed, or remembered but had forgotten. Woven throughout will be personal stories that maybe you can relate to. What you will not find are chapters devoted to the likes of Allen Iverson or Charles Barkley or Andre Iguodala. Their stories have been documented through countless articles, books, and documentaries. While they feature heavily in the backdrop of these stories, they're not the stars of this show. You will also not find essays devoted to players that are still in the NBA today, as their stories are not yet finished.

Everyone else is fair game. Any other Sixer who suited up at the Spectrum, the CoreStates Center, the First Union Center, the Wachovia Center, or the Wells Fargo Center is on the table. Whether they played one game (Tom Chambers) or hundreds (Willie Green). If they scored one basket (Casey Shaw), or were an All-Star (Hersey Hawkins). Countless players from the last thirty years are covered in this book, but not all. If 80's horror films have taught me anything, it's that you always leave room for a sequel.

So without further ado, the floor's yours, Kevin Ollie.

The Floor General

Name: Kevin Ollie

Height: 6'2"

College: UConn

Sixers Tenure: 1999-2000; 2000-2001; 2004-2008

When I was 7 or so, my mom signed me up for a weeklong basketball camp. I had only played on eight-foot nets up until that point. I was probably the youngest person in camp, and without question, the smallest. The camp counselors just babysat me really. Made sure I didn't drink too much soda at lunch or fall into the toilet, stuff like that. One of the events of camp that week was a 3-on-3 tournament. The counselors assigned captains, and by captains, I mean they let the youngest (see: worst) kids in camp draft their team. Forget dribbling with my off-hand - I was barely potty-trained - so I was given the #1 overall pick. I was terrible, but I had an eye for talent. A young Ed Stefanski, some would later call me. I selected, according to my big board, the best kid in camp. I think his name was Alejandro, but he said, "You can call me Al," JUST LIKE THE PAUL SIMON SONG.

There were about 15 teams. After the first round of picks, the counselors just assigned the other kids to teams so no one would get picked last. That was never part of the deal. Al and I had already been strategizing. We were targeting a 3 & D second grader in LA Gear's. There was no snake draft in 1991. As far as we were concerned, we were back on the clock at pick #16. But instead, we got saddled with a complete jabroni. The #1 overall pick tried to hide his disappointment. Al was stuck with some 9-year-old stiff and a little kid whose primary concern was whether he had enough change for an afternoon Sprite. He was a competitor though. Al rallied the troops and assigned us roles.

"Dave, you're gonna be the "steady check-in'er," he told me. I nodded quickly.

"What does that mean?"

"Anytime we have to check in the ball up top, that's your job," he instructed. "Your job is to pass it to me."

I think I understood, but I asked some clarifying questions.

"Can I dribble?"

"No," he said quickly.

"Can I shoot?"

"Definitely not. Besides, the person who checks the ball in isn't allowed to shoot. That's why I need you to check it in."

"What about *him*?" I whispered, pointing to Big Township, our teammate in jean shorts.

"Don't pass it to him," Al said. "Ever."

Al carried us to a few wins, but our lack of depth hurt us. Teams studied the scouting report. They double, triple-teamed Al. Big Township didn't make a basket all week. Every time I tried to dribble, I buckled under my own weight like a baby goat just learning to walk. But I took my duties seriously. When the other team scored, and we had to check up top, I sprinted to the top of key. I looked off BT and found Al double-teamed on the wing. Sometimes Al just took the ball out of my hands. It was just easier that way. My job wasn't to score, he explained. I knew my role.

If Mo said Kevin Ollie is the point guard, I couldn't be happier," Webber said. "He just reminds me of the Kevin Johnsons, the Derek Fishers ... he's the guy if you're picking a team in the park you wouldn't even look at him, but if you want to win, [he's a guy] you have to have. A great roleplayer is way more valuable than a player that could be good on a talented team ... Kevin Ollie's a leader and I'll follow him." (Schuler 2006).

Kevin Ollie was the consummate point guard. Or, if we're being technical, Kevin Ollie was the consummate back-up point guard. He was heady. He wasn't flashy, no, but he was steady. And the intelligence - my god, the basketball IQ - Kevin Ollie got his Master's in help defense and his doctorate in the defensive shuffle. Dr. Kevin Ollie made only nine threes in his NBA career, just two during his numerous stints in Philadelphia. Kevin Ollie was a throwback - a throwback to 6-on-6 girls basketball in the 1950s when only forwards were allowed to shoot.

Kevin Ollie was a true student of the game. We know this, because someone told us so. We believed it, because we weren't given any other option. The media, the announcers - someone - someone told us that having Kevin Ollie on the court was like having a second coach out there. That coaches trusted him. That Ollie had this heightened sense of enlightenment on the court, like he was the Voltaire of back-up point guards. And who were we to question that?

Kevin played twelve seasons in the NBA across twelve different cities for eleven different franchises (He played for both Seattle and then Oklahoma City seven seasons later). Ollie wasn't well-traveled. He was omnipresent. At one point in the mid-2000s, Kevin Ollie was simultaneously employed by half the NBA, two English Premier League teams, the Idaho Stampede, and the Winnipeg Jets. Any one-year deal Ollie signed was just 36 ½ ten-day contracts strung together. It was like Ollie got work from a temp agency.

"Exciting opportunity! Client is a middling NBA team that seeks a dependable, defensive-minded point guard for a temporary position - potential to become full-time. Click on the link below to apply!"

In November '99, the Sixers signed Ollie after Iverson went on the injured list with a broken thumb (Long 1999). His first stint in Philly wasn't particularly memorable, but Ollie fortunately would have two more cracks at it. A year later, right before the Christmas holiday, the Sixers signed Ollie again. In just his second game since rejoining the club, Ollie was thrusted into a starting role. Playing in Utah the day after Christmas, the Sixers were without both Iverson and Snow. Needing someone to soak up minutes, Larry Brown turned to his own Clay Condrey. Ollie played close to 40 minutes, chipping in 7 points and 7 assists in a surprising road win. In an April home win over Cleveland, Ollie finished one-point shy of a triple-double. He recorded the 'ol 9/10/10 stat line. Ricky Davis famously tried to orchestrate his own triple-double. Couldn't we post up Ollie in the final minute or something? Run him off a few screens for a patented Ollie fifteen-footer?

A few seasons later, he and the Sixers crossed paths once more. You haven't truly lived until you see the "Sixers acquire Kevin Ollie" ticker flash across the bottom of the screen while watching ESPN2. In '04, the Sixers traded Eric Snow to Cleveland for Kendrick Brown and Ollie. He started out the '06-'07 campaign sharing the same backcourt with Iverson. The pairing made sense. Let Iverson do his thing while Ollie handled the grunt work. Iverson would be moved to Denver not too long after, however. With Andre Miller now in the fold, Kevin was relegated back to the bench where he toiled for the remainder of the year. Ollie stuck around the league for two more seasons, retiring from the NBA at the age of 37. He had an unexpectedly lengthy career, perhaps best known for his time in Philadelphia. He was a Larry Brown Guy, if there ever was a Larry Brown Guy. Every team had a Kevin Ollie. In fact, every team did have Kevin Ollie.

The Night in Pittsburgh

Name: Warren Kidd

Height: 6'9"

College: Middle Tennessee St.

Sixers Tenure: 1993-1994

"It's questionable whether we showed up for the second half," said Shawn Bradley, who was 4-11 from the floor and finished with 16 points, 5 rebounds, and 0 blocks.

Clarence Weatherspoon had 16 points for the Sixers. Warren Kidd had 11 rebounds. (Ford 1993).

I remember that October contest vividly. It was a clear black night, a clear white moon. The preseason game was being played in Pittsburgh. It only added to the mystique. It was a surreal atmosphere. The tension inside the Pittsburgh Civic Arena was palpable. Everyone was a little on edge. I was anxious. So was my mom. She was in the kitchen playing Tetris on Game Boy. Blocks were stacking up without a semblance of order. Time was running out.

The story of the night was the rise of Warren Kidd. Who was he? Where did he come from? And why were the Sixers playing the Bulls in Pittsburgh? For me, Warren Kidd's journey from undrafted rookie to NBA player was both inspiring and heroic. At the age of nine, nothing else mattered. I engrossed myself in Kidd's quest to secure a roster spot. The telecast that night discussed his chances of making the team - this game being one of the final dress rehearsals before the regular season started. And I ate it up. I loved it. This underdog story played out right before my eyes, and in late October, Kidd's journey was the perfect cure for my Joe Carter home run-induced hangover.

"Kidd has really played well in training camp, really pushing the starters. I like that. The coaches are raving about his hustle. I think that's what we need. Our big men have to play more physical this year. We got killed on the glass last year. We gotta be better in that aspect. What do you think, mom?"

"Remember to wash your hands before dinner, sweetie," she responded.

Mom's apathy was frustrating. Kidd's been working his ass off in training camp. Why didn't she care? Why was she glossing over our frontcourt woes? Why were we eating dinner at 8:45? Kidd became my pet project. If he made the team, it was like me, a nine-year-old diehard Sixers fan, also made the team. He battled. He tried. I battled. I tried. Warren exceeded expectations and I'm thrilled to report that Kidd, unheralded and determined, rose from the rugged mountains of Parts Unknown and made the Sixers roster.

And he actually started the first fourteen games of his career. In a win over the Bullets on opening night, Kidd went a perfect 5-5 from the floor and hauled in nine rebounds. And because he was an overachiever, he also chipped in two steals and two blocks. (No other Sixer registered 2 steals and 2 blocks in their rookie debut until Matisse Thybulle).

Simply put, the former NCAA rebounding champion from Middle Tennessee State looked to be the best rookie on the floor that featured two of the top six draft choices: Shawn Bradley and Calbert Cheaney.

"I thanked Warren at half because he got us off to a great start, and you need someone to do that," Coach Fred Carter said. (Lawlor 1993).

Warren-Mania swept through the city.

@TimPerryTruther

I will always have love for #TP23, but this is now a Warren Kidd Appreciation Account. Please respect my family's privacy during this difficult time. #MyNewAdultSon

10:57 PM · Nov 5, 1993

143 Retweets 308 Likes

@KeithByarsIceCream

Hey @GoldMedalSportingGoods when does the shipment of @Wkidd43 jerseys come in? Asking for me and the entire city of Philadelphia. #ROY

9:02 AM · Nov 6, 1993

226 Retweets 417 Likes

In a victory over Utah a few games later, Kidd again went 5-5 from the floor and finished with 12 points and 12 boards. Karl Malone had no answer for the future Rookie of the Year. Warren's career looked promising. Here was this hyper-efficient guy who crashed the glass with reckless abandon. Maybe the Sixers had discovered a gem. Maybe my mom would now care.

I always latched on to these types – these underdogs who hit the ground running. It's why I had a three-week obsession with Ricky Otero and clung to every pitch thrown by Mike Grace during his 6-0 start in '96. Was Otero the next Rickey Henderson? Was Mike Grace gonna finish 24-0? Did Kidd suddenly morph into Moses Malone? I knew it was unlikely, but it was fun to dream.

That game against Utah was the peak for Kidd. He soon conceded minutes to Tim Perry and Orlando Woolridge and was relegated to a bit role. He slowly faded further and further away from my consciousness and my fandom. The clock struck midnight for Warren Kidd and his NBA career shortly after the season. For one month, though, he was a starter. Warren Kidd was a thing.

I was certainly pulling for him.

The Six Years

Name: Greg Buckner

Height: 6'4"

College: Clemson

Sixers Tenure: 2002-2004

It appeared Buckner was the Sixers' No. 1 priority this offseason as Brown and King wooed him from the beginning of free agency. (Moser 2002).

Greg Buckner is still on the books. There will come a point when Buckner's deal transitions from albatross to trade chip, but we're not there yet. Buckner was like a Blockbuster membership card. You haven't rented a movie since 2004, but they're still collecting late fees from your checking account. In a cabinet full of head-scratching and curious deals doled out by GM Billy King, Greg Buckner's contract was perhaps the most puzzling. In July 2002, King and the Sixers inked Bucker to an astonishingly long six year (six!), $18 million dollar deal.

Giving Buckner six years? What was he, a senator? Buckner wasn't an unknown. He had been in the league for three seasons and that's what was so perplexing. If Buckner was a mystery, then the gamble may have been justified. If he was some guy tearing up the Serbian League, and the only grainy footage of him was locked in a safety deposit box owned by Fran Fraschilla, then ok. Let's roll the dice on upside. Let's get nuts. The Clemson product was fresh off a season where he averaged under six points per game. Certainly, there's value in a defensive wing, but for a half a dozen years, you'd hope he comes with at least one made jumper a week. Six years was a long time to wait for a player to develop an offensive game. Six years was a long time by any measure.

Larry Brown's fingerprints were all over the Buckner acquisition. Coach Brown ended up abandoning the Sixers for the Pistons job after Greg's first year with the team. Not to play conspiracy theorist, but have we considered this was all part of Larry Brown's strategy? Hamstring the Sixers with all these bad contracts and mediocre players, and then jump ship to an Eastern Conference rival? This was an inside job. I'm not accusing anyone of anything. Actually, I am accusing someone of something. Larry Brown enjoyed a cake walk to the Finals, while Sixers fans were stuck contributing to a GoFundMe to hire Buzz Braman to fix Buckner's jump shot.

Early on, Buckner had an impressive five steal performance against the Cavs, which made fans briefly forget there were still five years and eleven months on his contract. He was ok in year one, but the limitations on the other end of the court were glaring. To justify playing a wing who brought so little offensively, they need to basically be Marty Brodeur on the other end. Buckner only shot 27% from behind the arc for the Sixers, so I'm thinking that GoFundMe that I contributed to never got off the ground.

Larry Brown then left and so did Buckner's biggest supporter. Greg's '03-'04 season was hampered by injuries. He missed close to thirty games, seemingly in and out of the line-up all year. There was a stretch in January where Buckner was held scoreless in five consecutive games. Teams obviously game planned - focused their efforts on slowing down Greg. It worked. He fell out of favor with Randy Ayers and then later Chris Ford. But in a season chock-full of disappointment, one lonely bright spot rose from the ashes. The Greg Buckner Game.

March 8th, 2004. Maybe you missed the game; maybe you had your reasons. Maybe you were mourning the Chris Therien trade to the Stars earlier that day. The banged-up Sixers, playing without Iverson, hopped on the backs of Buckner and *thee* Zendon Hamilton. The one-two punch sparked a 4th quarter comeback and the Black Shirts defeated the Milwaukee Bucks. Greg dropped 20 points and knocked down four triples in victory. It was the high watermark of his tenure here.

"I must be a dummy," Sixers interim coach Chris Ford said when asked why Buckner hadn't played the previous four games. (ESPN 2004).

With four years remaining on his contract, and the Bucks game safely in the rearview mirror, Sixers management decided to cut their losses. The organization was still on the hook for the remaining years but decided that the Buck-ner stops here. (Oh, come on. That wasn't that bad). The Sixers bought out his contract, making him a free agent. Greg Buckner's Sixers tenure wasn't long, but it seemed to last forever.

The Clear Out

Name: Gerald Henderson Jr.

Height: 6'5"

College: Duke

Sixers Tenure: 2016-2017

Overheard at The Skeller – State College, PA:

Date: November 5, 2016

Time: Approximately 4:37 PM

"You like the Sixers tonight, Beau? We're double-digit dogs."

"Love the Sixers tonight, Blake. They're 4-2 lifetime against the spread at home when Penn State plays Iowa."

Talk about checking all the boxes.

Local product? Yes.

Son of a former Sixer? YES.

Named his dog "Delco?" MAYBE. Does Henderson have any pets?

A graduate of Episcopal Academy, Gerald Henderson Jr followed in his father's footsteps and reached the professional ranks, getting drafted by the Charlotte Bobcats in the first round of the 2009 Draft. I appreciate that Gerald Henderson Jr is a junior, and would like to petition all incredible athletes across all sports to name their first child junior. It makes their kin easy to identify and alleviates some of my pre-draft homework. I'm a big 'pedigree' guy. I'd draft a broomstick if I knew its mom ran the 400m in the 2008 Summer Olympics.

Two seasons in Gerald Henderson Sr's lengthy thirteen-year career were spent in Philadelphia, which got me thinking. How many father/son combos played for the Sixers? I only counted three tandems, The Robinsons (Glenn and Glenn III), The Grants (Harvey and Jerami), and the Hendersons. But while researching, I actually discovered a shocking fourth father/son combo that will be revealed later in the book. Ooh, the mystery! The intrigue! So the total number is actually five if you account for our max contract offer to Bol Bol in a few years. It's an absurd accomplishment to have two family members reach the NBA. If I play the Six Degrees of Kevin Bacon for my closest connection to an NBA player, then it's Scott Brooks, who my second cousin met at Sixers Camp one summer.

Gerald Henderson Jr. joined a 2016-2017 team that was transitioning from bottom-feeder to eventual Eastern Conference contender. Rookie Joel Embiid joined Dario Šarić in the front court, and recent draftee, Ben Simmons, was taking the customary Sixers rookie gap year. Philly struggled to find their footing in the early going - beginning the year with four consecutive losses - when the undefeated, LeBron James-led Cavs entered the Wells Fargo Center in early November.

There was an energy in the arena that night. The celebrities were out. Ryan Howard, Meek Mill, and Nicki Minaj were in attendance (Bracy 2016). Vegas penciled Cleveland as 12-point favorites. But if Jason Kelce taught us anything, it's that hungry twelve-point dogs run faster. And the home dogs were barking that night. The Sixers bounced back from a double-digit first half deficit and took a lead late in the fourth quarter. Channing Frye buried a triple late to push the Cavs back in front. The Sixers had a final opportunity, trailing by one with 7.3 seconds on the clock. Let me check my playbook; see what I would've called there.

Ah, that's right. I would've called the only youth rec league basketball play in existence. I would've called "Stack." High-pitched screams from third graders echoed throughout the gymnasium when there was an inbound underneath the opposing team's basket.

"Stack! Stack! Stack!"

Like there were any other options. Let's go to the diagram:

Kid #1

They always ran to the opposite corner. He or she had no chance of getting the ball. Zero. It was basically a James Thrash seam route. They might as well have just run straight to the water fountain.

Kid #2

Kid #2 would backpedal to mid-court. They *maybe* had a chance of receiving the pass, assuming the inbound pass didn't ricochet off the backboard. That happened 40% of the time.

Kid #3

One player ran to the short corner, yelling, "Here, here, here," over and over. We get it, Billy. You think you're open.

Kid #4

Then there was the tallest kid, who didn't move, and just held his hands above their head. They were option #1, #2, and #3. The pass almost always resulted in a loose ball tie-up. If possession stayed, the kids would scream "stack," and we'd do it all over again.

Brett Brown didn't call "stack." He didn't draw something up for Embiid, or even Ersan Ilyasova. The designed call looked to be a clear-out for Gerald Henderson. Gerald to that point was 5-8 from the floor. The -19 +/- he carried was elementary at that stage of the game, so maybe Brown was rewarding the veteran and the hot hand. He threw it in at half-court, and if every announcer of every NBA game ever is to be believed, it's that the most dangerous man is the inbounder. Henderson quickly got it back. If you missed the game and are now reading about it for the first time here years later, keep your expectations low.

Gerald drove to his right and drew a double by LeBron. Henderson, now facing two Cavs defenders, threw up a running prayer that was deflected backwards. The Cavs escaped. Before heading back to the tunnel, Henderson watched the final sequence again on the jumbotron. Upset with how things unfolded, he threw his towel in disgust and accidentally hit teammate, Dario Šarić. Now, there was a lot of contact on that play - A LOT of contact. Was Gerald Henderson Jr fouled? YES, GERALD HENDERSON JR WAS FOULED. But sometimes the bad guys get away with it. Regardless, good teams win. Great teams cover (+12).

The Pinball Wizard

Name: Todd MacCulloch

Height: 7'0"

College: Washington

Sixers Tenure: 1999-2001; 2002-2003

There was a point last night when the five Sixers on the floor included Raja Bell, Rodney Buford, MacCulloch, Kevin Ollie, and Eric Snow. With all due respect, that is not a lineup destined for Springfield, Mass. Somehow, they had a one-point lead. (Lyon 2001).

Todd MacCulloch didn't exactly pass the eye test. He was that goofy dude from your high school – the kid who walked into first period in a pair of Zubaz pants and a Papa Roach t-shirt. The kid, we all knew one, who would yell "doorknob" when someone farted, and "safety" when the gas was his own. He dipped his pizza in ketchup. He wrote out "boobs" on his TI-83 calculator and laughed for hours. He wasn't popular, but he wasn't unpopular either. He was just Todd.

MacCulloch had a well-known and unhealthy obsession with *Dumb and Dumber*. He could quote every line from the film, an endearing parlor trick albeit a nerdy one. Who did Todd hang out with on the team? I like to imagine that Big Mac and AI bunked together during road trips. They'd order room service and watch TBS' *Dinner and a Movie*. Sure, they both have seen *10 Things I Hate About You*, but neither of them knows where the remote is and their favorite scene is coming up anyway. In the spring of 2020, MacCulloch appeared on Tom McGinnis' Podcast, *TOM's Talks*. Todd told this story about how he heard his teammate always hung out at T.G.I.Friday's, which the Canadian mistakenly thought was some nightclub (NBA 2020). Don't be so cynical, Big Mac. Our franchise player was just trying to get some apps, not bottle service.

MacCulloch wasn't athletic by NBA standards. He took up space. He didn't run. He lumbered. He had the lateral quickness of one of King Koopa's mushrooms. But MacCulloch was serviceable and extraordinarily efficient. They say you can't teach height or hands. Big Mac had both. He was all of 7'0" and 280 pounds, and his hands were soft, very soft, like two-week old bananas.

The Sixers selected MacCulloch #47 overall in the second round of the 1999 NBA Draft. He always surpassed the modest expectations placed upon him. Fans labeled him a 'pleasant surprise.' Paired with the highly paid and frustrating Matt Geiger, and it's easy to see why fans gravitated to the big man from Winnipeg. MacCulloch was drafted around guys like Tyrone Washington, J.R. Koch, Galen Young, and Venson Hamilton. Unlike his draft counterparts, Big Mac became something. He was useful. (He was also drafted around Manu Ginobili, but that didn't help my narrative).

Injuries to Matt Geiger and Tyrone Hill to begin the year forced MacCulloch into action (Associated Press 1999). He responded. In a November home win against the Sonics, Big Mac recorded 12 points and 10 rebounds in just 18 minutes of action. That game was a microcosm of his career. MacCulloch was efficient to a fault. He just couldn't give you that many minutes. He would haul in a pass from a penetrator, lurch towards the basket, and get an awkward shot attempt to drop. In '00-'01, he converted from the field at almost a 59% clip. I personally never saw Big Mac miss. Now, he did miss. I'm not denying that. I just never saw it. In his second season, he broke the single season record for right-handed lay-ups by a Canadian, 7'0" or taller. Eat your heart out, Bill Wennington.

In Game 3 of the 2001 Eastern Conference Finals against Milwaukee, the Sixers – without Iverson – trotted out one of the worst playoff line-ups in NBA history. It was a summer league team. The game should've been played in the Thomas & Mack Center, not downtown Milwaukee. But alas, the Bradley Center was rocking that day. I was nervous. Back home, the Philly sky was ominous. No, really. The

Fightins were rained out. Bruce Chen's start was pushed back a day.

The Sixers laid a dud, but MacCulloch performed admirably. Big Mac scored ten points on four shots - more economical than a 24-pack of Ramen Noodles. The Sixers lost a tight, low-scoring affair, 80-74. Replace Tyrone Hill's -21 +/- with some more Big Mac and the Black Shirts would've finished off George Karl and co. in five. In today's NBA, Big Mac would've been exposed. These smaller line-ups would've isolated MacCulloch in a pick and roll and had their way. But in 2001? Plodding big men had full carte blanche to roam the court like Brachiosauruses.

After the '01 playoff run, MacCulloch signed a free agent deal with New Jersey. He was the starting center for a Jason Kidd-led Nets team who advanced to the finals. That's all MacCulloch seemed to do. Shoot over 50% and breeze through the Eastern Conference. Big Mac came back to Philly along with Keith Van Horn in a trade for Dikembe Mutombo, but foot injuries derailed his season and eventually his career. The '02-'03 campaign was his last year in the NBA (News Service Reports 2003).

After retirement – and this is surprisingly well-documented – he turned his sights towards the International Flipper Pinball Association. Mostly a small man's game, McCulloch tore down barriers in the IFPA. As of 2020, he was ranked #3,462 in the world, but a strong result at next year's prestigious Northwest Pinball and Arcade Show Tournament could vault him back inside the top #3000 (International Flipper Pinball Association 2020).

I wouldn't bet against him. From what my scouts in the pinball field tell me, the kid has a great feel for the flippers.

The Juice Man

Name: Michael Cage

Height: 6'9"

College: San Diego St.

Sixers Tenure: 1996-1997

Cage is 34 and has played with three teams in his 12-year odyssey across the NBA. He is 6-foot-9 and a concrete-hard 248 pounds, and though he describes his talent as modest, the center-forward has hung around on such winning teams as Seattle and Cleveland through intelligent play, consistent effort, maniacal rebounding, and a zealous health regimen. (Cawthon 1996).

In 1997, I had a brush with greatness.

My mom and I had these amazing tickets for a Sixers/Trailblazers game in '97. We were fortunate enough to sit a few rows behind the scorer's table (I think she won a WIP contest). Michael Cage was about to check in, and clearly, I found this substitution very exciting. I screamed out, "Hey Juice Man!" as he used the powder on the scorer's table. He looked up, startled, and I screamed again. "Hey Juice Man!" He flashed me a confused look, raised an eyebrow, and took off his warm-ups. The 13-39 Sixers punked the Blazers that night, 97-80.

Michael Cage's default and more common nickname was "The Windex Man," due to his propensity to clean the glass. But I don't know, that was a bit vanilla for my tastes. "The Windex Man" doesn't pack a punch. But "The Juice Man?" Come on, now. That's gold. And the origin story of the moniker was so innocent, so pure. Michael Cage liked juice.

"You also have to take care of your insides: I drank a lot of water and a lot of natural juice. My teammates would call me the "Juice Man": my portable juicer

back then weighed about 50 pounds and when I would turn it on at the hotel the lights would dim. My 1st year in Cleveland I gave everyone a juicer for Christmas." (HoopsHD 2019).

Michael Cage was a man's man. Even his juicer was the size of a small child. Rugged and gritty, the Juice Man would've looked just as comfortable with an axe in the forest as he did in the paint. Cage's reputation was built on low-block positioning and hard work. No one called Michael Cage "soft." No one accused the Juice Man of lacking intensity. If you needed a defensive rebound in the late 80's, Cage was your guy. Oh, and the hair, man, that hair. He had a fantastic salad. His Jheri curl could have stopped traffic on Broad Street.

The Juice Man had his own brush with greatness. He played his collegiate ball at San Diego State with baseball Hall of Famer Tony Gwynn. Gwynn was basically Ted Williams, if Ted's cryogenically frozen body was successfully cloned. Gwynn made a living hitting 'em where they ain't, so avoiding a couple of WAC conference defenders to find the Juice Man underneath was child's play. Cage had a very lengthy and productive NBA career that spanned over fifteen years and five teams. In '87-'88, he led the league with thirteen boards a game, snatching the title on the final day from Charles Oakley by grabbing 30 rebounds in Game 82.

The Sixers signed the then 34-year old Cage in August of '96. His best days were behind him, but he offered that veteran presence that teams covet. The organization hoped that Cage would mentor the young Sixers, keep the likes of Iverson, Stackhouse, and Coleman in line through juice, nature's mediator. His numbers in Philadelphia were modest, but that wasn't the point. Management should have slapped the Player/Coach tag on Cage, because he walked into a dysfunctional family run by rookie head coach Johnny Davis. The Sixers needed the Juice Man more than he needed them, but Cage made smoothies, not miracles.

He was part of a bizarre saga in the June of '97 that would've sent the veteran big man to Boston. The Sixers agreed to send Cage and Clarence Weatherspoon to the Celtics for European sensation, Dino Radja. It was a hectic four days. Radja had an injured knee, or claimed he had an injured knee anyway. No problem, right? Just bring him to Philly and let the doctors give him a physical. Case closed. Except Dino Radja refused to come to Philly and undergo testing. The Sixers could've waived the physical, but if a player claims his knee hurts, that's not very prudent. Then there were reports of Radja having misgivings about the destination itself. It wasn't his knee. It was Philly. Dino Radja wanted to go to a playoff contender or a city with a pleasant climate. Well, aren't we picky? I guess a 22-60 team and Philly's humid subtropical climate isn't good enough for you, Dino. Noted.

"Dino, so far, has decided not to come to Philadelphia," Fleisher said. "[The Sixers] call frequently, and I've told Dino how Philly feels. He believes Larry Brown is one of the better coaches, has the utmost respect for him, and feels the team is headed in the right direction. But ..."

Radja supposedly told the Celtics he only wanted to go to a contender or a warm-weather city.

"We explained to him it's not Club Med," Pitino said. (Jasner 1997).

The team eventually got Radja in for a physical, which he failed. The trade was later rescinded, and Cage and Weatherspoon rejoined the Sixers. Not for long, though. Three days later, the 76ers traded Cage again - this time for good - along with Lucious Harris, Don MacLean and Keith Van Horn to the New Jersey Nets for Jim Jackson, Eric Montross, Anthony Parker and Tim Thomas. And that was it. With one forgettable trade after one forgettable season, the Juice Man was gone. Just another center traveling through Philly in the twilight of his career.

The Emergency Call

Name: Donyell Marshall

Height: 6'9"

College: UConn

Sixers Tenure: 2008-2009

"Hey, I'm always going in with us down 15 points or whatever," Marshall said. "It's easy. I have no conscience." (Hayes 2009).

"Stairs rips one into the night."

Without having a decibel meter hanging on my living room wall like a Dr. J poster, it's difficult to quantify my loudest scream for one individual play. Brandon Graham's strip sack of Tom Brady is definitely up there. So is Jimmy Rollins' walk-off double in Game 4 of the 2009 NLCS. The Stairs bomb though, sticks out. 3-1 count. Broxton had to challenge him. And the call - Joe Buck, the much-maligned Joe Buck, brought the goods. I sprung off the couch with a fist pump that would've made Jimmy Connors proud.

Around that same time, in October of 2008, the Sixers were preparing the start of their season with very little fanfare. The Eagles were the Eagles - and eventually made an unexpected run to the NFC Championship - but the Phillies were the toast of the town. You're forgiven if you missed the Sixers September signing of UConn great Donyell Marshall. There was a better chance of hearing sports talk radio discuss So Taguchi's lunch order than anything Sixers related.

"Hey Ang, first time long time. Before I get to my Phillies point, I just wanted to get your thoughts on Royal Ivey's impact on the second unit."

Those phone calls didn't happen. But regardless of the city's underwhelming reaction, the Marshall signing was a good one. Donyell was a pro's pro with a lengthy career that included stops in Minnesota, Golden State, Utah, Chicago, Toronto, Cleveland, and Seattle. He covered a lot of ground. If I saw someone wearing a Donyell Marshall San Diego Clippers jersey, I wouldn't even bat an eye. Up to that point, Marshall was best known for dropping a dozen threes on the Sixers in a March 2005 game as a member of the Raptors.

"The basket just looked humongous out there today," Marshall said. "My teammates kept telling me to shoot it. They kept saying no matter what play we run we're going to look for you in the corner." (ESPN 2005).

Who left Donyell Marshall open on twelve separate occasions? Were the Sixers that preoccupied with Rafer Alston? Marshall didn't even start that game. He only played 28 minutes that night, but when your jumper is as pure as winter's first snow fall, you don't need much time to inflict maximum damage. Donyell was the prototypical stretch 4. He would stretch you from the corner elbow to the Tacony-Palmyra. The Sixers brought him in hoping for that spark, that big triple off the bench. Defenses always had to account for a Donyell Marshall - that night in March of 2005 notwithstanding.

He appeared in just 25 games for Philly, meandering throughout the year - exiled to the bench in his final tour of duty. But that's not to say he didn't have his moments. In March, he chipped in 10 4th quarter points in a win at home against Miami. The next game, he contributed 9 points – all once again in the 4th - in an enormous road win against the future champion Lakers. (Iguodala hit a game-winning three as time expired). The Sixers, though, frustratingly average, limped into the playoffs with the #6 seed and a 41-41 record.

Game 1 of their playoff series against the heavily favored Orlando Magic had a weird start time. Sunday at 5:30. It wasn't natural. I should've been winding down with some raviolis and *60 Minutes*. Instead I'm blowing a gasket because Rashard Lewis' foot was on the line during a corner three and I'm apparently the only one who saw it. The Black Shirts trailed by 18 points in the second half. Dwight Howard was having his way underneath the basket, camping out in the lane longer than a

Scott Williams contract. After the Matt Stairs home run, there were these "Use Stairs in Case of Emergency" t-shirts created (great slogan by the way). A desperate Tony DiLeo reached into his bag of tricks, looking for his own Matt Stairs. He unleashed little-used Donyell Marshall - hey, he was fresh at least. Marshall didn't play in the first three quarters. Marshall hadn't played in the last four regular season games. He could've taken a cab from Epcot at halftime for all we know.

Before the start of the 4th quarter, Dei Lynam announced on the telecast that Donyell Marshall was checking in. She said that when the Sixers were down double-digits and needed a scorer, they turned to Marshall. On that night, Tony DiLeo's prayers were answered. Marshall buried three monster triples in the final quarter, no bigger than a three to tie the game with 34 seconds remaining. The shot prompted a classic Marc Zumoff, "YESSSSSSSS!" (Eight S's for Donyell's jersey number). The Sixers went on to win that game on the back of another Andre Iguodala game-winner. For the next 48 hours, "Big Homie" was the talk of the city. In case of emergency, dust off your grizzled stretch four.

In case of emergency, kick it out to Donyell Marshall.

The Hawk

Name: Hersey Hawkins

Height: 6'3"

College: Bradley

Sixers Tenure: 1988-1993

Hawkins has been around for four years, but it's doubtful you've heard of him unless you are an NCAA statistics nut. He's a basketball player and an outstanding one. But he doesn't do his business at North Carolina's Blue Heaven or Rupp Arena or Pauley Pavilion. New York City is quite a ways up the road. He prances around in Peoria, the dark side of the moon as far as members of the media are concerned.

People have begun noticing, though, that the Bradley senior is leading NCAA Division I in scoring, searing opponents for a 37.8 average. That tends to get the attention of the big guys, even if you have to scream it out from Peoria. Marty Blake, the college superscout for the NBA, has noticed. Says Blake, simply: "He's big-time." (White 1988).

If you're expecting to read one negative word on "The Hawk" Hersey Hawkins, just skip ahead to the next chapter right now. I will do no such thing. I loved the Hawk. Hersey Hawkins is admittedly probably a little too good for this book, but I couldn't write 1,000 words on B.J. Mullens so here we are. Hawk was a stud, an absurdly underrated talent who doesn't get his just due even in Philadelphia. So let's give the man his due now.

A few years back, I stumbled upon a gorgeous Hersey Hawkins Bradley University jersey. God, I wanted to be buried in this thing, marry my wife in this kit. Instead, I settled for an off the rack suit from Men's Wearhouse and wrote in my will my desire to be cremated. I didn't purchase the Hawkins jersey, and I can't give a good reason why not. Maybe rent was due? It was another regret in a lifetime full of 'em. Someone in this world has that jersey, and unless it's Hersey Hawkins himself, it's in the wrong hands.

Hawkins put up video game numbers in college. Like any poor sap from Evansville or Indiana State, or anyone else from the Missouri Valley Conference for that matter, had any chance of slowing Hawk down. He carried his Bradley squad to the NCAA tournament as a #9 seed. They lost to Chris Morris and Auburn, 90-86, despite 44 from Hawkins. 44 points in the NCAA Tournament? Can our hero get a little help here, Bradley University? (Apropos of nothing, but Matt Geiger was also on that Auburn team).

In the 1988 NBA Draft, the Sixers had the #3 selection and took Pittsburgh's Charles Smith. In a shrewd move and taking advantage of a decade's worth of Clippers futility, Philly flipped Smith to Los Angeles for the #6 pick (Hawkins), and a future first. The Sixers used that future first on Kenny Payne, but let's just table that little footnote. Hawkins became an instant starter in Philly. He averaged over 15 points per night and secured a spot on the NBA's All-Rookie Team. He was a worthy complement to Barkley, a legitimate scoring threat who could both shoot and slash. Hawkins shot 87% from the line for his career, seemingly missing just one foul shot a month. There is this old tall tale passed down from generation to generation. In October of 1992, Hawkins and Jeff Hornacek, a prolific shooter in his own right, started a game of "PIG" after practice. When Hersey was traded in September of '93 eleven months later, the score was tied, "P" to "P." Nobody missed.

In the '89-'90 season, Hawkins improved on his initial campaign. He also saved his best scoring outputs for the biggest stage. In the first-round playoff match-up with the underdog Cavaliers, Hawkins dropped 35 in a victory in Game 1, and then in the deciding Game 5, Hawk sunk Cleveland with a career-high 39 points. He treated Mark Price and Craig Ehlo like his old Missouri Valley Conference foes. Mark, you can be Southern Illinois. Craig, how does Drake suit you? Hawk got to any spot on the floor he wanted that night.

The Cleveland Cavaliers couldn't beat the four H's yesterday.

The Philadelphia 76ers had history, home-court advantage, and Hersey Hawkins all on their side and the latter played the biggest role of all in a resounding 113-97 victory over the Cavs in the fifth and deciding game of their opening round playoff series. (Groller 1990).

Hawkins and the Sixers then ran into the Bulls. The following season was Hawk's best. He averaged 22 a game and secured his one and only All-Star nod. A Hawkins '91 All-Star jersey is my white whale, but there's a better chance of spotting the Loch Ness Monster lurking in the Delaware. Those jerseys just don't exist. I've looked. After dispatching the Bucks in round one, the Sixers once again bumped into Michael Jordan. Hawkins had some nice moments, scoring 29 in their lone win against Chicago - including the game-winning three from the corner. It would be Hersey's last playoff series with the club.

Hawkins soldiered through his last two seasons in Philly. He missed just two games in that span. Attempting to expedite their rebuild, the Sixers traded their team captain to Charlotte for Dana Barros, Sidney Green, Greg Graham, and a future first (Sharone Wright). It was a big haul, and on paper, certainly a strong return for the popular Hawkins. His legacy in Philly is largely a forgotten one. Hawk played in the giant shadow of Charles Barkley, but he was more than competent.

If Hawkins dropped 39 in a deciding playoff game today, we'd create a mural or build a statue in his honor and raise thousands of dollars for his favorite charity by lunch (Hawk's Heroes?). Instead of cats, Sixers Twitter would #RaiseTheHawk, which means every pet parakeet in the greater Philadelphia area would be perched above their owner's head in solidarity. But back in 1990, with no social media and little notoriety? Hawkins just flew to Chicago to cover Michael Jordan.

The Savvy Vet

Name: Carl Landry

Height: 6'9"

College: Purdue

Sixers Tenure: 2015-2016

Carl Landry had a huge hand in the victory, scoring 22 points on 9-for-10 shooting off the bench. With just four games to play, he and the Sixers can look in their rearview mirrors and see the 1972-1973 Sixers, who remain the worst team ever at 9-73. The current Sixers snapped a 12-game skid to improve to 10-68. (Pompey 2016).

Carl Landry looked out of place. Survey the 2015-2016 Sixers roster, and it's full of rookies and castoffs and guys trying to carve out any sort of role in the league. Throw out the brief second stint of Elton Brand which fans barely acknowledge (like Iverson's return to Philly in 2009, which fans refuse to acknowledge), and Landry was the exception on that roster, not the rule. In the movie, *Necessary Roughness*, Héctor Elizondo, head coach of the Texas State Armadillos, sees 40-year-old Scott Bakula walking onto the field. Elizondo asked his assistant if he hired another coach without telling him. Defensive coordinator, Coach Wally Riggendorf, replied, "No, but I got you a quarterback without telling you." (Also starring Sinbad, as university professor turned defensive lineman, Andre Krimm). Landry, an eight-year vet, was the elder statesman of the group. An "all of the above" answer to the SAT question, "What intangibles does Carl Landry bring to the young Sixers?"

A) Veteran Presence

B) Locker Room Leadership

C) NBA Experience

D) All of the above

Landry made the rounds. He was effective during his numerous NBA stops - Houston, a couple of tours in Sacramento, Golden State, and New Orleans. He averaged double digits in four consecutive seasons, doing most of his handy work off the pine. "The Microwave" Carl Landry provided a spark. Give him the ball on the low block, and he had more moves in his arsenal than Garry Kasparov. He wasn't a superstar, but he wasn't just a guy either. Carl came over to Philly from Sacramento in a July 2015 trade. The haul the Sixers received was widely praised, and arguably Sam Hinkie's best move as GM. The Kings wanted to shed salary - Landry's contract being one such example - and Hinkie offered Sacramento the NBA equivalent of a predatory loan. Hinkie took back Landry, Jason Thompson, and Nik Stauskas, but also a first-round pick, and the right to swap first-round picks (which was exercised in 2017, when the Sixers jumped from #5 to #3). The contracts of Thompson and Landry were barely blips on the ledger. The Sixers had cap space hand over fist. They could've purchased a cruise ship and still had enough money to give someone a max offer sheet.

Landry missed the start of the season with a wrist injury (Pompey 2015). His hopes, I imagine, were for the Sixers to tread water until his return. Philly didn't have these grandiose ideas about the postseason in '15-'16, but there must have been a happy medium between being a playoff contender and one of the worst teams in existence. The Sixers were 1-29 when Carl made his debut in late December. Or, glass half-full, the Sixers were 0-0 when playing with Carl Landry. They lost his Sixers debut at Milwaukee, before trekking out to the west coast for a showdown with the Phoenix Suns the day after Christmas.

People bet the over of the Heart of Dallas Bowl earlier that day and needed the Sixers to cover for the final leg of their parlay. So I've heard anyway. Landry led the way. He recorded 16 points and 8 boards on a tidy 7-10 shooting, and the Sixers, your 76ers, grabbed their second win of the season. At 2-30, momentum was sky high. There were 50 games left to make a run. The Sixers were knocking on the door of the playoff picture - a few more wins, a couple of lucky bounces, maybe the Pistons or Pacers hit a March swoon, who knows - stranger things have happened. Alas, it wasn't meant to be. The odds were too long. The Sixers finished the season strong. They won every game but forty-two of them yet missed out on the postseason.

Landry, though, was a bright spot. Incredibly efficient, he shot over 55% from the floor albeit in just 36 games played. He had a wildly proficient month of March, consistently hitting double-digits with little wasted effort. Fans probably missed most of Landry's outings, spending most of March scouting college prospects and sorting out the Steve Mason/Michal Neuvirth goalie controversy. But Landry got his. He was a dynamo offensively. His last two games in a Sixers uniform included 41 points on 16-20 shooting. He was as automatic as grabbing a soft pretzel by the register at Wawa. Those were his final two appearances in the NBA - not a bad way to go out. Carl Landry was a veteran on a team looking towards tomorrow. He performed admirably even in constant defeat.

The Pure Shooter

Name: Jason Kapono

Height: 6'8"

College: UCLA

Sixers Tenure: 2009-2011

Fans assumed the team had finally found its outside shooter. Kapono entered this season as a niche-market commodity, an assassin-for-hire to teams wanting that outside weapon. For much of the season, Coach Eddie Jordan had no use for him, cutting him completely out of the lineup. Now he's playing more because of Thaddeus Young's injury, although it feels like too little, too late. (Fagan 2010).

My biggest memory of the Eddie Jordan Era was the rims. Coach Jordan came to Philly to install his Princeton Offense, trying to back cut his way into the city's heart. The Princeton Offense is great if you're trying to win the Ivy League, but Sixers fans wanted to aim a little bit higher than the #15 seed in the NCAA Tournament. The year was a complete debacle. On December 11th, 2009, the Sixers were 5-18 and fresh off their twelfth consecutive loss. I would say that was rock bottom for Philly sports at that time, but we were less than a month away from Donovan McNabb's air guitar performance at Dallas' AT&T Stadium. The Sixers did something different that season, or perhaps it was just more noticeable that year. They had microphones installed near each Wachovia Center basket. The problem was there were only a couple of thousand fans in attendance. The viewer heard everything. Every noise from the court was magnified. Each time a Rodney Carney jumper clanged off the rim, my dog ran and hid underneath the coffee table.

From a three-point shooting standpoint, Jason Kapono brought the greatest résumé to Philly since Kyle Korver. The Sixers have never had an All-Star Weekend Three-Point Contest winner. Kapono won back-to-back titles in '07 and '08. He was just a couple of years removed from a massive 51% shooting season from beyond the arc. On paper, he was a welcomed addition to a team starved of pure jump shooters. The previous season, the Sixers were 29th in the league in three pointers attempted, and 30th in shots made. Noted three-point specialist, Royal Ivey, was second on the team in percentage. So, yeah, it was a need, even if acquiring Kapono meant dealing the popular Reggie Evans in exchange. Fans, however, should've known this was a failed experiment as soon as Kapono rolled out his new jersey number. #72. What were you thinking, Jason? No team, not in the history of sport or mankind, has ever uttered the words, "Hey, we can't leave #72 open." No one is scheming against the Fumblerooskie. #72 is designated for the offensive line. Tra Thomas? He's #72.

*The Sixers told us Kapono had hoped to wear number 24 which he has worn throughout his NBA career, but as Sixers fans know, a 24 jersey hangs in the rafters of the Spectrum, retired for the great Bobby Jones. Since Kapono couldn't get his number of choice, he reasoned that he was brought in here to drain three pointers so he'd simply multiply his old number times three. Yes, I double checked on my scientific calculator: 24*3=72.* (NBC Sports 2009).

That logic gave me all sorts of Vince Young's "Dream Team" vibes. In his first season in Philly, Kapono had a frustrating year that was highlighted by DNP's and 36.8% from behind the arc. The shooting percentage was fine. It was certainly an acceptable mark, but not for one of the purest jump shooters on the planet. It's like acquiring a 6'10" Chris Webber, only to find out he doesn't play on the low block anymore - hypothetically speaking anyways. From December of that season to March, Kapono was an apparition. The Sixers took one of the most prolific shooters in the game and made him obsolete. Kapono didn't compete in the 2010 Three-Point Contest. But no one would've been surprised if he showed up in a generic NBA jersey like Craig Hodges back in '93, because they thought he was out of the league.

Jason started a string of games towards the end of the season, logging some good minutes, but good April regular season basketball is like foreplay. It's nice, but does it really matter? Entering the next campaign, Kapono should've changed his jersey number, gotten a fresh start. #72 was clearly bad juju. He could've politely asked Bobby Jones to unretire #24, or gone really, really high, and picked like #183. What the hell, right? With new coach Doug Collins at the helm, there was reason for optimism. Maybe Kapono would be better suited in a new system, a change of scenery of sorts. Fans clung to any sort of hope, any cliché.

"He had to get used to the Wachovia Center rims. They can be tricky."

"Jason should thrive in Doug's system."

"He just needs to find his sea legs."

There were no sea legs to be found. Kapono started the first two games for Doug Collins and then completely fell off the grid. His last known whereabouts were with D.B. Cooper in the Pacific Northwest. He appeared in just 24 games that year, zero in the postseason. In his final season in Philly, Jason Kapono shot 12.5% from beyond the arc.

He made 1 of 8.

The Boston Massacre

Name: Jeff Ruland

Height: 6'11"

College: Iona

Sixers Tenure: 1986-1987; 1992

Yep, as unbelievable as it may sound, Jeff Ruland is back. Until yesterday, if you said, "Jeff Ruland" to a Sixers fan, it probably would've been taken as an insult. But when Ruland is announced tonight in the Spectrum, he's likely to draw a thunderous roar - maybe even a standing ovation. (Groller 1992).

None of this was Jeff Ruland's fault. He didn't ask for the nagging foot injuries that derailed a promising career. Ruland didn't ask to be traded to Philadelphia from Washington in 1986 for...

checking my notes

Moses Malone. Oh my god, the Sixers traded Moses for Ruland? Take a breath, Dave. Take a breath.

Let's try this again.

None of this was Jeff Ruland's fault. Getting traded to Philadelphia for a Hall of Fame center, and then being forced to retire after just *five games* is just stupid, terribly bad luck. And besides, at least Ruland *played* five games for the Sixers. I have an Andrew Bynum "Pressure Makes Diamonds" t-shirt that I use to clean my baseboards. This debacle falls on Sixers management. They never should have acquired a big man with foot injuries, or, they could have - I was only two years old at the time and powerless to stop them - but not at the expense of our beloved Moses.

Ruland was an All-Star with Washington. He was legit. He dropped 30 points,

15 boards, and eight assists on the Celtics in the '84 Playoffs but was plagued by injuries his final two seasons with the Bullets. You don't 'buy high' on a player like that. You can't just slap some Dr. Scholl's inserts into Ruland's Converses and expect him to play 82 games the next year.

He announced his retirement in June of '87 due to a chronic knee issue. It was a disappointing conclusion for both Jeff and the Sixers, especially after trading one of the most popular players in franchise history just a season earlier. But after a five-year absence, an absolute eternity in the NBA world, bah gawd, that's Jeff Ruland's music! He rejoined the Sixers in early January of 1992. The rehab in itself was a huge accomplishment and a testament to Ruland's resolve. I have a half bathroom that I can't work up the energy to finish painting. It's been like a decade. The can of paint is sitting right there. I respect Ruland for wanting to finish on his own terms, and there has to be a happy ending buried in here somewhere, right? Maybe Ruland played a few injury-free seasons and sailed off into the sunset or something? Well, not quite. This book is about to move from the sports genre to True Crime, because Jeff Ruland was run down with a cart by a Boston Celtics ball boy. Let me repeat that again for emphasis. Jeff Ruland was run down with a cart by a Boston Celtics ball boy.

Ruland has said he was hit from behind by a luggage cart directed by an employee of the Celtics while he was waiting to board the team bus. Finally, after some earlier delays, Ruland has filed suit against the Celtics, the Garden and three John Does, seeking $370,000 in damages for the missed games and additional damages for pain and suffering and possible loss of future income.

"Jeff has absolutely given the Celtics every opportunity to try and resolve this without going to court, but that hasn't happened," Plunkett said.

Said Ruland: "I expect to go to court and win." (Jasner 1992).

Details were murky. Johnny Dawkins reportedly had to dive out of the way of the murder cart (Kelly 1992). Was Ruland even the intended target, or was it in fact Dawkins, or maybe even someone else? Shackleford got 19 and 14 that night - who knows – maybe the Celtics wanted to chop Shack down to size? And who drove the cart? A Celtics ball boy? A team employee? A hired hitman? Was it a ball cart, a luggage cart, a golf cart, a shopping cart? A Mario Go-Kart? The only thing we know for certain was that this was premeditated. This hit was intentional. I would've declared war on the Boston Celtics, the city of Boston, the state of Massachusetts, and all of New England, just to cover my bases, right then and there.

You looking at me funny, Maine?

What are you hiding, New Brunswick, Canada?

I would've taken my revenge tour right up the coast. This was the real Boston Massacre. Of course this was intentional. The cart rammed right into Ruland's achilles. It didn't run over his foot. Jeff Gillooly and Tonya Harding were more subtle in their attack of Nancy Kerrigan. The next time the Celtics were in Philly, I would've hired someone to run a soft pretzel cart, or one of those Fudgie Wudgie coolers, straight into Kevin McHale's shins.

"Revenge, Kevin, is a dish best served ... ice cold. Fudgie Wudgies! Get your ice cold Fudgie Wudgies here!"

Can you imagine if this incident happened today? Social Media would've been all over this. Facebook would've been littered with conspiracy theories.

"I heard it was Manute. He was vying for more playing time."

"Really? I'm hearing that Sherman Douglas is actually the mastermind."

"The General? Really?"

"Yeah. My friend texted me. His dad works for Homeland Security..."

We would've seen absolutely crazy shit posted, and I would've been liking, and retweeting, and favoriting all of it. Except for the Manute Conspiracy. Bol was a sweetheart. I know cheating is ramped up there in Boston, but I thought Bill Belichick was in Cleveland in '92?

The case went to trial in '95. The defense attorney's opening statement focused on Ruland's past injuries, suggesting that compounding leg issues throughout the years ended his career. The defense said there was no correlation between this single incident in Boston and the end of Ruland's NBA tenure. Ruland's team claimed that Jeff was fully healthy in early '92 and had completely recovered from the knee injury from his first Sixers run. Then there were doubts raised about the Celtics ball boys themselves, and if ball boys were even considered team employees. Were these goons on the take? Maybe? Investigators later found drawers full of cash, passports, marijuana cigarettes, and countless Kevin Gamble memorabilia inside the ball boys' homes. Ok, I made that part up.

Now, Ruland's career didn't end after that Celtics game. He appeared in four more games that week, four games, the defense concluded, which proved this incident didn't end Jeff's career. The Sixers trainer and their equipment manager were all called to the stand. Both sides were steadfast in who they felt was responsible, or in the case of the defense, who wasn't responsible (Gun 1995).

A week and a half after opening arguments, the jury, which, it should be noted, was from Boston, awarded the decision to the defendants after six hours of deliberation. Three jurors wore Larry Bird jerseys during closing arguments - so I've heard anyway. They concluded that the Boston Massacre was not the reason for the abbreviated end to Ruland's comeback (Daily News Wire Service 1995).

Justice, sadly, was not served that day.

The Aussie

Name: Mark Bradtke

Height: 6'10"

School: Redcliffe State High School - Redcliffe, Queensland (Australia)

Sixers Tenure: 1996-1997

Overheard at junior high gym class:

Date: October 18, 1996

Time: Approximately 10:45 AM

"What do you think of the Bradtke pickup?"

"Should help solidify the middle – low risk move. Oh hey, you want to come over Sunday for *In Your House: Buried Alive*? My dad got a Pay-Per-View descrambler from a guy at work. Supposed to work pretty good."

"Oh damn, really? Yeah, I'll ask my mom."

They say that two thirds of the Southern Hemisphere is covered by the Indian Ocean. The rest is covered by Mark Bradtke. Bradtke was a basketball god in Australia - a 6'10" towering presence who dominated the National Basketball League, the premier hoops league Down Under. He was a staple of the Australian Men's National Team (The Boomers). Mark played with The Boomers in four separate Olympic Games, a longevity not seen since the Fabulous Moolah's Women's Title reign. He and Luc Longley teamed up to form the largest tandem west of Bol and Shawn Bradley. Or maybe east of Bol and Shawn Bradley. (I recently watched a documentary on the Flat Earth Society). Bradtke and Longley were two behemoths, 4.213 meters of rim protection. I heard some poor sap from the New Zealand National Team tried a left-handed lay-up in '91, and the ball was found seven years later washed ashore the Fiji Islands. The Dream Team ducked The Boomers in the '92 Summer Games. Team USA had no problem disposing of overmatched Angola or Croatia (twice), but Mark Bradtke didn't travel to Barcelona to fawn over a bunch of over-the-hill stars. A fortuitous draw in group play for the Americans and four losses by the Australian Team deprived the international audience of this dream match-up. The Boomers would've covered.

Mark Bradtke appeared in a little-known video game for Sega Genesis called, *Team USA Basketball.* It's the only video game ever centered around Olympic and international hoops. Arvydas Sabonis, Šarūnas Marčiulionis, Toni Kukoc, Drazen Petrović, Rik Smits, and the like all appeared. I found the game manual while helping my parents with a yard sale a few years back. An interested buyer approached me about the manual, but I told him it wasn't for sale. I redirected his attention to the VHS copy of *Vanilla Sky* my mom was asking $.50 for. EA (Electronic Arts) wrote an analysis of each country and assured us gamers that, "You can count on forward, Mark Bradtke, a superb athlete, shooter, and rebounder, to be a major force." EA Sports wasn't sleeping on Mark Bradtke. So why was everyone else?

Bradtke made the jump to the NBA and signed with the Sixers in October of '96. First, though, there was some unfinished business with his club team, the Melbourne Tigers.

If the Tigers lose in the semis, Bradtke could arrive in the U.S., receive his physical and suit up for the team's final preseason game, Oct. 26 at home against the Golden State Warriors. If the Tigers reach the championship and go to the final game of that three-game series, Bradtke, 28, would suit up at the earliest for the third game of the regular season, a Nov. 5 home game against the Pistons. (Deitch 1996).

I don't mean to come off as *that* high school football coach. "Hey, son, you either play quarterback for my team or you do Hamlet or do stage crew or whatever it is they do, but you can't do that and play football for me." But, Bradtke, come on. Wish your Melbourne Tigers the best of luck and Show Ya Luv. Bradtke used three weeks of PTO right out of the gate. He signed with the Sixers in October - prorated - he probably only had like 3.5 days paid time off and one floating holiday for the rest of 1996. He'll definitely have to speak with HR about that. The speed of the NBA was always going to be a huge adjustment for the big Aussie. Not having the time to acclimate put Bradtke behind the eight ball before he even stepped foot in the States. What further complicated the situation and elongated Bradtke's steep learning curve was Johnny Davis' opinion on the big man. Or lack of an opinion anyway.

Mark Bradtke, the mystery man from Australia whom 76ers coach Johnny Davis has never seen play, will be in uniform tonight against the Phoenix Suns. (Cawthon 1996).

Can we get coach some Melbourne Tigers game film? Bradtke played just 36 games with the Sixers. The signing was a gamble by Philly, an interesting one, but neither party had the patience or commitment to see it through. Bradtke is royalty on his home continent, but in the NBA, he was a small fish, albeit a 6'10" one, in a very, very large ocean. Fans are excused if they don't know Mark Bradtke. Sounds like half the organization didn't know him either.

The Gunslinger

Name: Vernon Maxwell

Height: 6'4"

College: Florida

Sixers Tenure: 1995-1996; 2000

"To hell with Michael (Jordan). To hell with Scottie Pippen," Maxwell said. "Those guys haven't done nothing for me, and you can print that." (Cawthon 1996).

They say Vernon Maxwell never saw a shot he didn't like. That his range began once he stepped into the gym. Legend has it that Vernon Maxwell pulled up for a jumper as soon as he touched down at Philly International Airport in 1995. The fact that his shot rolled meekly down I-95 was beside the point. Maxwell played with an admirable and blatant disregard for shot selection and efficiency. He was a cavalier - not in the Cleveland sense - but in the vigilante one. Shoot first. Ask questions later.

Vernon made you a believer, a dreamer. Area boys and girls from as far west as Altoona could be seen practicing off-balance 18 footers on their driveways and Nerf nets. Your teammate was open down low? Who cares. There was room for a few more dribbles inside the three-point line, said your rec league coach? Didn't matter. Run the offense? Nope. Work the clock? Fuck that. "If Mad Max gets hot..." was the "If Ben learns to shoot..." Giving Mad Max the reins was like handing a child a brush and an open can of paint. Most likely it's going to be a disaster, but there's also a chance the kid could be Michelangelo. As a Houston Rocket, he dropped 51 on the Cavs in '91. He also went into the stands a few years later and smacked a heckling spectator. It was a give and take relationship. Maxwell was a ticking time bomb, a loose cannon, a volume scorer - he was a ton of things - but he certainly wasn't boring.

Maxwell has a championship to his name. In fact, he has two (technically). During the '94-'95 season, the defending champion Houston Rockets acquired Hall of Famer Clyde Drexler. After the first playoff game against Utah in the opening round, Maxwell quit the team, claiming a hamstring injury. The Rockets later cited an absence from the team for personal reasons. A month later, he admitted to making up the ailment. A girl pulled a similar stunt at my 7th grade dance. I asked her to slow dance and she told me about her lingering turf toe injury. Five minutes later, she was busting a move with her friends to "Return of the Mack."

His frustrations, Maxwell confessed, was due to a decrease in playing time after the arrival of Drexler (Associated Press 1995). The Rockets went on to sweep Orlando and capture another title without Mad Max. Given the recent events, Houston predictably cut ties with the much-maligned guard. Maxwell entered free agency looking for another home and a second chance. Enter John Lucas.

Sixers head coach John Lucas, who overcame his own personal demons, was a lifeline for NBA players seeking another opportunity. Lucas had signed Lloyd Daniels and Richard Dumas, two other ostracized players, so pursuing Mad Max wasn't unexpected. Maxwell's talent was never questioned, and he proved a capable, albeit not often willing passer from the two-guard spot. Katz and Lucas signed Vernon to a low-risk one-year deal with the hopes he could defend opposing shooting guards and transition to the point. Vernon Maxwell, Point Guard, was certainly an idea. Mad Max never played the point his previous seven years in the NBA, but a team doesn't sign Vernon Maxwell to play it safe. Give the keys to Max and enjoy the journey.

"Making the move to point guard will be very interesting for me," Maxwell said. "Like John said, we're going to be very up-tempo and put a lot of pressure up front on the ball."

Maxwell said he could've gone to Charlotte or Indiana for more money. That can't be confirmed and seems unlikely. Whatever, he chose the Sixers. (Jerardi

1995).

Vernon didn't ease into his Sixers debut. He didn't just dip his toe into the water. Maxwell leapt off the high dive and cannonballed right into Spectrum. In a home win over the Bullets, he scored 18 on 6-17 shooting and added 5 steals, 7 boards, 14 assists, and 6 turnovers. He proved you could accomplish anything, like become John Stockton overnight, as long as you can put up your obligatory seventeen shot attempts first. The next game he added 12 assists. Two games later, he recorded another 13. One of those 13 assists, in a home win over the Hornets, came from a half-court heave by Mad Max at the end of the first half. The shot was errant, off-right, and fell directly into the long arms of Shawn Bradley for an alley-oop. Players nowadays dribble out the clock in the backcourt to end each quarter, preserving their field goal percentage. Not Uncle Vern. You miss every shot you don't take - even those from 47 feet away. Sometimes you even get an assist out of it.

The Sixers started the season 2-2, but by New Years, they sat in the basement at 5-22. In a December 30th loss in Denver, Lucas benched Maxwell.

And Maxwell, Lucas said, "was having a horrendous night and I didn't want to look at that anymore." (Cawthon 1995).

In a win at Milwaukee in February, Lucas called Maxwell "outstanding." (Associated Press 1996). It was the Vernon Maxwell Experience. Watching Mad Max was like watching *Inception*. After two and a half hours, you're asking yourself, "What the hell just happened?" The Sixers season was a lost one. Buried at the bottom of the standings and with Stackhouse sidelined, the Sixers' intent to merely play out the string was transparent. Philly fans turned their sights towards Ricky Botallico's all-star campaign, the Atlanta Olympics, anything - anything else other than the Sixers. Nobody was supervising the proceedings. We're all culpable. It happened on all our watches. Vernon Maxwell went rogue, and we just sat idly by. On April 8th, 1996, you were probably sidetracked. You meant to switch to the Sixers during commercials, but you were beguiled by the unique delivery of Sid

Fernandez, who dealt five strong innings against the Pirates. Next thing you know, you're falling asleep to *Action News*. Vernon and the Sixers defeated the Nets that night. Maxwell hung 41 points on 15-33 shooting. He shot 17 threes and recorded one measly assist. That's a 17:1 three pointers attempted to assist ratio if you're scoring at home. Just another day at the office for Mad Max.

The Sixers and Vernon parted ways in the offseason, and that figured to be the end of the Maxwell/Philly romance. But in 2000, Philly brought in Maxwell once more. No wonder the Sixers ran through the Eastern Conference. Mad Max sprinkled a little championship dust on them before he exited stage right. Maxwell played 24 games with the Sixers, registering 6 starts after Eric Snow was sidelined with an injury. It was a tamer, more refined Mad Max. He was cut in December for Kevin Ollie, the only free agent point guard ever available on the market. There was a bit of drama surrounding his departure, but this time, he wasn't the instigator.

Iverson was visibly upset before the game because Brown cut his best friend on the team, Vernon Maxwell.

I'd be surprised if he didn't react," Brown said of Iverson. "[Maxwell] was his best friend."

Iverson didn't speak to reporters after the game. (Maaddi 2000).

Maxwell's NBA tenure ended after that season. He had a colorful career, highlighted by the highest of highs and also quitting on his team and taking a swing at a fan. Sandwiched between those milestones were almost 10,000 field goal attempts. Some, maybe most, were considered a bad shot for a mere mortal. But there was nothing normal about Mad Max. The next shot was always his best shot.

If Mad Max gets hot ...

The One-Hit Wonder

Name: Jumaine Jones

Height: 6'8"

College: Georgia

Sixers Tenure: 1999-2001

Everybody was sore, everybody was spent. But there was courageous play after courageous play, the Raptors rallying from a big deficit, the Sixers answering every challenge with a clutch shot by Snow or Aaron McKie or the inspired Jumaine Jones. (Whittaker 2001).

There's this running gag on Twitter where someone tweets at a famous athlete, like a Bryce Harper or an Embiid, and says something like, "Decapitate me and then use my skull as a chip and dip bowl." I know, I know. It makes little sense, but it's actually a huge compliment and a tweet of endearment. I'm a sucker for it. I imagine these athletes checking their mentions saying to themselves, "What the hell? They want me to do what now?" Twenty years ago, these same Sixers fans/masochists would've BEGGED Jumaine Jones to dunk their carcass straight into a briar patch.

Sixers PA Announcer and national treasure, Matt Cord, gave Jumaine Jones the star treatment. Jones' intro and Cord's annunciation was folklore in this city. It became part of the student curriculum, like a teacher asking you to diagram a sentence.

A 6'8" forward, from Georgia, #33... Jumaine Jones.

"What is wrong with the above, class?"

"There's no emphasis on 'Jumaine,' Ms. Applebee. There's no dash in his first name, and where's the capitalization?"

"Great job, Melissa! You're exactly right! The sentence should read like this."

A "6'8" forward, from Georgia, #33... JU-MAINE Jones."

No one talks about the 2001 Sixers team and says, "Oh, hey, remember that Jones guy?" Address him properly - it's 'JU-MAINE Jones' - or GTFO.

An uber-athletic forward from Georgia, Jumaine - pardon - JU-MAINE Jones wasn't a Flight Brother, but he could've been a close relative. A Flight Cousin or a Flight Next Door Neighbor maybe. The 2001 Finals team was gritty, hard-nosed, and very sound defensively, but outside of Iverson, they weren't super athletic. Jones was the outlier. Jumaine Jones was a late first round pick of the Atlanta Hawks, but traded to Philly for another future first. The strategy of acquiring a player on draft night taken late in the first round by giving up a future first is a dicey one - I still have Arnett Moultrie flashbacks - but I suppose this move served its purpose.

Larry Brown had planned for his vets to do the heavy lifting in the postseason. George Lynch, however, fractured his foot during Game 4 of the Raptors series, leaving Brown scrambling. There weren't too many small forwards in his arsenal. Outside of Larry dusting off Roshown McLeod, or coaxing Mark Davis out of retirement ala Birds tight end Jeff Thomason for Super Bowl XXXIX, options were limited. So Brown turned to Jumaine Jones, who was told his rookie year that scoring the basketball was no longer his sole purpose in life.

"It was a transition for me because I came from being a scorer and I led the SEC in scoring [at Georgia], and I thought that was one of the reasons why I got drafted to go to Philadelphia," he said. "And it was funny, the first day I got to practice, [head coach] Larry Brown came up to me and he was like, 'Look here, Jumaine. You want to play for me, you've gotta find something else to do, because we've got a little guy on our team who's going to shoot 50 times a night.'" (Levick 2020).

Jones responded, providing a key tip-in or a monster dunk at just the right time. In the excruciatingly close series with the Raptors, Jones chipped in 16 points on 6-9 shooting in Game 7. The Sixers needed every bit of those sixteen points, as they clung to an 88-87 victory. Jumaine was serviceable in the Milwaukee series, but saw his playing time wane against the hated Lakers in the Finals. With George Lynch requesting a trade in the off-season, many expected Jumaine to absorb a larger role in the '01-'02 campaign. Jones, though, joined Tyrone Hill in a trade to Cleveland for Matt Harpring that summer. Cavs GM, John Paxson, wouldn't agree to the deal (Hill's career was nearing an end) without the inclusion of Jones, who had just torn up the Boston Summer League. (Associated Press 2001).

It was a brief Sixers stint for Jumaine, but his heroics in the '01 Playoffs are still fondly remembered. Jones was a Philly sports one-hit wonder. He paved the way for guys like Freddie Mitchell and Corey Clement. JU-MAINE only had one hit, but it was a banger.

The Nerf Game

Name: Rex Walters

Height: 6'3"

College: Kansas

Sixers Tenure: 1995-1998

My brother and I played a lot of Nerf basketball growing up. I rarely won because he was five years older than me, and I, blessed with great court vision, was a pass-first point guard. That skill set didn't translate in one-on-one. For the sake of competitiveness, I implemented the "no blocking three pointers" rule. It changed the landscape of the game, like the three seconds in the lane violation or Vatican II.

A quick aside: Our Nerf rim was bent forward from excessive dunking. In a brilliant stroke of engineering, I wedged a cardboard pizza coupon underneath the rim to prop it up. This little trick lasted eleven years. Over winter break in college, my friends and I had scrounged up nine coupons and needed one more for a free medium pie. I turned to the Nerf net still hanging from the basement door. The coupon had one final task. We were told, unfortunately, that coupon had expired ten and half years ago.

The 'no blocking threes' rule was the great neutralizer. While my brother did his work on the low block, courageously posting up a defenseless seven-year old, I floated around the three-point line like a prepubescent Mike Scott.

In one of our more ridiculous ideas, we decided to play out every NCAA Tournament game. We each chose a team. We would play as our favorite/the team's best player, using the NCAA Tournament Preview provided by the *Philadelphia Inquirer*. Well, I did anyway. My brother lacked my imagination.

"Look! This guy on Coastal Carolina shoots 41% from three-point land. I'll be him."

We took a blank bracket and wrote in each winner. This tournament is when all hell broke loose. See, I hated being a top seed. I didn't want to lose (which happened quite often) and be stuck with a South Alabama/Mount Saint Mary's championship. I wanted to maintain the integrity of Nerf March Madness. I wanted big television ratings. The casual fan wants UCLA/Duke, not two mid-majors battling it out in my parents' living room, I told myself, a protégée of Billy Packer. That's why I always took the lower seed in the early rounds. Give the fans what they want. There was just one exception.

Kansas. My guilty Midwestern pleasure. I was confident. Playing as a sharp-shooting Rex Walters, I planned on holding serve as the #1 seed in the Midwest Bracket. Who cares if my brother was taller, stronger, and five years older? He was Howard University, a pathetic and lowly #16 seed.

Well, Kansas had an off day.

Was it the early start time (8:15 A.M.)? Was it overconfidence? Lack of preparation? A bad shooting night? Lack of interior defense? Playing in socks? I don't know, probably all of the above. Kansas lost to an upstart Howard team – a talented squad who played much better than the #16 next to their name. While my mom did her crossword puzzle, I addressed the media after the loss.

"They did some things today that we didn't see in the game film."

"Tip my hats to those guys. They played loose. They were well-coached."

"Despite today's outcome, I'm still proud of my guys. We had a great season. We overcame a lot."

"Sure, the loss hurts. All losses do. But I told the guys in the locker room that they have nothing to be ashamed of. Of course, Rex is devastated. He's a competitor. I told him to keep his head up."

And then my brother spoke.

"What a win! What an upset by the Bison of Howard! The #16 seed has shocked the world! The fans can't believe it! The Jayhawks are stunned!"

He ran around the kitchen in jubilation. I was livid. I didn't want to address the media anymore. I wanted to strangle my brother. I wanted to kick him in the shins. Jump off my couch and drill him with a double axe handle. How could he say that? How could he play the upset card?

"You're twelve," I fired back. "You were supposed to beat me!"

"A huge win for the Bison!" he countered. "Without question, the biggest upset in tournament history! Nobody thought they could do it! Nobody believed in Howard! A 34-point underdog!"

The 34-point line was especially obnoxious since we only played to thirty. I ended the post-game press conference prematurely. I looked towards my mother. Do something. Make him stop! Can't you hear him?

"Do any of you know a river in Eastern Europe? Six letters..."

I resorted to my only defense, a failsafe that got me through the darkest of Nerf basketball losses. I charged at my brother like Bald Bull from *Mike Tyson's Punch-Out*. I swung wildly, fighting back tears. I kicked and screamed and punched and hollered.

"It wasn't an upset! You were supposed to win! Howard was fabored! Howard was fabored!"

Yes, I said 'fabored.' My mother finally intervened. Not so much because of the fighting, but because we were dangerously close to the spice rack. I don't remember how far Howard advanced, or who eventually won that tournament, but Rex Walters and the Jayhawks deserved better.

"When I was traded there, it was something they had to do," Walters said of the Sixers. "It wasn't like they wanted Rex Walters. So I never felt like Philadelphia was my home." (Smith 1998).

Few Philadelphia athletes were more polarizing than Rex Walters. He was a lightning rod of controversy that divided the city at the seams. A mid-90s Sixers fan always had an opinion of ol' Rex, and it was firm. It was unwavering. Now, there were two distinct sides to the Rex Walters debate - a debate mind you - that helped shape your political affiliation and social status.

Camp #1: Rex is an integral part of the rebuilding process. He can play both guard positions. He can stretch the floor with his range. He's a poor man's Jeff Hornacek.

Camp #2: Rex is undersized. He can't defend. He's not athletic enough. He talks in the third person.

The Rex Walters issue didn't just affect the employees inside the Spectrum. It extended to the streets of South Philly, to the radio, to the once comfortable homes of Suburbia.

"Honey, we need to talk about this. I think Rex is stunting the growth of our young backcourt."

"Can you please pass the spaghetti?"

"Alan, I'm not just going to sweep this issue under the rug. We need to see what we have in Trevor Ruffin."

"I'm not getting into this now, Amy. Not in front of the kids. Now, can you please pass the spaghetti?"

Walters came over to Philly along with Derrick Coleman in November of 1995. With the Sixers fighting for extra lottery balls, Walters went from little used guard to workhorse, suddenly playing 35 plus minutes a night. In his first start for Philly, he recorded 17 points and 7 assists in a road win at Atlanta. He also chipped in five fouls. Make Mookie Blaylock earn it, Rex. I appreciate the physicality. His next start, a win against the Nets, produced newspaper leads like this:

After checking with the league office last night to ensure that what John Lucas put on the Spectrum court qualified as an NBA team, the Nets' 82-79 loss to the lowly Philadelphia 76ers was without doubt their worst this season. (James 1996).

Before Walters was inserted into the line-up, the Sixers were 14-60. Since, 2-0. Just puttin' the numbers out there. People can draw their own conclusions. The Sixers eventually did lose a Rex Walters start, and the selection of Allen Iverson that June moved the former Jayhawk back to the bench. In January of '97, in a thrilling overtime win in Boston, Rex dropped a Lebronesque 27, 11, and 9. But those performances were few and far between. Walters survived the '96-'97 season and yet another coaching change. Rex hung on to a roster spot until January of '98, when the acquisition of Eric Snow led to his release.

Back in 1996, I convinced this kid on my travel basketball team that my $20 sneakers from Value City were in fact, "the new Rex Walters." I guess he forgot about the endorsement deal Rex signed with Stride Rite. But looking back, I guess a lot of people forgot about him. He had no attachment to Philadelphia. Like he said, *"It wasn't like they wanted Rex Walters."*

The Lefty

Name: Kareem Rush

Height: 6'6"

College: Missouri

Sixers Tenure: 2008-2009

NBA Live was my favorite video game as a kid. *NBA Jam* was great, ridiculously entertaining, but also cartoonish. You enter in the code, "DIS," then press the C-button, and you're running through the competition with George Clinton, front man for the P-Funk All-Stars. Which was cool and all, but with *NBA Live,* I could send Bradley to help on Weatherspoon's man in the post. And what's more exciting than a good weak side double-team? There was also *Tecmo NBA Basketball* for Nintendo. It was the first NBA game that featured all the teams, full rosters, season mode, etc, but gameplaywise, it was a poor substitute compared to its NFL counterpart, *Tecmo Super Bowl.*

NBA Live was groundbreaking. The courts were custom to each team. The Celtics had the parquet floor. The Nets, Mavericks, had their retro logos at midcourt. I was so excited when *NBA Live '96* came out. Now, you could play with the expansion Toronto Raptors and Vancouver Grizzlies. Clogging the middle with Bryant Reeves was previously just a pipedream. The entire world was suddenly at my fingertips. The left-handed players in these games, their jump shots just looked prettier. They looked crisper. You always thought their shots were going in. Half of my childhood was spent chucking up threes with left-handed players in *NBA Live.* Brad Lohaus and Stacey King practically raised me.

When the Sixers inked free agent Elton Brand to a monster five-year deal in the summer of 2008, the narrative changed. The Sixers were no longer some team just treading water in the underbelly of the league. They were instant contenders, a force to be reckoned with in the East. It's interesting how the roster management changes at that point. Once you have that star player, once that starting line-up is cemented, the focus instantly moves to the fringes.

"We just need that spot-up shooter now to keep defenses honest. Cap space is tight but hopefully Stefanski can do some bargain bin shopping."

"Paper or plastic?" asked the ACME cashier.

The '08 offseason was a puzzle, and every piece seemingly fit nice and snug like Mickey Morandini's second baseman's mitt. The July 29th, 2008 Kareem Rush signing may have been buried in the headlines though. The Phils defeated the Nationals 2-1 that night, thanks to a Chase Utley two-run homer. Utley sported a .290./.369/.566 slash line at the time, but enough about Utley's slam dunk Hall of Fame candidacy. The Rush acquisition was tidy; the fit was seamless. The Missouri product with the smooth lefty stroke entered the league in 2002, and had stints with the Lakers and the Bobcats, before playing a year in Lithuania. He signed with the Pacers for the '07-'08 season, where he shot a career-best 39% from behind the arc. It was a low risk move by the Sixers that most expected would reap some sort of benefit. Rush would stretch the floor. It would provide Brand some real estate to operate down low in the half-court. Surround your best frontcourt player with some shooters. It was a simple strategy, Basketball 101.

Except Kareem Rush didn't play at all. The Google Images search of "Kareem Rush + Sixers" is a wasteland. There are no highlights of Kareem Rush in Philly. There was no "Kareem Rush Game." There is actually a Kareem Rush montage on YouTube that even includes clips from his time in the Baltic Basketball League (Longer01 2008). But the video was created in 2008, before he inked his one-year deal with the Sixers. A sequel was never produced.

If I wasn't staring at a couple of rogue box scores from the '08-'09 season, I wouldn't even believe Rush was a Sixer. He appeared in just 25 games for Philly. He was a forgotten man. While the fit was there, the opportunity was not. Kareem Rush was definitely a Sixer at one time. I'm almost certain of it.

The Waiver Claim

Name: Thomas Robinson

Height: 6'10"

College: Kansas

Sixers Tenure: 2015

Robinson had been placed on waivers Sunday by the Denver Nuggets. He agreed to play with Brooklyn on Monday but had to clear waivers Tuesday evening before signing a contract. The Nets are upset over the Sixers' actions, according to multiple league sources. (Pompey 2015).

What we had here was a good old-fashioned cock block. Normally, I'd be above the fray, the pettiness of it all, but I enjoyed the drama at the time. NBA waiver wire claims are pretty uncommon. This wasn't like fantasy football, where you put in seven waiver claims Tuesday night and woke up with a second kicker and Jason Avant. It's more nuanced than that. To claim a player on waivers, a team has to have either a trade exception, or be able to absorb that player's salary into their cap. Very few teams were swimming well under budget. Like Billy King never had $5 million lying around, burning a hole in his pocket, waiting for Samaki Walker to land in his lap through waivers. Most players just clear waivers, and then sign with whatever team they choose. Cap space was a rarity - that was except for Sam Hinkie's Sixers.

"Salary Cap Floor" wasn't even in our nation's lexicon until the Hinkie Era. The Sixers were working on an Arena Football League budget. 99% of the league is shopping at Whole Foods, while Sam was getting his produce from Aldi's. That season Philly got a first-round pick from the Nuggets just for paying the remainder of JaVale McGee's $11 million salary. The Sixers were loan sharks. Absorb a few bad contracts and get some draft picks for their monetary efforts. It was a nice trade-off.

Thomas Robinson entered the league with a big pedigree. He was an athletic power forward, a ferocious rebounder, who was a walking double-double at Kansas. The Kings selected him 5th overall in the 2012 NBA Draft, but Robinson never saw much time behind DeMarcus Cousins and Jason Thompson. Sacramento wasn't a great landing spot for him. In his precious few minutes with the Kings, though, Robinson did manage to elbow Detroit's Jonas Jerebko square in the jugular. So that's something? (Jones 2012). The Kings bailed on Robinson half-way through his rookie year - he was moved to Houston, then Portland, then Denver for a few days. Two and half years into his career and Robinson was one more boarding pass away from being Tony Massenburg. When he was waived by the Nuggets in February 2015, the rest of the league, and Robinson and his agent, too, expected him to sign with Brooklyn. Welp.

The Philadelphia 76ers have acquired forward Thomas Robinson through a claim in the NBA's waiver process, league sources told Yahoo Sports.

Robinson had reached agreement on a deal with the Brooklyn Nets should he have cleared waivers and become a free agent. For the Nets to sign Robinson for a possible playoff appearance, the Sixers would have to waive him by Saturday.

The Sixers needed the sum of Robinson's remaining salary to honor the obligations of the collective bargaining agreement that dictate a team needs to reach within 90 percent of the NBA's salary floor before season's end – or pay out that shortfall amount equally among the rest of the players on the roster. (Wojnarowski 2015).

Did the Sixers claim Robinson because absorbing his rookie contract put them over the salary floor? Did they want to gamble on a high lottery pick - see what Robinson offered in extended minutes? Yeah, I'm sure both factors played a role. Did they want to stick it to Brooklyn for no real reason at all? I'D LIKE TO THINK SO. The Thomas Robinson Drama was a silly, quirky side plot and I was here for it.

Two months prior, the Sixers acquired Andrei Kirilenko from Brooklyn in another salary dump. There supposedly was a handshake deal between the three parties. Kirilenko had no interest in joining the losing Sixers, and Philly apparently had agreed to release the athletic Russian after acquiring him. The Sixers reneged on that deal, or there was a miscommunication, or something. Either way, Kirilenko never reported, citing a family matter. The Sixers never released him, and Philly eventually suspended Kirilenko. There was speculation that Hinkie hoped to flip Andrei for a draft pick, but that never came to fruition (Ford 2015). The Kirilenko story just added another layer to the tense Sixers/Nets relationship. Around the same time, Bob Diaco, the former coach of UConn football, fabricated this rivalry with Central Florida, their fellow compatriots of the American Athletic Conference. Diaco dubbed the rivalry, "The Civil Conflict," and sanctioned a trophy for the winner and everything. The whole thing was goofy - neither team cared about the other - but sometimes you have to create your own drama. Were the Sixers/Nets suddenly Lakers/Celtics? No, but it was something.

Philly fans enjoyed antagonizing Brooklyn supporters over the Thomas Robinson claim, because some Nets fans really seemed bothered by it. They felt the move was unethical, immoral, or just shady. Sure, the Sixers were 12-45 at the time, but that was no matter. Sixers Twitter waved their waiver wire claim like a winning scratch-off.

It was glorious and fun and really all so dumb. Robinson actually played well in his 22 games with the Sixers. Per 36, he averaged 17 points and 15 boards. If you squinted hard enough, Robinson was basically Artis Gilmore. Robinson played hard in Philly, finally getting the opportunity to show his potential. A free agent that offseason, Brooklyn finally got their man. The Nets inked Thomas Robinson to a contract.

No waiver wire claim required.

The Hot Plate

Name: Ron Anderson

Height: 6'7"

College: Fresno St.

Sixers Tenure: 1988-1993

Early on, the acquisition of Anderson from Indiana for second-round draft pick Everette Stephens was regarded as a steal. Now that the 6-foot-7 forward is averaging 17.9 points in just 23 minutes per game, the crime has been upgraded to grand larceny. (Ford 1988).

Today, the mid-range jumper has been shunned from society. If a player is caught on camera shooting a sixteen-footer, their family's restaurant gets flooded with one-star reviews on Yelp and their life gets canceled.

"Hey, what ever happened to Flip Murray?"

"Last I heard he took a seventeen-footer in a road game at Dallas."

The early 90s were a simpler time though. Back before the mid-range jumper became a lost art, Ron Anderson was our Picasso. His jumper was neither abstract nor expressionism, however, because Ron Anderson would not be labeled. His game was smooth. It was refined. There were no wasted motions with Ron Anderson. He was a suave small forward who would have been just as comfortable playing in cuff links instead of his trademark wristbands.

Oh, did I mention wristbands? Those wristbands, those glorious, beautiful wristbands. Every bartender in the country tucks their bottle opener into their wristband because they graduated from the Ron Anderson School of Mixology. There would've been a mad dash to secure the Twitter handle, @RonsWristBands.

@RonsWristBands

Looking good and feeling good. 'Like' if you prefer me on Ron's wrists. RT if you want me on Ron's forearms. #BeatDetroit

6:56 PM · Dec 8, 1989

236 Retweets 341 Likes

What a cult following Anderson would've had - it would have been the second coming of Mike Scott Hive. Ron Anderson lookalike contests during tailgates. We'd call it the "Battle of the Bands." Get it? T-shirts, koozies, headbands, wristbands (duh), merchandise opportunities galore. Little red, white, and blue wristbands for dogs. Half the rescue pups in Fishtown would be named "6th Man" or "Ron Ron" or "Midrange."

But it took our hero a couple of years to find his calling. Ron Anderson's origin story is something out of a movie. He didn't play high school basketball in his native Illinois. He stocked shelves at a local grocery store after graduation. He played pick-up hoops, and the guys he teamed with decided to register for some tournament. A brother of a teammate, who played at Santa Barbara Junior College, saw Anderson play and convinced him to go out west. From Santa Barbara, he transferred to Fresno State and eventually became a 25-year-old NBA rookie (Jauss 1985). Remember, bench scoring ages like a nice Cabernet Sauvignon. A second-round draft pick by the Cavaliers in 1984, the Sixers later acquired Anderson in '88 and the move paid immediate dividends.

Anderson's first year in Philly was arguably the best of his career. Coming off the bench, a role that fit him like a tailored suit, Anderson averaged a touch over 16 points per game in 31 minutes. Ron didn't pay much mind to defense, because he couldn't be bogged down by such trivial things. Anderson's job was to fill it up and fill it up he did. If Vinnie Johnson was "The Microwave," then Anderson was, well, something else that heats things up quickly. Ron "The Hot Plate" Anderson? He flourished in his role as the Sixers' 6th man, averaging double digits in each of his five seasons with the club. Many pointed to Anderson as a main factor for the Sixers' big turnaround in the '88'-89 season.

"Ron has been extremely effective. We're getting used to him coming off the bench and delivering big performances for us," said Lynam. "We like him in that role. Bench scoring was a major problem for us last year, and it's now an area we feel we're much improved. Ron just seems to flourish coming off the bench." (Groller 1989).

For us Ron Anderson aficionados and 6th Man connoisseurs, that quote is NSFW. Talk dirty to us, Jim Lynam. The Sixers could never get over the hump in the Eastern Conference, but Anderson was a stalwart. He was beloved by fans for his scoring prowess off the bench, his trademark wristbands, and, funny enough, his introduction. Thanks to former Sixers PA announcer, Jim Wise, Anderson checked-in with the flare of a bride and groom reception entrance.

"Let's stand up and put your hands together ... let's make some noise ... introducing for the very first time ..."

Ron AN...DER-son checks-in...for the Hammer, Armen Gilliam.

This substitution was not so much a catch phrase, but a battle cry. It worked with any combination.

Going small?

Ron AN...DER-son checks-in...for the G-Man, Mike Gminski.

Going big?

Ron AN...DER-son checks-in...for the Hawk, Hersey Hawkins.

See? Anderson could adapt to any situation. Ron Anderson left the Sixers in 1993. It was the worst Philadelphia sports moment of the year.

The Basket

Name: Casey Shaw

Height: 6'10"

College: Toledo

Sixers Tenure: A handful of games

Overheard at a Wawa:

Date: February 26th, 1999

Time: Approximately 7:15 AM

Man pulls an Arctic Splash iced tea from the cooler

"That rookie Shaw got his first bucket last night, Jim."

"Saw that. Should be plenty more where that came from."

My older sister was on Nickelodeon's *Double Dare*. Years and years later, I was speaking with my brother about it. We had this great idea to track down the episode and put it on a DVD. Give it to her on Christmas. YouTube had tons of old *Double Dare* clips - should be a quick pull, we figured. Or so we thought. Traditional *Double Dare*, *Family Double Dare*, episodes as far as the eyes could see. I fell down the rabbit hole. I watched complete episodes, hours upon hours of general knowledge trivia and physical challenges on an endless loop. I couldn't step away. I stopped shaving, stopped showering. This quest consumed me. But our YouTube search came up empty. So I called up Viacom. They owned Nickelodeon. I got hold of a nice woman and explained my plight. She laughed, and then told me that "*Double Dare* episodes aren't in the vault." Seemed fishy and worthy of a deeper investigation, but I was on a deadline. Christmas was just a week away. My brother backpedaled, mumbled something about a Yankee candle. But I was undeterred.

I went back to the internet, but this time, I bypassed YouTube. I went to the deep, dark underbelly of the World Wide Web. Lurking in the shadows were *Double Dare* super fans. Tape collectors. I treaded carefully. I found a fan site that was hosted on like an old Angelfire or Geocities platform. This site listed all the episodes the collector had for sale. Was there a big market for old *Double Dare* tapes, I wondered? No matter. I surged on. I recognized my sister's episode by her team name. I emailed the guy, asked if he had the episode on VHS. I explained our intent to burn it to a DVD as a Christmas gift. He emailed me *right* back, like alarmingly fast, like he had been waiting his entire life for my email.

"I have the episode. Did your sister ever become a teacher?" he wrote.

Oh god, what have I done? I stared at the email for a while. Do I cut my losses? "Hey sis. We got you a candle. Apple cinnamon scent. It may look nice in your downstairs half bathroom." Do I roll the dice, exchange emails with this stranger on the internet, whose intentions may or may not be pure? Well, you don't visit an Angelfire site to play it safe. I told the seller that my sister was "in business," as if she was in the mob. And the guy was great! Said he was happy to help. He wouldn't accept any money. He burned the tape on to a DVD for me and overnighted the episode in time for Christmas. He was incredibly nice. He was a rock star. These *Double Dare* tape collectors are a fine breed it turns out. My sister, though, didn't love the gift. There was a reason why there was no video evidence of the episode. She wanted it that way.

Casey Shaw went to Toledo. Like Shaw, "The Mayor" Steve Mix, the former color man for Sixers broadcasts, was also a fellow Rocket. Mix went out of his way to mention this bond every time Casey Shaw checked into the game. As the old saying goes, find someone who loves you as much as Steve Mix loves Toledo University. It was a bit of a running gag from the broadcast team, like when Chris Berman would tee up Tom Jackson with, "From ... Louisville," on ESPN's *NFL Primetime*. In a way, Casey Shaw was Steve Mix's Ernest Givins.

A former 2nd round pick of the Sixers in 1998, Casey Shaw played just nine games for the Sixers and scored a grand total of two points. Surely, in the advanced technological age we live in today, I would've been able to find video proof of this Shaw bucket in a road victory over the Bulls on February 25th, 1999. Just a couple of clicks, a quick search, and I should be face-to-face with a Shaw hoop, right?

"Casey Shaw Sixers two points"

Nothing.

"Casey Shaw basket 76ers 1999"

Nada.

"Sixers Bulls February 25th, 1999"

Nope.

"Philly Special Super Bowl LII"

What do you want from me? I needed a win to build back up my Google search confidence.

But no, there is no video evidence of this basket because we live in the Dark Ages. In *Back to the Future II,* they referenced flying cars in 2015. Hardly. Not only can I not fly my two door sedan through the Delaware Valley, but I'm left wondering if Casey Shaw's lone bucket in the NBA was a routine lay-up, a monstrous dunk, a jump hook, a sky hook, a baseline jumper, or a step-back sixteen footer. I have no idea. Your guess is as good as mine.

The Third Wheel

Name: Andrew Lang

Height: 6'11"

College: Arkansas

Sixers Tenure: 1992-1993

The majority of Intell readers responding to this week's People Poll question think the Philadelphia 76ers came out on top Wednesday when they traded star Charles Barkley to the Phoenix Suns.

In return, the Sixers received guard Jeff Hornacek, forward Tim Perry and center Andrew Lang.

This week's question was:

Do you think the 76ers made a good trade?

Here is how the voting went:

185 or 69 percent of the 269 voting - Think the Sixers made a good deal in trading Sir Charles for the Phoenix trio.

84 or 31 percent of those voting - Think that Phoenix was the shrewder trader in acquiring Barkley. - A 1992, *Intelligencer Journal* reader poll (Intelligencer Journal 1992).

Oh no, what are we doing *Intelligencer Journal* subscribers?

No player from the Barkley haul drew more of the fans' venom than center Andrew Lang. Hornacek was the best of the bunch. Perry was a local guy. Then there was Lang. It's a tradition as old as time. All else being equal, and if there's no Wes Helms within arm's reach, boo the unproductive Sixers center. Lang played just one season in Philly. The Sixers then renounced his rights, making him a free agent. A month later, Lang signed a deal with the Hawks. A key member in the return for the beloved superstar gone, just like that. Both parties said the right things. "We're not ruling anything out. We'd entertain an offer, etc, etc." But those were just words. It's like bumping into someone from your past, and the conversation ends with, "We should get coffee sometime. Catch up." It's just something you say. Lang didn't necessarily underachieve in Philly, not to the extent that fans believe all these years later anyway. He was fresh off a 7 point, 6 rebounds per game campaign in Phoenix. For Charles Barkley, fans expected an All-Star in return, or at least a quality starter. Instead, they got Kwame Brown.

Despite acquiring a young center, Lang's arrival to the Sixers didn't generate any buzz. There was no John Clark on assignment hanging outside Philly International Airport, awaiting the big man's arrival. Modell's didn't stock their showrooms with Lang jerseys.

"Excuse me. I'm looking for the Andrew Lang jerseys? I didn't see any."

"Do you mean Andy Ashby?"

"No, no. Andrew Lang."

"Dmitry Yushkevich?"

"No, Lang. The center. He plays center."

"Oh, center. Yes, of course. Sorry, I misheard you. David Alexander jerseys are in the back corner, right-hand side."

Mention Andrew Lang in 1992, and the best you'd elicit was a shrug. There is no return policy in the NBA. The Sixers traded Barkley for peanuts. It was just best to never speak of it again, like the Cliff Lee return from Seattle. That summer not only marked Andrew Lang's arrival, but also new Sixers head coach, Doug Moe. Moe famously utilized an up-tempo, freelance-style offense, and for bigs like Lang, the new approach could leave the frontcourt players feeling like fish out of water. Playing one night against Hakeem Olajuwon and the Rockets in a losing effort, Lang tried to lure the Hall of Famer outside of the lane. And we'll let Moe take it from here.

Particularly noteworthy was Andrew Lang's 5-17, an uncharacteristically high number of shots.

"I don't know what Andrew Lang was thinking about," Moe said. "I guess he thought he was a jump shooter. He took more shots than anybody in the first half." (Weiss 1993).

The expectation, or the hope anyway, was that young Andrew Lang would take the lion's share of the minutes at the five spot. He'd easily outperform the three other centers on the Sixers roster and cement his future with the team. Offensively, Lang was limited but brought with him a reputation as a capable defender and a prolific shot blocker. But his potential never materialized. Moe played musical chairs with Lang, Manute Bol, Charles Shackleford, and the venerable Eddie Lee Wilkins. Four tall reasons why Coach Moe ended practice early to attend the afternoon matinee with his wife. Sure, the Sixers were abysmal, but Jack Nicholson gave a riveting performance as Col. Nathan Jessup in *A Few Good Men*. The warning signs on Lang were there right from the jump. In the second game of the season, Lang played 40 minutes in a loss to the Knicks. He went 0-4 from the floor and pulled down 8 boards. Think of what Lang could've accomplished in 42 minutes if he didn't get into foul trouble. A terrific 18-point, 20-board, 5-block effort against Miami later that month was a rarity. Lang never did take ownership of that center spot.

Doug Moe was relieved of his duties in March, after a 56-point loss to Seattle. That may seem like a lot, but the Sixers trailed by 84 (!) at one point in the third quarter. I'm kidding, but I had you there for a second. While many players openly expressed their frustrations with the line-up changes and rotational philosophies of Moe, perhaps no group was more disgruntled than the centers (Fernandez 1993). Seemingly everyone over 6'10" griped about their role at one point or another. Except Manute. Manute was an angel.

Player morale improved under interim coach "Mad Dog" Fred Carter, but the writing was on the wall. The Sixers moved on from Lang, Shackleford, and Eddie Lee Wilkins in the off-season. Lang was a 12-year NBA veteran, a big man who carved out a respectable career. But to most, fair or not, Andrew Lang was just a guy who was part of one of the most lopsided trades in NBA history.

The 40% Shooter

Name: Hollis Thompson

Height: 6'8"

College: Georgetown

Sixers Tenure: 2013-2017

The name of my original blog was called, Where Is Ben Rivera. For the uninitiated, Ben Rivera was the 5th starter for the '93 Phillies World Series team. He won 13 games that season at the tender age of 25, pitched a handful of times the following year, and then completely vanished. Never pitched in the majors again. And what I found so fascinating was that no one ever questioned Rivera's whereabouts. He was seemingly erased from Philadelphia's consciousness. I'm walking down Market Street holding a sign saying, "Where Is Ben Rivera?" and I can't even get a honk or a wave or even a head nod.

Anyways, where is Hollis Thompson, and why is he not in the league? Hell, even Joel Embiid asked that same question on a recent Rights to Ricky Sanchez Podcast episode (Eskin and Levin 2020).

Thompson was a decent wing defender who shot close to 40% from behind the arc. Every team in the league craves that type of player. The demand, frankly, doesn't meet the supply, and teams will throw cash at any wing-type that flashes the smallest kernel of that potential. In most cases, it's the jump shot that's missing. In three full seasons with the Sixers, Thompson never shot below 38% from three. At the age of 25, Hollis Thompson was out of the NBA.

The Process Trusters inflated the talent of some of these Hinkie Era players. I'm just as guilty of it. In a group of loveable losers - and there was a lot of losing - we hitched our wagons to these castaways because we had no one else. Heck, I used to keep track of Doug Glanville's stolen bases inside a notebook. Fans learned to look past the assembly line of defeats. The Sixers losing by 30 to Indiana and getting outscored 36-18 in the third quarter was just window dressing, parsley on an entree. Hollis Thompson hitting 2 of 5 from deep was the ribeye steak.

Those Sixers teams were our Bad News Bears. And while there may not have been a Kelly Leak on the roster, there were a handful of Engelbergs and Tanner Boyles. Very few players from that era hung around though, and I wonder if the stigma of the rebuild, the losing, "The Process" branding played a factor. A player can bathe in a vat of tomato juice and still not shed the stench of perceived tanking.

By NBA standards, Hollis Thompson had a relatively quiet college career at Georgetown, but a 44% clip from beyond the arc was a very promising indicator. He went undrafted, spent a year in the Developmental League before catching on with the Sixers. It's worth mentioning that Hollis was a key cog of that dominant 2014 Sixers Summer League Team, who ran roughshod through the competition in Orlando. The team celebrated the Summer League Championship with a parade - the victory float made two full loops around the Philadelphia College of Osteopathic Medicine (PCOM) parking lot. Light refreshments were served afterwards. I couldn't attend the festivities, but I heard it was nice.

A month into the '13-'14 season, Hollis Thompson carved out a starting spot and became a staple in the rotation through 2016. Thompson played for the Sixers for 3 ½ seasons, and in Process Years, that's like 182 years. He didn't create on offense, didn't have the ball in his hands often, yet he was efficient. Death, taxes, and Hollis Thompson shooting 40% from three. The fact that Hollis never really progressed in other aspects of the game was inconsequential. Thompson could've missed every shot attempt from Halloween to President's Day; yet turn the page to April: 40%. It became a thing on Sixers Twitter. Put Hollis Thompson on a mountain or in a desert. Put him inside ECW Arena with Tommy Dreamer. The environment didn't matter. Thompson could make two out of every five threes on the South Pole, even with the loss of feeling in his extremities. As long as there was a hoop and a ball, Thomson would shoot 40%. In the '15-'16 season, Hollis shot 38% from behind the arc, but that was just fuzzy math, a clear rounding error. If you round up from the seventh decimal point? That's right. 40%.

In his final season in Philly, Thompson saw his playing time decrease with the arrival of Gerald Henderson. Hollis was perhaps just too one dimensional for the coaching staff. The rest of his game never caught up with that jump shot. He was released in January and signed with the Pelicans. But that was the end of the road. Thompson hasn't gotten back to the NBA ranks. In a league that pays a premium for shooting, it's surprising. He seemed destined to crawl out through the Process Years and linger as a contributor for a contending Sixers team. But it was not to be. In an era of countless players shuttling in and out, Thompson managed to stick around - for a while anyway. Hollis Thompson could shoot, and 40% of the time he was perfect.

The IMDb Credit

Name: Eric Leckner

Height: 6'11"

College: Wyoming

Sixers Tenure: 1993-1994

"Culturally, being in Italy was terrific," Leckner said. "But the basketball experience was so bad, I'd rather play one minute in the NBA than be a star over there." (Jasner 1993).

My dad held a grudge against all Phillies bullpen pitchers. Left-handed, right-handed, closers, middle relief, it was all the same. He hated all of 'em. Whenever they sprinted out from the 'pen, my father would wake up from his green recliner and shout at the TV.

"Bedrosian!? Anybody but Bed Rock!"

"Not Wild Thing, Fregosi! He can't throw a strike! Leave Mason in!"

"Cormier? You've got to be kidding me!"

I was my father's son, so I followed suit. Sure, I was only 9 but I had opinions. Every time I saw Leckner at the scorer's table, I voiced my displeasure.

"Come on Mad Dog! Leckner? Leckner!? Don't you have anyone else!"

Eric Leckner looked like an actor on TV - some sleazy guy with nefarious intentions who was dating the main character's sister. In the early 90s, if you told me Leckner was the lead singer for a rival band on *California Dreams*, or if *he* played Jeff, and not Patrick Muldoon, the new manager of the Max who seduced Kelly Kapowski and then eventually two-timed her with some blonde co-ed at the hot new club, *The Attic*, I wouldn't have questioned you. In fact, I was *sure* that Eric Leckner was actually an actor, so I searched for him on IMDb. And I got a hit. He has one credit to his name. He appeared in the TV series, *NBA on CBS*, playing himself, a Utah Jazz center/forward, in a December 25th, 1988 episode titled, "Jazz vs. Lakers." (IMDb 2020). Vindication.

Leckner cut his teeth in the WAC at Wyoming, pairing with former college stud, Fennis Dembo. The Cowboys had some very successful teams during Leckner's time there. His junior year, as a #12 seed, Wyoming advanced to the Sweet 16, beating UCLA's Reggie Miller and Pooh Richardson (pride of Ben Franklin High School) in the process. In Leckner's final collegiate game one year later, they had a wild affair with Loyola Marymount in the first round of the NCAA tournament. Leckner recorded 23 points and 8 boards but was outdueled by Bo Kimble and Hank Gathers (R.I.P.), 119-115.

Given his collegiate production, it wasn't a reach or a surprise to see the big man selected by the Utah Jazz #17 overall in the '88 NBA Draft. He saw little time in Salt Lake City though, firmly entrenched behind gargantuan center Mark Eaton on the depth chart. He bounced around the league for a couple of seasons and played one year in Italy, before the Sixers came calling. Before signing a deal, Leckner spent four days scrimmaging with the team (Jasner 1993). Was that standard practice - a week-long job interview? Did Leckner work pro bono? Did he get some sort of daily stipend? It shouldn't have been that complicated. One phone interview, maybe a Zoom call, then you fly in Leckner for a few wind sprints, a couple of jump hooks over a folding chair and draw up the paperwork.

The Sixers may have been on to something with this extended try-out though. There could be money there. A team of traveling journeymen touring the country, scrimmaging NBA teams during the summer or training camp. Maybe a player gets hot and lands a deal with that team. Bring in someone fun like Don Nelson to coach. It could be a reality show. The camera focuses on the bus sitting idly in the parking lot of the Target Center. The next shot is inside the bus, panning to one empty seat. Coach Nelson stands up, steps into the aisle with a solemn look. He tells his team that Dan Dickau won't be joining them on the road to Denver. He's now a

Minnesota Timberwolf. The bus erupts into a cheer as Nelson flashes a huge grin. They're happy for Dan, but also fighting back a hint of jealousy. ESPN could televise it on ESPNU after a replay of like the 2006 Liberty Bowl. We'll call it, *Last Stop*.

Along with inking a back-up big, these summer runs were designed to get rookie, and the anointed face of the franchise, Shawn Bradley, some NBA competition. Those workouts were a who's who of 80's and 90's big men, guys rotating in and out, all taking their best shot at the big man. Leckner, Rick Mahorn, Greg "Cadillac" Anderson, and Sixers assistant coach, Jeff Ruland, all took part in grooming Bradley for the rigors of the NBA (Jasner 1993). They were like the guys in a video game you fought before you reached the final boss. Leckner eventually joined Bradley in a frontcourt that included a 38-year-old Moses Malone and undrafted rookie, Warren Kidd. The Legion of Gloom didn't exactly generate much buzz.

Behind Bradley, the Sixers have Moses Malone and veteran backup Eric Leckner. If Bradley remains healthy, neither probably will play much, although using Leckner, a hard worker and good defender, occasionally at forward wouldn't be the worst idea. Malone might have a little something left, but his continued health is a question mark.

And there they are ... your Philadelphia 76ers.

Maybe anonymity isn't such a bad thing. (Ford 1993).

With the wounds of the '93 World Series still fresh and the Eagles hosting the Cowboys on Halloween, most fans glossed over the idea of Eric Leckner, power forward. (The Birds lost that day, thanks in part to a pedestrian performance from Eagles QB Ken O'Brien). The frontcourt had a lot of holes, but such was life in 1993. You started Bradley, then you put in Leckner when Shawn picked up two early fouls. Early in the year, Leckner threw down a vicious dunk on Shawn Kemp of all people. After getting a nice pass from Hornacek in the middle of the lane, he rose up and flushed a one-handed slam right on the superstar's head. Leckner was fired up and got a chest bump from teammate Orlando Woolridge. The Spectrum crowd went bananas. The Sixers lost by 12 that night at home. Kemp and starting center Sam Perkins combined for 40 points on 16-25 shooting, but whatever. Big Leck threw it down.

When Bradley went down with a season-ending injury in Portland, Leckner was moved into the rotation. He started every game from there on out, but outside of a few highs - an 11 and 17 performance at Minnesota stood out - Leckner labored through the remaining part of the schedule with few highlights of note. After the season, the Sixers flipped Leckner to Detroit for a future second round pick. That pick turned into Jamie Feick who, from my research anyway, never posterized Shawn Kemp.

The KG Stopper

Name: Lavoy Allen

Height: 6'9"

College: Temple

Sixers Tenure: 2011-2014

It's not like Lavoy is the KG stopper or anything," Sixers coach Doug Collins said. (Frank 2012).

To hell he wasn't, Doug.

Before the start of the 2011 NBA Season, ESPN created a ranking of the top-500 players in the NBA. They crowdsourced this project, collecting votes from their staff, their blog network, TrueHoop, and various other outlets. They ranked rookie Lavoy Allen last at player #500 (ESPN 2011). The list was certainly not an exact science, especially considering that the ageless Uwe Blab ranked in at #496 and Master P was slotted one spot above. Please don't fact check me. The rankings were arbitrary - once you get past #300, you're just pulling names out of a hat, treating the list like Day 3 of an NFL Draft. Clayton Thorson? Sure, why not? Call it in. But where I come from, that's called bulletin board material. I'd hang a Post-It Note that says "#500" in my locker and let it fuel me. The expectations for Lavoy Allen were non-existent, so any contribution was an unexpected gift.

Allen was a local kid, the pride of Bucks County, PA. He played at Pennsbury High School then took I-95 southbound to Temple. Lavoy wasn't really considered an NBA Draft prospect - most figured he'd latch on to a team's summer league roster or maybe get a training camp invite down the road. The Sixers, though, selected Allen #50 overall in the second round of the 2011 Draft. Perhaps the Allen pick shouldn't have been a huge shock, considering the organization's propensity to take local talent. If you lined up two hypothetical prospects side by side, the Sixers will always defer to the guy that spent two years at Penn State Abington or spent his summers in Sea Isle. Allen was caught in a unique position, however. With the NBA in a lockout, he signed overseas with Strasbourg IG. Most Bucks County kids got a summer job at Sesame Place. Allen went to the French Pro A League.

With an opt-out clause in his contract once the NBA strike ended, Allen traveled back to the States to join the Sixers. Early on, Lavoy was either inactive or registered a DNP. But an achilles injury to Spencer Hawes in late January propelled Allen to a larger role. He offered a toughness defensively that Hawes and fellow rookie, and current NBA offensive standout, Nikola Vucevic, did not. As the Sixers sharpened the edges of their rotation entering the postseason, there was still a giant question mark at the five spot. Collins rotated Hawes, Vucevic, and Allen, trying to find the right combination to couple with Elton Brand.

Allen provided valuable minutes in his first ever playoff series, including an 11-point, 9-board effort in Game 2 at Chicago. But the Celtics series was where Lavoy found his calling. Lavoy Allen: Kevin Garnett Stopper. KG steamrolled Spencer Hawes in the early stages of the series. Face-up jumper, face-up jumper, turnaround, face-up jumper, turnaround. Like Chad Lewis in the back of the end zone, the defense knew what was coming but was powerless to stop it. Hawes was never going to be mistaken for Ben Wallace and being asked to guard a Hall of Fame player was a difficult task for anyone.

Enter Allen. Garnett won a boatload of accolades in his career, but he never got *First Team All-Bucks County Courier Times*. Were we even convinced Garnett could start in the Suburban One League? Allen invaded KG's personal space the rest of the series. Terrific defense on Garnett in the final moments of Game 2 - locked all windows and doors, obviously - helped clinch a big Sixers road win (not to mention a desperation heave from Lavoy at the end of the shot clock late in the 4th quarter). Allen excelled where every other teammate before him had failed. While some chalked up Lavoy's defensive performance in Game 2 as a fluke, it soon became a pattern. After Game 4, Allen had become a problem.

With the Sixers needing to contain Kevin Garnett - who finished with just 9 points on 3-of-12 shooting - those duties fell to Allen, who performed admirably, especially as the game wore on and the Sixers drew closer.

"Lavoy, once again, defensively just did a tremendous job," Collins said. (Benjamin 2012).

The worst player in the NBA was suddenly the X-factor. ESPN owned up and issued Allen an apology.

We called Lavoy Allen the 500th best player in the NBA. We were wrong. (ESPN 2012).

The Celtics held on to win a tightly contested series in seven games, but the Sixers had found something in Allen. They re-signed Lavoy in the off-season, a no brainer given his postseason success. But Allen never again recaptured that magic. His play was inconsistent. His offensive game never evolved. Whether he was just a one-hit wonder or simply the victim of greater expectations, Allen was no longer Mr. #500. Now he was a known commodity. Now he was appropriately paid, and now more was expected from him.

In one bizarre exchange with the media, Allen was asked what he had learned in then his second season in the league. It was a softball question, one ripe for a cliché or six.

"Just preparation, you know? Learning to adjust to the grind of a long season."

See? Say anything. Literally anything, Lavoy. The world's your oyster.

"What have I learned? I mean, what have I learned? That's a good question." Allen said the other day.

"Uhh, nothing really," he said. "I didn't have to do any rookie duties this year, so that's good, I guess." (Levin 2013).

Ok, don't say that. With the bloom officially off the Bucks County rose, Lavoy Allen was moved to Indiana at the 2014 trade deadline.

The Sheriff

Name: Rodney Buford

Height: 6’5”

College: Creighton

Sixers Tenure: 2000-2001

Allen Iverson is out for the next one to three weeks. His replacement is some guy by the name of Rodney Buford. (Smith 2000).

Every conversation about Rodney Buford (and there are many currently taking place in the greater Philadelphia area) begin with his nickname.

The Sheriff.

She's a beaut, ain't she? She packs a punch. It's a nickname you remember. It stays with you. It's embedded in your consciousness like *Contra's* thirty lives cheat code. Up, Up, Down, Down, Left, Right, Left, Right, B, A, Start. Rodney Buford was the Sheriff. The Sheriff was Rodney Buford. The origin story, though, that’s a bit of a mystery. The internet doesn’t tell you anything; just countless confirmations that Rodney Buford, yes, is the Sheriff. No one is disputing that, World Wide Web. The consensus is that “The Sheriff” was dubbed by Marc Zumoff. Now, I had thought Zumoff pulled “The Sheriff” from Jackie Gleason’s character, Sheriff Buford T. Justice, in *Smokey and the Bandit.* But according to Buford, that’s not the case.

Rodney Buford earned the nickname from TV commentators during his NBA days in Philadelphia, when he would come off the bench for perennial all-star Allen Iverson.

"I came off the bench and took no prisoners. I was always ready to shoot," Buford said. "The (coaches) told me my role was to shoot so I became the Sheriff." (Colgan 2012).

No disrespect to the Sheriff, but that explanation seemed a bit flimsy, a bit too convenient. So I went right to the source. I tweeted Marc Zumoff. Zoo, a man of the people, tweeted me back. Turns out I was right. He pulled 'the Sheriff' from *Smokey and the Bandit* (Zumoff 2020). Nicknames have seen a bit of a resurgence recently, but for a while, the 21st century was littered with monikers that were just a series of letters and numbers - D12, KD, CP3. Those aren't nicknames. That's where I parked my car at the mall. Back then, nicknames had substance. Michael Cage was the "Juice Man" because he liked juice, man. Steve Mix was "The Mayor," because he ran for Toledo City Council back in '88 under the *Two for One If They Hurry* platform. He lost. It was a bit too progressive for Toledoans who preferred the safety and comfort of milking the shot clock.

Buford was a 2nd round selection of the Miami Heat, before being shipped off to Charlotte and eventually waived. In December of 2000, the Sixers brought in the free agent Buford to restore law and order on the second unit. Buford was an athletic, quick-triggered mercenary, but no one knew it at the time. The Sheriff was an unknown. You were left to your own devices. You had to form your own opinion; rely on the ol' eye test. There was no kid wandering the halls of junior high twenty years ago reciting Buford's summer league true shooting percentage (TS%). Rodney Buford liked to spot up, and he went by "The Sheriff." Boom. Opinion formed. Philly loved him. No one had a bad word to say about Rodney Buford.

"What do you think of this Buford kid, Greg?"

"Haven't seen him play yet, but I heard his nickname is 'The Sheriff.' I think he dunked once?"

"Yep. He's like my favorite player after Iverson."

"Same."

The Sixers, per tradition, were banged up a couple of months into the season. With Iverson dealing with some aches and pains, management brought in Buford and Kevin Ollie. Despite the injuries, the Sixers kept winning. In a January 19th victory over the Nets without AI, Buford pitched in 16 points in just 18 minutes of action. Rodney played about a quarter a night for that Finals team. Never enough to completely frustrate you, but just enough to keep you intrigued. Like 2012 Bryce Brown. Buford was used sparingly in the playoff run, mostly relegated to a cheerleader and designated chest-bumper for Iverson as he came off the court. Not a bad gig in all honesty.

The Sheriff played just one season in Philadelphia. He bounced around the league for a few more years before enjoying a lengthy career internationally. Rodney Buford's nickname transcended his talent, but, man, what a nickname it was.

The Amphibian

Name: Charles Shackleford

Height: 6'10"

College: North Carolina St.

Sixers Tenure: 1991-1993

"Where's the gamble?" Fred Carter, the 76ers' assistant coach, asked before the Knick rookies and free agents defeated their 76er counterparts, 99-90, tonight at the Kutsher's Sports Academy, with Shackleford scoring 8 points and getting 9 rebounds.

"Shack is a bona fide 6-11, has extremely long arms and can rebound," Carter said. "No one has ever questioned his ability to chase down the ball. Who was our starting center last year, Rick Mahorn? Shack is a much better rebounder." (Goldaper 1991).

Despite Mad Dog's confidence, Charles Shackleford was an enormous gamble. With two pedestrian NBA seasons to his name and one year overseas, Shackleford was expected to come in and solidify the middle. Like the Sixers brass knew something that no one else did. Shack was yet another center brought in to help exercise the demons created by Moses Malone's departure five years prior. Shackleford was listed at 6'10", 6'11", but was actually 7'5" if you include his flat-top haircut that made him the third tallest structure in Philadelphia behind Manute Bol and One Liberty Place. Along with his height and great hair came a checkered past. Actually, Charles Shackleford had a really checkered past. His college career covered every major plot point of the movie, *Blue Chips*.

Former N.C. State University basketball player Charles Shackleford and three teammates allegedly took part in point-shaving with a New Jersey gambler during the 1987-88 season, ABC News reported Wednesday.

The television network said three "informed sources," including an unidentified teammate of Shackleford's, claimed Shackleford shaved points in a game March 6, 1988, against Wake Forest and in as many as three other games. ABC didn't identify the other players or the other games.

According to point spreads released by the Associated Press, N.C. State was favored to beat Wake Forest by 15 points and won by four, 86-82. Shackleford scored 16 points in the game. The player he was guarding, Wake Forest center Ralph Kitley, scored a career-high 22 points. Kitley averaged three points that season. (Chandler and O'Brien 1990).

Was Shackleford on the take, or did the dynamic Ralph Kitley just get hot that night? Charles, it should be noted, denied all allegations and in September of '93 the investigation into Shack and the alleged point shaving ended without any charges. So maybe Kitley did just catch fire. Shackleford did, however, admit to taking $65,000 from two people while at North Carolina State. While not all allegations against Shack proved to be true, a stigma hovered over him as he exited Raleigh for the NBA (Jasner 1993). It was a difficult burden for any rookie to shoulder entering the '88 NBA Draft, whether human or amphibian. Despite all the controversy and allegations that surrounded Shack in school, it's the quote he gave when asked if he was left or right-handed that everyone remembers. "I can shoot with my left hand. I can shoot with my right hand. I'm amphibious." (Associated Press 2017).

Before the Shackleford signing in July of '91, the Sixers were also linked to two other relatively safer choices - veteran big men Moses Malone (of course) and Jack Sikma. Moses played all 82 games in the '91-'92 season for Milwaukee, averaging 15 and 10. But a herniated disc sidelined him most of the '92-'93 season. Jack Sikma ended up retiring (Jasner 1991). So maybe Shackleford was the path of least resistance? Besides, Charles Barkley famously asked for Shaq, not Sikma.

The Shackleford Experiment didn't go well. Concerns surfaced instantly, even before the start of the season. During training camp, players labeled him as foul-prone and suggested he had trouble picking things up (Ford 1991).

"Don't like what I've been reading, AJ. I'm hearing the new guy Shackleford is foul-prone, and he's having trouble picking things up."

"Still 82 games left to work out the kinks, Paige. Shack had a big year in Italy last season. Refs call things a bit tighter over here. He'll adjust."

Barkley did not think highly of Shackleford's body of work and voiced his concerns to anyone within earshot. After Shack's first season in Philly, Charles was asked about recently hired Sixers coach, Doug Moe. Barkley was still a Sixer, temporarily anyway, and said it didn't matter if Knute Rockne was coaching. Without better players, the team wasn't going anywhere.

Barkley said the Sixers "have got to get a starting center. Charles Shackleford just can't play center - he's not a center." (Associated Press 1992).

Except Shackleford *was* the center. He started 62 games at the position in his first season with the club. He averaged 6 points and 6 pulls in just under 20 minutes of action. Per 36, those numbers don't look half-bad, but Barkley, his teammates, and the fans had already drawn their own conclusions. The fans really gave it to Shack. Barkley even suggested on *The Mike Missanelli Show* that Shackleford would purposely commit fouls to get pulled from the game - to spare himself from the wrath of the home crowd (Hudrick 2019). Entering the '92-'93 season, Andrew Lang had replaced him at the five spot. Just to cover their bases, fans booed Lang, too. Shack's numbers, including minutes, decreased across the board. Predictably, the Sixers declined his team option in the offseason. He went back to Italy where, per his agent, his talent and presence was more appreciated.

"In his first game back in Italy, he received a five-minute ovation, as opposed to Philadelphia, where he received boos any time he was introduced," DiFazio said. "He rewarded the fans in Italy with 29 points and 21 rebounds in his first game." (Jasner 1993).

The Bench Scorer

Name: Don MacLean

Height: 6'10"

College: UCLA

Sixers Tenure: 1996-1997

"I'm no savior, but I wanted to be part of a team that was trying to build something special. I think that's what's taking place here, so I'm pretty excited." (Smith 1996).

Don MacLean got buckets. With apologies to Abdul-Jabbar and the "freshman rule," it's MacLean, not Kareem or Bill Walton or the O'Bannon Brothers or George Zidek, who is UCLA's all-time leading scorer. If you needed a bucket on the west coast in the early 90s, you didn't call James Worthy. You got the ball to Hollywood MacLean in the short corner. Getting points was never an issue for MacLean. Now, that's not to say there weren't *some* issues.

If you search YouTube for Don MacLean NBA highlights, it's with a heavy heart that I report there is no compilation of drop-step low post moves or elbow jumpers. The video cupboard is bare. YouTube offers just two clips of Grant Hill blowing past MacLean and dunking on noted rim protectors, Gheorghe Muresan and Oliver Miller, respectively. Muresan and Miller were salvaged from the title though: "Two times Grant Hill abused Don MacLean then dunked on two of the NBA's biggest dudes" (Van Dusen 2019). We could've left MacLean's name out of it. "Two Monster Grant Hill Dunks" is much more succinct. Don was never going to land on an All-Defensive Team. He didn't have the quickness to keep up with small forwards and lacked the strength to consistently defend the fours. Injuries were also a concern. After a career year in '93-'94, where he averaged over 18 points per night and captured the NBA's Most Improved Player Award, MacLean missed 69 games the next two seasons before becoming a free agent.

His appeal was obvious. Since the beginning of time, humans have been trying to find food, water, and a consistent scorer off the bench. The Sixers formerly had that in Ron Anderson, and now entering the season with a three-headed monster of rookie Allen Iverson, Jerry Stackhouse, and Derrick Coleman, the organization landed a scoring punch to alleviate the workload. When asked about MacLean's injury history and committing to a five-year deal, GM Brad Greenberg downplayed any concerns.

"Doesn't faze me," Greenberg said. "Don MacLean is a proven double-digit scorer. He's competitive, mentally and physically tough, and dedicated to helping the 76ers create a positive and winning attitude. My hope is that he'll end his career as a Sixer." (Smith 1996).

MacLean played 37 games with the Sixers and was traded after one season.

So ... how about those Birds?

Outside of a 16-point performance early on at Chicago (in a 29-point loss), Don had difficulty finding the freedom offensively he enjoyed in Washington. MacLean was part of a second unit that included Lucious Harris, Doug Overton, and Michael Cage. Opponents keyed in on MacLean, living by the old adage, "Make Doug Overton and Lucious Harris hurt us."

"Teams are aware of my role," he said. "I'm supposed to score. When I come in, they put their best defender on me. The other night, I came in and Detroit put in Stacey Augmon." (Cawthon 1996).

"Plastic Man's checking in, Dino."

"Probably to check MacLean, Greg. You watch *Seinfeld* last night? Jerry has all these royalty checks -"

"I taped it! No spoilers!"

Knee tendinitis sidelined MacLean for eight games in November, and a hip flexor shelved him for all of December. The injury concerns, which the organization had chalked up to bad luck or hoped were safely in the rearview mirror, reared their ugly head (Long 1996). Don returned to the line-up in January and played well. He had a monster five game stretch as the calendar moved to February. Don MacLean Week™, as it was affectionately called by locals, was the precursor to Shark Week in terms of must-see television. MacLean captivated the Philly audience. I wrote out his nightly scoring outputs with the number magnets on our refrigerator. He scored 24, 21, 24, 29, and 21 all off the bench, as the Sixers scratched out a few wins. Don looked like he had turned the corner, flexing that offensive prowess the Sixers desperately needed. Yet another injury, however, derailed his season. He suffered an ankle sprain in early March and was shut down for the rest of the year.

Desperate to free up cap space and escape the long-term deals that handcuffed their roster, the Sixers traded MacLean to New Jersey. It was a quick end to one injury-riddled campaign. Don had some short stints with other clubs, before garnering national headlines for testing positive for steroids. Asked about MacLean's steroid use, Charles Barkley said, "Don MacLean? I've seen Don MacLean naked, and he doesn't use steroids." (Fleischman 2001). When healthy, he wasn't bad. He averaged just under eleven points per night, but a rash of injuries dominated his Sixers tenure. Don MacLean had range, but it didn't extend as far back as the training table.

The Saboteur

Name: Andre Miller

Height: 6'3"

College: Utah

Sixers Tenure: 2006-2009

In my first job out of college, I would go to Quizno's for lunch with a colleague. This was right thick in the Andre Miller Years. My colleague was, and still is, a great guy and a huge Sixers fan. Mike was an eternal optimist though. He was the guy checking the standings in late March with the Sixers 5 ½ games back from the final playoff spot saying, "The schedule lightens up in April. And the Wizards just dropped two of three." I tried to have an honest dialogue with him - explain the top heaviness of the NBA power structure - but this was a man who ordered a broccoli and cheese soup in a bread bowl for nine months straight. He was beyond reason.

Andre Miller was good. Known for his terrific court-vision and a throwback, 'old man game,' Miller enjoyed a terrific seventeen-year career. He backed down his smaller opponents at a snail's pace, like the dude at the Y who rocked black high tops and a sleeveless No Fear t-shirt. You weren't trying defensively unless you ate a few of his armpit hairs. Miller's play at the point position caused fits for other teams. While playing for Portland, he dropped 52 points on the Mavs in 2010. I had completely forgotten Miller's half a hundred yet can recite every play of the Eagles/Cowboys "Tommy Hutton Game," because I'm a masochist and didn't have NBA League Pass at the time. Andre's trademark wasn't his scoring, though. He was a great passer, incredibly durable, and took care of the ball.

Andre Miller was good, and that was the problem.

The '06-'07 Sixers were a team dead on arrival, playing out the string as soon as they broke camp. The Black Shirts actually started out 3-0, but it was fool's gold, like a Samuel Dalembert made seventeen-footer after the opening tip. Reality soon intervened. The losses mounted. That hot start quickly morphed into 5-12. Iverson was told to stay home or chose to stay home depending on who you ask, and the Allen Iverson Trade Watch commenced. Kevin Ollie and Rodney Carney headed the backcourt. Loss after loss after loss piled up like shore traffic on 76. By December 20th, the Sixers were 5-19, their last win coming before Labor Day, or maybe Arbor Day. Can't recall at the moment. They had the worst record in the NBA - a game ahead of Charlotte and Memphis in the loss column.

Half-way across the country, on that same day in December, a lanky, 6'10" freshman forward from the University of Texas named Kevin Durant* scored 28 points and recorded 13 rebounds in an 80-76 win over Arkansas. Philadelphia is 1,669 miles away from Austin, TX, but at that moment, on that night, the two cities were never closer. All the Sixers had to do to lock up this transcendent talent was nothing at all. Stick to the plan. Run the offense through Rodney Carney and let nature take its course.

Then Andre Miller happened. Traded along with Joe Smith and some picks for Iverson, this white knight galloped down from Denver to, I guess, save us - to carry the Sixers limp carcass to 35 wins. Why? Nobody asked for this. LET US DIE, ANDRE. Ollie and Carney were flourishing in their new roles. We needed to give them time to build chemistry. I think 58 was the perfect number of games to find out what we had in this young backcourt. I already had "Broad and Ol-Ney" t-shirts printed out and had plans to sell them outside the arena. One for $20, or two for $30 with the purchase of a soft pretzel.

There is no Good Samaritan Law in the NBA. Andre Miller wasn't obligated to salvage the Sixers season. We weren't hurting anyone. Andre was what the kids call a 'try hard.' He spawned a bunch of coach speak from talking heads like, "he brings a winning attitude," and "Miller's effort is contagious." By April, the Sixers were back in the mix. Fucking Bread Bowl Mike asked me if I wanted to go halfsies on playoff tickets.

What is surprising, however, is that it took until April 14 - not April 1 or March 14 - to be presented with a do-or-die game. After all, the Sixers were 5-18 when they traded Allen Iverson on Dec. 19 and 10-29 after they lost at fellow doormat Memphis on Jan. 17.

Even Maurice Cheeks seems amazed. (Juliano 2007).

Playoffs? We're talking playoffs? Playoffs? With each meaningless win, Kevin Durant went from potential franchise centerpiece to pipedream. There had been rumors of Andre Miller being flipped at the trade deadline, but Billy King put the kibosh on that. King said simply, *"I like Andre."* (Schuler 2007). Everyone liked Andre, Billy. Everyone respected Andre. Philadelphians just at that moment needed him 5,000 miles away from team facilities. Couldn't we bring in Ric Flair or Harley Race to challenge Miller to a "Loser Leaves Town" match? It was nothing personal. Miller and the Sixers kept playing well. By spring, they would have needed a telescope to see Kevin Durant from their current draft position. Philly finished the season going 30-28; their competence over the second half of the year was grossly negligent. They selected 12th in the 2007 draft, which was basically one pick above Mr. Irrelevant.

Miller was back to his old tricks in '07-'08. He dragged the Sixers to the postseason once again. That accomplishment, however, was slightly diminished when you realize the team finished just 40-42, and back then, everyone in the East not named the Knicks made the playoffs. Those Sixers teams were cannon fodder for the Eastern Conference heavyweights - getting bounced in the first round by Detroit, Orlando, and Miami, respectively. Andre Miller was called, "The Professor," (no relation to "The Professor" from the And1 Mixtape Tour), and he taught the city of Philadelphia a very valuable lesson. No one likes a try hard.

*I don't know who Greg Oden is.

The Dunk Contest(s)

Name: Tim Perry

Height: 6'9"

College: Temple

Sixers Tenure: 1992-1995

Fellow Sixers forward, Tim Perry, also competing in the dunk contest, didn't fare as well. He missed an early attempt, and then came up short on a running from-the-foul-line attempt.

"Somebody moved the basket," Perry said. (Ford 1993).

Temple alum are very protective. They'll defend Aaron McKie and Eddie Jones like they were their own kin. Criticize Mark Macon or Rick Brunson, and Temple faithful will hurl you in front of traffic on N. Broad St. Politely suggest that Pepe Sánchez' inconsistent jump shot limited his upside, and the Cherry and White will give you repeated swirlies until you repent. Mark Karcher never got a fair shot in the NBA. Marc Jackson was absurdly underrated. There was no one better in crunch time than Lynn Greer. The list goes on. Except for Tim Perry. Perry is the anomaly. Temple folks don't defend Perry with the same ferocity. Talk to a Temple grad about Tim Perry, and they're like, "Yeah. He was ok, I guess. Hey, remember when Johnny Miller dropped 30 on Cincinnati in the NCAA tournament?"

Tim Perry will be forever linked to the wretched Charles Barkley deal that buried the Sixers franchise for half a decade. The return for Barkley seemed light at the time, and one, two years after the deal, it was confirmed. But I wonder, is the Barkley trade the sole reason why Tim Perry's legacy in Temple lore is cast aside? Or was it something else? Were there other factors in play? We're not going to rehash the Charles Barkley trade in this chapter. There are much more important, much more urgent issues to address. We need to discuss Tim Perry's NBA Slam Dunk Contest performances.

When you were a kid, there was nothing better than NBA All-Star weekend. My best friend's little brother's birthday party was always on All-Star Saturday. We had a dunk contest every year in their unfinished basement. Our dunk contest itself was lame, mostly just variations of the same Statue of Liberty Dunk. I tried the Cedric Ceballos blindfold slam one year and crashed into a pillar. There was blood everywhere. Blindfolds were quickly banned by his mom, and that really stifled our creativity. The Dunk Contest nowadays is more condensed. There are only four participants, each judge seemingly has their favorite, and it feels more scripted than an Erik Kratz Godschall's turkey bacon commercial. Every dunker has a prop or a celebrity helping out. I miss the purity of the contest - when it was less pomp, less circumstance. In the late 80s, early 90s, eight participants battled it out. Tim Perry was a combatant on three of those occasions.

As a member of the Suns, Perry participated in the '89 Contest. He had a decent performance, finishing 5th out of eight dunkers, but failed to qualify for the semi-finals. In 1993, now a member of the Sixers, Perry was back. Our guy, Philly pride, Fight, Fight, Fight for the Cherry and White. The Sixers actually had two participants in the '93 Dunk Contest, and as an eight-year-old - soon to be nine - I seized the opportunity. I called my bookie.

"Nickel on Spoon at +210, and a nickel on Perry at +185. My mom has a line of credit," I told him, using my friend's landline. Perry was a veteran of the dunk contest circuit, I told the six year old birthday boy. "He's been here before. The moment won't be too big for him." Little Brian agreed, nodding between pieces of chocolate cake.

Perry's first dunk was a run of the mill two-handed reverse. The cameras panned to the All-Stars in the front row where there was little reaction. Clyde Drexler held up a half-hearted "9" sign, but I think it was just a "6" turned upside down. The commentators labeled his dunk as "unenthusiastic," like getting a summons in the mail for jury duty. On his second attempt, Tim Perry took off from just inside the foul line. He didn't quite have the elevation and his dunk banged off the rim. Dr. J, a contest judge, shook his head in displeasure.

For his third attempt - and I've watched this about eighty-three times now - Perry dribbled around the perimeter for a bit, buying time. Either he was milking the shot clock or he was out of ideas. He attempted a bounce pass off the backboard, but the ball fell awry. He walked off the court sheepishly, as I threw my Tim Perry '93 Slam Dunk Contest Winner bet slip into my friend's fireplace. But since he didn't attempt a dunk - there was no missed slam - NBA officials ushered him back. The nightmare wasn't quite over. It was like clogging someone's toilet, but then having to go back to their house because you forgot your phone. After some deliberation, Perry started his next attempt from the wing and did a dunk so basic it came with a Starbucks cup. If you watch this dunk enough times, you start to see the appeal of Darrell Armstrong's lay-up in the '96 Contest. At least we'll never have to watch that again, I thought.

And then two years later, Tim Perry was back. Did the NBA have a hard time finding eight dunkers – maybe Joe Wolf already had a fishing trip planned with a nonrefundable deposit? Was there like an NBA Slam Dunk Contest participant distribution list or something and they forgot to remove Perry? Did Tim not click on the 'unsubscribe' link? Was Perry invited by accident, like getting an RSVP for your wedding from your strange cousin twice removed?

"How did Creepy Kevin get an invite?"

"I have no idea, but he's bringing a plus one."

Despite my reservations, value was value. I seized the opportunity. I called my bookie. "Nickel on Tim Perry at +4700. Uh huh. Yep, Tim Perry, the Sixers' Tim Perry. A nickel. Yep, I'm sure. Uh huh. Yep, I'm her son," I told him.

Perry was a veteran of the dunk contest circuit, I told the eight year old birthday boy. "He has learned from his mistakes. This year will be different." Little Brian agreed, nodding between pieces of chocolate cake.

The '95 Contest presented a different format. Each participant was given ninety seconds to complete three different slams. Tim Perry dunked only twice. They were fine, passable dunks, but then he pulled up limp after the second slam. He stretched at mid-court, nodded off for a few seconds, and then attempted a very similar dunk from the '93 contest - a two-handed reverse from the corner. He missed the initial try. With the 90-second clock winding down, Perry dribbled between his legs a few times, like he was waiting for a ball screen from Sharone Wright. His next attempt clanged off the rim and ricocheted into the front row as the buzzer sounded.

And that was it. Forget the dunks and the execution. The lethargic performance is what baffled me then and haunts me still today 25 years later. Have we considered that someone slipped Ambien into his water bottle? That's what I can't wrap my head around. Perry looked like he was being held hostage, like outside forces TWICE kidnapped Tim Perry and forced him to dunk on national TV. This was *Abducted in Plain Sight* without the hand jobs. Tim Perry never appeared in another NBA Dunk Contest. But, hey, know who could fly? That Terence Stansbury. He could really get up.

The Big Beers

Name: Lorenzo Brown

Height: 6'5"

College: North Carolina State

Sixers Tenure: 2013-2014

There was this incredible beer vendor at the Spectrum. I can't speak for the beer - I was seven at the time - but the dude had charisma. His, "Beer here! Get your cold beer heeeere," bellowed throughout the section. He had a presence about him. The guy owned the room. During time-outs, he asked the fans what play the Sixers should draw up. It was a great gimmick. People ate it up. After a spectator gave an answer, he would repeat it to the rest of the section.

"This young lady says we should get the ball to Barkley! You hear that Lynam! Maybe you should listen! Get it to Charles!"

One night, during a Sixers/Pacers game, this vendor stopped by our row and asked me what the Sixers should do defensively. I had been preparing for this moment my entire life.

"Stop Reggie Miller," I told him, shoving cotton candy down my gullet.

"Stop Reggie Miller!" he shouted out. "Did everyone hear that? Did you hear that Lynam? They're gonna give the ball to Miller! Everyone knows it! Even the little man knows it!" I was so proud of myself. I looked over at my dad with a smile from ear to ear. There I was, a first grader by day, defensive guru by night. After the timeout, Miller came off a few screens and knocked down a jumper. The vendor threw his hands up and said, "We told ya! We told ya Miller was gonna get it. You never listen! You never listen! Who needs a beer? Beer here! Get your cold beer heeeere!" On the way home that night, I threw up into a plastic bag. I had eaten too much cotton candy. It was the last time I ever touched the stuff.

Years later, of age now, I went to a Sixers game with my wife. The Sixers were in the early stages of their rebuild in 2013 and attendance was scarce. It was her first game at the Wells Fargo Center. I planned to ease her into Philly sporting events. I figured Sixers/Raptors in November with plenty of seats available was the gateway drug to Eagles/Cowboys and an eight-hour tailgate at the Jetro Lot. We met our friend at the seats who strolled in with the largest beer I've ever seen. He was holding a Rolling Rock filled in like a milk jug. It was gargantuan. I pointed to his beer.

"Right outside Section 211," he said. "They got big beers."

Yeah they did. Section 211 was a game changer. The beer sizes came in Theo Ratliff (large), Shawn Bradley (extra-large), and Manute Bol (they just hand you an oil can filled with High Life). The Sixers lost handedly that night, but the journey was more important than the destination. We had a blast. I danced to Fatboy Slim. I created a makeshift Philly Taco (Cheesesteak rolled up into a pizza slice). I ate a second Philly Taco. In the final minute of the game, North Carolina State rookie and newly acquired Lorenzo Brown checked in for his first NBA action. We witnessed history. We just didn't realize it at the time. I wish I did. I wish I was prepared. I wish I had some poster board, construction paper, colored markers, something. Randy's Wolfpack. Omar's Daal House. Lorenzo's Giant Slices? Do they sell cosplay pizza costumes down the street at Condom Kingdom? I'm just spitballin' here.

Lorenzo Brown was not intimidated by the 2,500 or so people still in attendance. Brown went off. He knocked down a triple, blitzed the Raptors with five points in 58 seconds of action. Give him 48 minutes and Brown was on pace for 240 points, which I'm pretty sure would've been an NBA record. Would he have gotten there? Maybe, maybe not. Raptors Coach Dwane Casey would've made some adjustments. But a 125, 130-point effort was on the table.

Lorenzo Brown only played 26 games with the Sixers. He traveled back and forth from Wilmington and the 87ers so many times that PennDOT adopted a stretch of highway in his honor. Mile marker 74 I think? After leaving Philly, Brown saw action in just over 100 games stretched across five seasons. But for those initial 58 seconds, Lorenzo Brown was a god.

The 53 Point Game

Name: Willie Burton

Height: 6'8"

College: Minnesota

Sixers Tenure: 1994-1995

"Free Willie" was a night-long feature last night at the CoreStates Spectrum and the 76ers had a whale of a good time.

Willie Burton scored a career-high and Spectrum record 53 points to lead the Sixers to an easy 105-90 win over the Miami Heat. (Groller 1994).

Pundits called Willie Burton a one-hit wonder - a flash in the pan who never before or after duplicated the performance on December 13th, 1994. They labeled Burton's game a statistical anomaly, the beneficiary of some tight officiating and 28 trips to the foul line. Critics tried to paint Burton with a broad brush, lumping him in with the likes of Tony Delk, Corey Brewer, and Chumbawamba. The signs for a monster game, though, were there all along. People just weren't looking in the right places. I'm not shocked Willie Burton dropped 53 on the Miami Heat. I'm just surprised he didn't do it sooner.

After a decorated career at the University of Minnesota, the Heat drafted Burton #9 overall in the 1990 NBA Draft. Burton could always score. In his final collegiate game, he dropped 35 points in an Elite 8 loss to Georgia Tech. In his very first NBA game, he scored 25 points off the bench in barely a half of action. That's why I'm not going to sit idly by and listen to this Willie Burton slander. "Click here for a slideshow of the Top Ten most unlikely 50-point scorers in NBA History!!!" Nah, I'll pass. I'm all set.

Burton battled some off the court issues while in Miami. He was eventually released by the Heat in early November of '94 and signed with the Sixers a few days later. Willie joined a particularly bad Sixers club, in a particularly dark time in Philly sports. The Sixers were already 0-3, and mathematically eliminated from the playoffs by Veteran's Day. Rich Kotite and the Eagles were in the midst of losing seven consecutive games after a 7-2 start. Willie Burton and his heroics weren't just a breath of fresh air. They were a lifeline. While Kotite was across the parking lot "weighing his options," Burton injected some excitement into South Philly. He demonstrated his knack for scoring immediately - consistently reaching double-digits - even when coming off John Lucas' bench.

Just four days prior, the Philadelphia Tribune ran a story about the spark he'd been giving the Sixers: "Whenever the club's offensive scheme becomes stagnated, [Coach John] Lucas is quick to holler, "Willie!" (Heisel 2015).

Clouds were forming. A storm was brewing. About a week and a half prior to the infamous night, Burton poured in 25 off the bench against the hapless Kings. Burton wasn't just part of the second unit. He was the second unit. Willie was the 6th, 7th, 8th, and 9th man. Then there was Derrick Alston. He was an advanced stats darling, if advanced stats were a thing back then. He ferociously attacked the basket, drawing fouls and getting to the charity stripe. Burton went to the foul line thirteen times against Sacramento, twelve times a few days later against the Knicks. Willie carved out a prominent role in the rotation, and he did so in a hurry. Burton was only playing in his 16th game with the club when his ex-mates, the Miami Heat, visited the Spectrum.

The stars were aligned. A hungry Willie Burton, clicking on all cylinders, playing against his former team who were on the second leg of a back-to-back. The Heat beat the Knicks in Madison Square Garden the night prior. Maybe Brad Lohaus and co. was feeling themselves a bit. Maybe they enjoyed the Manhattan nightlife after the game, got a few steaks from Smith and Wollensky. Maybe New Jersey Transit broke down, and they didn't get to their team hotel until the early morning. Like I said, the stars were aligned.

Burton torched the Heat. Miami's Bimbo Coles, Billy Owens, Matt Geiger, John Salley, Kevin Gamble - everyone - they all took a crack at Burton. Burton put 53 on 'em, masking a 4-20 performance from my guy, Clarence Weatherspoon (Spoon must've been under the weather). Willie did his damage on just 19 field goal attempts. It was an economical performance, the Prius of fifty plus point efforts. His 24-28 outing from the charity stripe just proved that in 1994, like a Heathcliff Slocumb fastball, you couldn't keep up with Willie Burton.

I watched the game with my brother and my dad – well my dad was physically there anyway. He was sound asleep on his recliner. He woke up to his sons cheering as Burton crossed the 40-point mark.

"Willie Burton has 40!" I told him.

"Willie Burton?" my dad said. His eyes still closed. "Never heard of 'em. He pitch for the Brewers last year?"

"No, no," I told him. "He was a standout at Minnesota, dad. Then he was drafted by the –"

Never mind. I didn't have time for this. Burton was now up to 43, 44 points. My dad's history lesson would have to wait. My job was to get back on defense and tally up Burton's buckets. In the fourth quarter, Willie hit a jumper on the right wing to give him 49. He high stepped back down the court like Deion Sanders on the final twenty yards of a pick six. I high stepped to my kitchen and back in solidarity.

"Willie Burton, baby," I screamed over and over. "You can't stop him!"

Moments later, he bowed to the Spectrum faithful. Coach Lucas took exception to the display of showmanship and tried to reign in Willie. Counterargument: I LOVED the showmanship. The night belonged to Willie Burton. He was our king and the 7,000 plus in attendance was his loyal subjects. Burton could do no wrong.

"Willie, if he continues to work on his game, has a chance to be special," said Lucas, the Sixers' Coach. It's a matter of [whether] he can keep that canary on his shoulders settled. Tonight, it had plenty of birdseed." (Jasner 1994).

A few years ago, some tweet popped up on my timeline regarding the aftermath of that performance. Someone recalled listening to WIP the morning after, and a caller, on a Willie Burton high, had anointed him the next Jordan. The tweet ended with something patronizing, like "lol" or the gif of that white dude blinking. That caller wasn't me, but it would've been if WIP had allowed 10-year-olds on air. Days later, my friend tried to capitalize on my Burton Fever. He tried to sell high – offered me a '92-'93 Fleer Burton – near mint – for my Ken Griffey Jr. Upper Deck rookie card.

Those Griffey cards are worthless now. I got caught up in the Burton hysteria. I basked in it. I regret nothing. Willie Burton, baby. You can't stop him.

The Seven-Year Itch

Name: Willie Green

Height: 6’3”

College: Detroit Mercy

Sixers Tenure: 2003-2010

“Thinking a Willie Green breakout season this year? Heard he’s looked great in camp.”

“Isn’t he like 34?”

For all intents and purposes, Willie Green was a nice guy. Highly regarded by his coaches and respected by his teammates, no one in Philadelphia questioned his character or his work ethic. People liked Willie Green.

But, boy, people also hated Willie Green. I don’t think it had anything to do with Green himself, but rather the idea, the concept of Willie Green. Sixers fans got Willie Green Fatigue™. If my math is right - multiply by four, carry the two - then Willie threw out the first pitch of the Phillies 1986 home opener and started in the same backcourt with Michael Carter-Williams. Officially, Green was in Philly for seven years, a painfully long excursion when every October you were reminded that, “Wait, Willie Green is still on the team?” Green was the person you went with on vacation. The first day or two are great - you’re having drinks, relaxing by the pool, taking selfies together. By day five, if you hear them ask the server if their fish is “locally-sourced” one more time, you’re going to have blood on your hands. Willie Green’s biggest crime was his longevity. It’s like if ol’ rubber arm Kyle Kendrick started every third day for the Phillies for ten consecutive years. You’re excused if you want a little variety in your life.

Green's career began innocently enough. A 2003 2nd round draft of Seattle, he was traded to the Sixers on draft night. His first two seasons were fairly nondescript. The organization liked him enough, though, to offer him an absurdly long six-year deal. Green agreed to the terms, but in a horrible stroke of luck, injured his knee playing pick-up before the contract signing.

Willie Green planned to go on vacation and relax after agreeing to a lucrative deal a few years ago with the Philadelphia 76ers.

But first, he wanted to stop by the famed St. Cecilia's gym in his hometown because that's what basketball players do each summer in the Motor City.

He played one game too many on July 9, 2005.

Green injured his left knee, and suddenly, the $20 million, six-year deal waiting for his signature was in peril. (Associated Press 2008).

He rehabbed for much of the '05-'06 season and saw action in just ten games. Billy King was determined, however. Locking up Willie Green was paramount. This time, King and the Sixers got their man, signing Green to a five-year deal. King tried to ink Willie to a 13-year deal, and he would've gotten away with it, too, if it wasn't for that pesky Collective Bargaining Agreement. Green was fine in '06-'07, I guess. Some games he dropped 20. Some games you forgot he was there. More often than not, Green chipped in 8. If this was *NBA 2K*, Willie was "Created Player" if you took no further action. Slap a 73-overall rating on him and plug him into your backcourt. Green saved his best performance for a meaningless contest that no one saw. I actually had no idea it even happened. KYW 1060 broke the news to me the next morning while I was trying to get an update on rush hour traffic. In Game 82, Willie Green poured in a career-high 37 points against the Raptors on April 18th of a Sixers season where they finished 35-47. Can you think of anything more obnoxious? The nerve of Willie. Nobody watched that Raptors game.

"Ah, Bob. Thanks for the extra ticket, but I'm sorry. I already have plans. Any other day, really, I would … I'd love to drink a bunch of beers and watch Ryan Howard mash homers against bad NL East pitching, but the 34-47 Sixers are trying to finish the season strong at Toronto. Build momentum for next season. They're ushering in a new era. The road to redemption starts Sunday afternoon at Toronto, Bob. You understand, right? Maybe next time."

If Willie Green scores 37 points in Canada in the middle of April, but no one sees it, et al. (The Phils lost 5-4 to the Nats in 13 innings on April 18th. Adam Eaton started. So maybe the Sixers/Raptors would've been a better option. Always skip an Adam Eaton start if possible).

Green played three more seasons in Philly, averaging over twenty minutes a game each year. He wasn't bad, but he wasn't coveted either. There weren't Spurs or Rockets fans conjuring up Willie Green deals on team blogs and message boards (This is 2008, mind you). Fans shouldn't hold a grudge over Willie for his contract length, or the amount of playing time he got. He wasn't Tree Rollins, Player/Coach. It wasn't his decision, but fans held it against him regardless. He was dependable, but Willie Green, starting two guard for the NBA Champion Sixers, didn't exactly roll off the tongue.

In 2010, the Sixers moved on from Green and his seven-year tenure, trading him and Jason Smith to New Orleans for Craig Brackins and Darius Songaila. Willie Green met the modest expectations placed upon him year after year after year, and that unfortunately was the problem.

The Big Nasty

Name: Corliss Williamson

Height: 6'7"

College: Arkansas

Sixers Tenure: 2004-2005

"It doesn't matter, it really doesn't matter whether you start or finish," O'Brien said. "(Thomas) is a pretty damn good player. They (Thomas and Corliss Williamson) play the same position. I've got to make a choice. Clearly, I'm more comfortable with Corliss at that spot in the fourth quarter." (Jasner 2004).

My memory of this era is a bit hazy. I was away at college at the time, and it was tough to budget NBA League Pass when my only source of income was depositing bottles and cans for five cents a pop. Outside of nationally televised games that didn't interfere with Thursday's $.50 cent mixed-drink night (I KNOW), I followed the Black Shirts blindly. I Yahoo Refresh'd. I would pull up the box score, gamecast, whatever, and frantically click refresh over and over. My most notorious Yahoo Refresh memory, and arguably the worst day of my life, was when I followed a September game between the Phillies and the Astros in 2005. Turncoat Billy Wagner served up a meatball to Craig Biggio in the top of the 9th inning - a three run bomb that was a death knell to the Phillies' playoff hopes. I just stared at the screen, hoping it was a glitch, a bad dream, anything, but no dice. Fuckin' Craig Biggio, man. Go wash your helmet. Yahoo and I have a complicated relationship.

Affectionately called "Big Nasty" - great nickname by the way - Corliss Williamson played a huge role in Nolan Richardson's "40 Minutes of Hell" Arkansas teams that ran opponents ragged in the mid-90s. He was a real problem in *Coach K College Basketball* for Sega Genesis, the step cousin of *NBA Live*. That Razorbacks team was the only one who could bottle up Virtual Kerry Kittles. Williamson had a solid, albeit unassuming NBA career before capturing the 6th Man of the Year Award in 2002. The early 2000s had seemingly an influx of power forwards. Everyone was a power forward. The entire league was seemingly 6'8" and couldn't shoot. Stretch 4s were still in their infancy at this time - Ersan Ilyasova was just getting his driver's permit - so there wasn't quite the liability in having a four, or even a small forward, who couldn't consistently hit a jump shot. Every team had the same handicap. Only a select few had Shaq or Tim Duncan.

In 2001, the Toronto Raptors traded Williamson and spare parts to Detroit for Eric Montross and Jerome "Junkyard Dog" Williams. You may remember Williams from the Sixers/Raptors '01 Eastern Conference Semifinals. He gained notoriety and TV time for being a glorified hype man on the Raptors bench. Broadcasts would seemingly cut to the Junkyard Dog after every Toronto basket, like he was Chris Christie at a Cowboys game. Williams, in kind, would wave his rally towel and yuck it up for the cameras. I hated it. Corliss Williamson, a no-nonsense guy in his own right, didn't take too kindly from being traded by Toronto - not for the second coming of Mark Madsen anyway. Williamson held a grudge. While playing the Raptors in the following season's playoffs, Big Nasty got an and-1 on the Junkyard Dog and shouted back at him, "Woof, woof, woof, motherfucker."

In their ongoing quest to complete an NBA forward bingo card, the Sixers acquired Williamson in 2004 for Derrick Coleman and Amal McCaskill. On the surface, it was a steal for the Black Shirts. DC was 37 years old at the time, was riddled by injuries, and would only play five more games in the NBA.

"I don't look at any deals as 'steals,'" King said. "I think people make deals based on what's best for their franchise. This was a fit for us. What [Pistons president of basketball operations Joe Dumars] did was a fit for what they wanted to do." (Jasner 2004).

While a nice return for Coleman, Williamson was an odd fit for a team who had just committed considerable resources to the power forward position. Corliss and Kenny Thomas played hot potato at the four spot. O'Brien designated Big Nasty as a closer of sorts - he rarely started but often finished games. He wasn't perfect, but he was more Brad Lidge than Jeanmar Gómez. He etched out his role in the half court when the offense broke down. Let Williamson face up his man from twelve feet and lower a shoulder. It sometimes produced points. It always created chaos. His style of play spread. Out of shape guys in Roxborough playing pick-up would dip their shoulder and put up a floater.

"Big Nasty!" they would scream, before trekking up to Dalessandro's for a post-game steak.

Williamson averaged just under 11 points per night in 20 plus minutes of action. He was useful, but his tenure in Philadelphia lasted only 48 games. Corliss played physical. He had a toughness and an edge to him. Big Nasty wasn't a 'Philly Guy,' but with a longer tenure? He would've been. Woof, woof, woof.

The Trentonian

Name: Greg Grant

Height: 5'7"

College: Trenton State

Sixers Tenure: 1991-1993; 1995

And point guard Greg Grant, 5'7", recently played a game in which two of his first three shots were blocked, but he finished by making 18 of 32 and scoring 51 points in summer league play.

"Greg's definitely shown he's resilient," said Suns assistant coach, Paul Westphal, who is directing the summer league group. "He has to be. If you're 5'7" and not resilient, you're a jockey, not a basketball player." (Shappell 1989).

Young Sixers fans loved Greg Grant. He was relatable. He had over a 98% approval rating from fans under the age of ten. (The 2% minority wanted to hand the keys to Brian Oliver). Here was this short player leading the break, getting steals, making these big guys look silly. It was the same reason why *Home Alone* and *3 Ninjas* were so popular. If Tum Tum was actually 6'0", would anyone care?

There is this incredible highlight reel of Greg Grant on YouTube set to Marky Mark and the Funky Bunch's "Good Vibrations" (Gscottdesign 2014). I'll pause a moment and let that sink in. Greg is all over the floor - getting to the hoop, disrupting passing lanes, and taking the lowly Timberwolves to task. Grant turned former Sixer, Scott Brooks, into a turnstile. It was the best 4:29 seconds of my life. Well, now the best 8:58 seconds of my life, because I just watched it again.

Greg Grant was a local kid who made good. The pride of Trenton, NJ, Grant was the best thing since sliced, well, pork roll. Taylor's pork roll to be exact. Greg stayed in his hometown and excelled at Division-III Trenton State (now The College of New

Jersey), which is not to be confused with Rowan College, which was formerly known as Gloucester County College. I'm expecting Rutgers to change their name to 'Beaver College' just to screw with us. The New Jersey Network (NJN) used to air Trenton State games, when they weren't showing Seton Hall hoops and reruns of *Mr. Bean.* They targeted a niche market and I was their exact demographic.

Grant was taken in the second round of the '89 Draft by the Phoenix Suns. You can't be 5'7" *and* slow in the NBA - heaven knows I tried - and Grant was anything but. He was pint-sized perfection. Nicknamed the "Water Bug," Grant flew around the court. He just wasn't on the court often. Greg saw limited minutes backing up the terrific Kevin Johnson in Phoenix before being waived in the summer of 1990. He bounced around with a few teams during training camp before beginning the season with Charlotte. The Hornets released him in December, and the Sixers pounced two weeks later. Christmas came early for the little boys and girls in the greater Delaware Valley.

On December 21, 1991, the Flyers beat the Capitals in OT on a Brad Jones game-winner (assisted by Rick Tocchet naturally) and the Sixers signed Greg Grant. Wrap a Byron Evans jersey and a Troll Doll under the tree and it was the perfect holiday season. Grant re-signed with the Sixers for one year in '92, but his agent wasn't happy with the terms. He suggested that Grant's size played a role in both the length and amount of the contract.

Keith Glass is not happy. Glass represents Grant, 26, who finished third in the NBA last season in assists-to-turnover ratio, behind Chicago's John Paxson and Charlotte's Muggsy Bogues. Grant had 217 assists and only 46 turnovers.

"I'm not happy with this deal, and I don't mind saying so," Glass said. "I don't think Greg got fair market value. I've represented a lot of players over the years, done a lot of deals, and, to me, a good deal is one that's fair on both sides."

"His alternative, obviously, was to get an offer sheet from another team. But let's be realistic: He's not 6-10, he's 5-7. Terry Mills could get a sheet worth nearly $10 million and go from New Jersey to Detroit, but nobody was going to do that for

Greg." (Jasner 1992).

I like this Keith Glass. He'll go to bat for you. People suggested I sell this book at a bargain bin price, but then my inner Keith Glass said, "Terry Mills wouldn't charge $2.99 for his autobiography, would he?" Grant's best two seasons as a pro were as a Sixer. He was a nice fit off the bench in Doug Moe's offense. Moe wanted his guards to push the ball and the Water Bug was more than happy to oblige. Lost in the heroics of Manute Bol's 18-point game against the Suns in Phoenix was Greg Grant's double-double. You have a lot more room to operate when your 7'7" center is knocking down jumpers from Flagstaff.

Not as well-known as his diminutive counterparts, Grant was Muggsy Bogues without the PR machine behind him. If the Monstars stole Greg Grant's talent instead of Muggsy's, they'd have beaten the Tune Squad by double digits. When the shorter players in the NBA are discussed, however, Grant is rarely mentioned. The Water Bug was the third wheel behind Bogues and Spud Webb. Muggsy was on the very popular expansion Hornets (everyone had a Charlotte Starter jacket). Spud Webb was the dunker, and Grant was the other one.

That's not meant to diminish Greg's achievements. A 5'7" Division-III player reached the NBA. It's as far-fetched as waking up from a four-month nap in mid-August and discovering that Ben Revere leads the National League in home runs (37; two via inside-the-park). While Grant never made the lasting impact in the league he may have hoped, sticking around for six seasons is an accomplishment in its own right. Trenton Makes. The World Takes Greg Grant highlights and sets them to "Good Vibrations" for all to enjoy.

(Seriously, go watch that video. Kenny Payne can wait).

The 2,000 Boos

Name: Kenny Payne

Height: 6'8"

College: Louisville

Sixers Tenure: 1989-1993

Payne's selection was booed immediately by the majority of the 2,000 or so season-ticket holders that showed up at the Spectrum to view the proceedings.

"They booed the selection of Dan Majerle in Phoenix last season," Philadelphia owner Harold Katz said between puffs of his cigar. "Majerle proved this season he's going to be one of the next stars in this league. We feel Kenny Payne can do the same thing." (Bostrom 1989).

I went to this summer day camp as a kid that was run by the township. You played stickball, kickball, and went to the pool a couple of times a day. I was an awful swimmer. I would just wade around in the shallow end, dodging rogue Band-Aids while other campers did cannon balls and can openers in the deep end. I was jealous of their aquatic skills, yeah, but my main focus was on Dave Hollins and his struggles at the hot corner. I had enough to keep my mind busy in three feet of water. The game, Mercy, was real popular at lunchtime. For those who weren't traumatized as a kid, Mercy is when two people interlock hands like a test of strength. The purpose is to try and push the other kid's fingers back towards their wrists until they scream, "Mercy!" One time at lunch, an older kid challenged me to a game. I was terrified, but also saw it as my ticket to instant popularity. I just had to tolerate the pain until a camp counselor inevitably broke it up – maybe ten seconds tops. The game was outlawed. The counselors always intervened. I accepted the challenge, and the entire camp circled around us.

It was a set-up. The game started, and the older kid and I locked hands. He didn't immediately try and bend my fingers back into my soul though. Something was up. I could sense it. My mind was quickly trying to reconcile "Why? What's his end game?" A few seconds later, I was pantsed. Someone else had come up behind me and yanked my swim trunks down. It was another fifteen years before I wore a bathing suit without underwear underneath. I was the "pantsed kid" for the remainder of camp. Sometimes you can't shake the one thing you don't want to be remembered for.

When you search YouTube for "Kenny Payne Sixers," one lonely Sixers-related video populates. It's an eleven second clip of Payne dunking off a dish from Hersey Hawkins. It's one of the only video remnants of Payne's time here - one isolated fossil that preserves a career and tenure that is otherwise erased from fans' consciousness. Payne's play wasn't what fans remember. Donovan McNabb was famously booed by Angelo Cataldi and his "Dirty Thirty" at the 1999 NFL Draft. But there was a precedent here. McNabb wasn't the first Philly sports draft pick to be rejected by the masses. Before there was Donovan McNabb, there was Mike Mamula. Before there was Mamula, there was Kenny Payne.

The only thing worse than Philly fans being wrong about a player is Philly fans being right about a player. It's hard to fathom a draft pick in the latter part of the first round (#19 overall) so universally panned. Every selection outside the top-10 is basically an "upside pick." Jay Bilas would greenlight the drafting of an octopus because you can't teach wingspan, but no one aside from the Sixers brass was on board with Payne.

"Hey Lance, you end up buying Val that House of Payne shirt?"

"Nah, she wanted Divac."

The overall consensus was that fans wanted Vlade Divac or Clifford Robinson or just about anyone else. The organization was forced to defend the pick just moments after the Payne selection was announced.

Lynam was clearly annoyed with the fans' assessment of the selection.

"At the end of last summer, when we made the deal for Ron Anderson, I was very excited," said Lynam, the agitation evident in his voice. "I'll let that deal stand on its own merits. I'm as excited with this pick as I was with Ron Anderson. There's no question the best guy the Sixers could have gotten with the pick was Kenny Payne." (Hilt 1989).

Payne was a left-handed swingman, and those guys always vault to the front of my draft board. But I knew Stacey Augmon. Stacey Augmon was a friend of mine, and, well you get the idea. Post-draft grade pieces were just as harsh.

Philadelphia - Kenny Payne, Reggie Cross, Tony Mack: Who??? How did the Sixers stumble on picking Payne when Roy Marble, Blue Edwards, Anthony Cook, Vlade Divac and Kenny Battle were left? Perhaps they'll have the last laugh, but the former Louisville player is a less-than-dazzling player. Grade: C. (Sefko 1989).

That "C" draft grade is a death blow. I know these grades mean very little, but a "C" doesn't make you feel good, does it? You have to hear about it from the talking heads and everyone on social media. The draft grade is a status symbol. The only "C" I want to see is on Eric Lindros' sweater. The blowback of this disastrous draft could've all been avoided incidentally three years prior. Forget Kenny Payne for a moment. In 1986, the Sixers acquired big man, Tim McCormick, and Danny Vranes from the Supersonics for Clemon Johnson and a 1989 first round pick. Seattle used that first rounder (#17 overall) to select Shawn Kemp.

"But what about the spacing issues!? Barkley and Kemp played the same position!"

Ah, shut up, nerd. Let me live.

In perhaps an attempt to silence their critics, Jim Lynam and the organization started Payne the first three games of his rookie season. It was a brief, failed experiment. Kenny was quickly relegated to the bench where he remained for the rest of his tenure. In August of '91, two Italian teams showed interest in Payne, who, per team officials, was considered "a summer league veteran" at that point.

"Summer league veteran" just meant that you've had the same job for years and can't get promoted. The Sixers actually encouraged Payne to consider the move overseas. Kenny, though, wanted to stick it out (Ford 1991).

Payne scored a career-high 24 points in a late February game in '92, but in a whopping 52-point loss to the 20-36 Charlotte Hornets, that high mark lost some of its luster. He was released in January of '93 and never played in the NBA again. Kenny Payne's story is a cautionary tale. On June 27th, 1989, the Sixers organization defied the consensus. They felt they were the smartest people in the room. On that night, they weren't. Vlade Divac would've looked great in red, white, and blue.

The Explorer

Name: Steven Smith

Height: 6'8"

College: La Salle

Sixers Tenure: 2006-2007

It became official after practice Monday, when the 76ers bookkeepers presented rookies Ivan McFarlin and Steven Smith with their tax forms to fill out.

"You do want to get paid in two weeks, don't you?" one asked Smith.

Smith nodded affirmatively.

He and McFarlin made the 76ers roster; which was finalized Monday for the season opener Wednesday. (Frank 2006).

I've always liked La Salle hoops. 'Nova had the pedigree. Temple had John Chaney. Penn was the Ivy. St. Joe's had the hawk (hey, it's something). La Salle was the underdog. They were the least discussed and received the littlest fanfare of the Big 5 schools. I gravitated towards them. I remember the "L-Train" Lionel Simmons, but his Explorer days were on the edges of my earliest basketball memories. Doug Overton and Randy Woods, they're closer to my wheelhouse. Kareem Townes, though, that was my guy. The Townes Era was my sweet spot. Townes took over twenty shots a game for three straight seasons. That wasn't enough. He should've put up forty, fifty shots. I saw La Salle battle Notre Dame and future (former) Sixer, Monty Williams, at Convention Hall. Townes dropped 38 in an 84-81 overtime win. Until Iverson entered my life, I never saw someone get so many buckets in person. I was mesmerized. In Houston that same night, the Sixers lost to the 27-4 Houston Rockets. Though I missed Orlando Woolridge chip in ten points off the bench, I think I made the right decision.

A graduate of Northeast High and later La Salle, Steven Smith was as local as it gets. You may as well start off every Steven Smith interview with, "Hey, so what's your favorite cheesesteak place?" Has to be Steve's Prince of Steaks off the Boulevard, by the way. Despite a successful four-year career with the Explorers, Smith went undrafted in 2006. Prospect evaluation shifted in a hurry. NBA Drafts in the 1990s were littered with four-year guys, but fast-forward a decade later, and their age was now considered a detriment. Their potential and their upside, teams felt, was already capped at age 21 or 22. College seniors may as well have been part of the cast of *The Golden Girls*, enjoying an unsweetened iced tea on the lanai with Blanche and Rose.

Despite not being drafted, Smith turned heads in summer league action. He joined the Golden State Warriors in Las Vegas, leading the team in both scoring and rebounding. He then took a red-eye flight from Vegas (who hasn't) back to Philly (Jasner 2006). He played for his local Sixers in the Rocky Mountain Revue Summer League in '06. Smith was terrific, making "First Team All-Tournament" in Utah along with Sixers teammate Lou Williams.

Besides MVP Marvin Williams, a five-member Revue team was chosen via voting by selected media, scouts and summer-league staff.

The honorees: Philadelphia teammates Louis Williams and Steven Smith; Utah teammates Ronnie Brewer and Paul Millsap; and Seattle's Andre Emmett.

Smith, undrafted out of LaSalle, averaged 15.7 points over six games and made scouts from at least one other NBA team besides the 76ers take notice. (ESPN 2006).

I've been an avid follower of the Rocky Mountain Revue Summer League since '74 and can confirm Smith's performance ranks right up there. Summer Leagues back then didn't carry the same notoriety as they do nowadays. Now, every Summer League game is on ESPN. Fans can take to Twitter, for better or worse. Have enough beers and you'll call one second round pick both David Robinson and Rafael Araújo in the same half.

Smith appeared in only eight games in the NBA, going scoreless in his first seven. In a December loss to the Pacers, Smith finally got in the books. He registered 5 points in a quarter of action, creating some separation between him and Casey Shaw. The game itself and Smith's first NBA bucket was overshadowed by the events of the previous day. The Sixers had traded Allen Iverson to Denver. The Indiana game was just background noise. Steven Smith remained on the team until early January before being waived. He never latched on with another franchise and later enjoyed a successful and lengthy international career. Smith was a local product, a La Salle guy, a hometown underdog who carved out his small place in NBA history.

The Red Paperclip

Name: Jeff Malone

Height: 6'4"

College: Mississippi State

Sixers Tenure: 1994-1996

Overheard at a sleepover:

Date: April 13, 1994.

Time: Approximately 8:50 P.M.

"Do you want to watch the 4th quarter?"

"Nah, Pacers are up 19. Let's play *Road Rash*."

"My mom said it was too violent. I rented *Ecco the Dolphin* instead."

There was this story fifteen or so years ago about a Canadian blogger who posted an ad on Craigslist. Not one of *those* Craigslist ads. This guy posted an ad offering to trade a single red paperclip. He eventually found a suitor and traded that paperclip for a fish pen, the pen then for a custom knob, the custom knob for a camping stove. Somewhere in this journey Alice Cooper makes an appearance, along with actor Corbin Bernsen (Roger Dorn from *Major League)*. A KISS snow globe plays a vital part. Eventually, a town in Saskatchewan, Canada offers this blogger a house for a speaking role in one of Bernsen's movies, *Donna on Demand.*

Jeff Malone is the red paper clip. Except the complete opposite.

In 1994, Philly traded Hornacek, the lynchpin of the Barkley return, to the Utah Jazz for a pick and 33-year-old Jeff Malone. In January of '96, Philly released Malone, the last branch of the Charles deal. But I wish they saw this through. The Sixers could've flipped Malone for Brian Stith, Stith for Felton Spencer, Spencer for

Cherokee Parks, and hey, who knows, five transactions later they could've ended up with a box of Clorox wipes and some fruit snacks (Sharks, ACME brand). Jeff had fallen out of favor in Utah and with their star player, Karl Malone. Over the '94 All-Star break, Karl had hinted that certain teammates were a bit lackadaisical night to night. While Jeff was never mentioned outright, reports concluded that he was the recipient of the Mailman's criticism. (Jasner 1994).

Years before his arrival in Philly, Jeff Malone thrived for the Washington Bullets in the 1980's. He has a game winner from his rookie season against Detroit to his name - a ridiculous, falling out of bounds triple from behind the backboard at the buzzer. It's a top-5 game winner. Malone was gifted offensively. He had a wide array of tricks in his repertoire, but perhaps none greater than his patented running jumper. Malone's runner was poetry, a gorgeous floater that can only be washed in the delicate spin cycle. People argue that the mid-range jumper is a lost art, but it's actually the running fifteen-footer. That shot was a staple in pee-wee hoops when a desperate kid would chuck a line drive up at the basket, hoping for a friendly bounce from the backboard gods. There was always some parent ready to yell, "Guess the bank is open on Saturday, Pete!" And if the other adults didn't laugh, he would just say it again.

Who decided that running jumpers were only designated for half-court shooting contests? You want free pizza for a year? Free tuition for a semester? You lean on the running jumper. Yet that shot's not good enough inside twenty feet? In this country, there are only like three people without any student loan debt. Relying on a made 47-foot running jumper isn't a sustainable debt relief plan, but that's all we got.

Malone arrived in February of '94 from a Utah team who routinely won 50+ games. Boy was he in for a surprise. Jeff Malone's first game here was a loss to the Hawks, then a loss to the Bullets, Cavs, Heat, Nets, the Magic, and then the Magic again. Then the Sixers turned a corner and won a game. And then they lost ten straight. Name a U.S. city: Portland, Chicago, Boston, Des Moines. Philly lost to all of 'em. The Sixers went 1-17 in Malone's first eighteen games here. Jeff Malone knew he was going east. He just didn't know he was going to the Washington Generals.

To his credit, Malone seemed like he wanted to be here. Or he portrayed that to the media anyway. Hornacek looked like he was being blackmailed. Outside of a clunker or two, Malone played well. It wasn't like Jeff forgot how to score. He just no longer had John Stockton or Karl Malone beside him. Jeff Hornacek was the younger, better player, but the first round pick the Sixers received in addition was the sweetener (#20 overall.) But when the team uses that pick to select BJ Tyler and his 55 career games, you're just one step above trading Horny for Malone and cash considerations.

Jeff joined Dana Barros in the backcourt for the '94-'95 season. It was a potent combo offensively, despite some big defensive deficiencies. He had a few big moments in the front half of the season - dropping thirty plus points a handful of times - but was plagued by health woes. An injury in late December sidelined him for three months. He returned to play exactly one other contest. Incredulously, Malone, fresh off rehab, played forty minutes that night in late March. Up until that point, Jeff had only reached the forty-minute mark three previous times. But, hey, the Sixers beat the Warriors that night to improve their record to 18-48. So ... it was worth it? Malone re-aggravated an injury and was shelved for the remainder of the year.

Jeff stuck around the following season, but with rookie Jerry Stackhouse now in the fold, Malone saw a vastly reduced role. In early January of '96, he was released and retired from the NBA later that year. He was a very good player for a very long time and the last remnants of the Charles Barkley deal. Malone's offense could mask a lot of flaws, just not the many flaws of the mid-90's Sixers.

The Situational Lefty

Name: Mark Hendrickson

Height: 6'9"

College: Washington St.

Sixers Tenure: 1996-1997

Trailing 3-0, the Phils used Chris Coste's three-run homer, Shane Victorino's two-run double, and Chase Utley's two-run homer to produce a seven-run second inning against shell-shocked lefthander Mark Hendrickson. Utley has four homers and 15 RBIs in his last five games. (Carchidi 2008).

When I was ten, like a lot of kids, I wanted to be a professional basketball player. But 4'7" gritty point guards with no off hand can barely sniff the court for their CYO team, let alone back-up Dana Barros. At age eleven, I switched gears. Told my parents I wanted to be a professional baseball player. I had just gone 3 for 4 against the ShopRite Cardinals. I was seeing the ball well. Turned out to be a mirage, however – just some shoddy Cardinals defense and a generous scorekeeper. Reality set in. I turned my sights to other careers. By age twelve, I wanted to be a doctor. A veterinarian. Then a comedian. Then a teacher. Maybe a firefighter. My goals then became more short-sighted. At age 14, I hoped the Phillies salvaged a split on their west coast road swing. At 20, I just wanted to see a girl in her bra.

Mark Hendrickson is a card-carrying member of the exclusive two-sport athlete club. He doesn't have the local ties of former NFL kicker and Philadelphia Atoms star, Chris Bahr. Hendrickson doesn't carry the clout of *Tecmo Super Bowl* legend Bo Jackson or Deion Sanders. Or even former Falcons cornerback and Cardinals outfielder, Brian Jordan, for that matter. But Hedrickson wasn't some guy who toiled in the minors. The label, 'two-sport athlete,' is used pretty liberally.

"Oh, so and so was a two-sport athlete in college. He was selected by the Padres in the 28th round, but never signed."

Bravo. Tom Brady was drafted by the Montreal Expos, yeah, but he never bunted Mark Grudzielanek over to third.

General manager Brad Greenberg had projected Hendrickson as a first-round pick. He was pleased that Hendrickson and Ryan Minor, a 6-7, 220 pound forward from Oklahoma with a deft shooting touch, were available as the draft reached the 31st and 32nd picks, both of which were owned by the Sixers. Greenberg contends that Hendrickson, Minor, and Allen Iverson, the No. 1 pick, give the team three draft choices with first-round talent. (Cawthon 1996).

Hendrickson was overmatched in the NBA, lacking the strength and athleticism to compete with the league's talent. He played sparingly in his lone season with the club, averaging just under 3 points per game. Hendrickson's biggest highlight in the NBA was being on a poster. There's an iconic photo of Michael Jordan rising up over him. I couldn't confirm the end result, but I like to think MJ dunked on Hendrickson so hard, it sent Mark all the way back to Single-A Dunedin in the Florida State League.

He started just one game for the Sixers, an April 12th loss to the Cavs. Hendrickson's insertion into the lineup dominated the headlines the next morning. It jammed up the phone lines on all the morning talk shows. The Philadelphia media wanted to know how it felt - to hear his name called during the starters' introductions, to take part in the opening tip. The press huddled around the locker of Iverson (50 points, 17-32 shooting), peppering him with questions regarding Big Mark's first start. It was a night to remember. Following the season, the Sixers made Hendrickson a free agent. He hung around the league for a couple years before transitioning to baseball.

The left-hander made his debut for the Blue Jays in 2002. Despite his towering presence on the bump, Randy Johnson he was not. Hendrickson was a bit of a soft-tosser - a guy whose high-80's fastball made even Chad Ogea blush. In baseball cliché speak, Hendrickson survived ten seasons in the Major Leagues on craftiness and guile – Don Carman Tested. Chris Wheeler Approved. Hendrickson retired from Major League Baseball in 2011 with 54 wins and a 5.03 career ERA. He also had four career sacrifice bunts. Four more than one-sport athlete, Tom Brady.

The Thump

Name: Rick Mahorn

Height: 6'10"

College: Hampton

Sixers Tenure: 1989-1991; 1999

Barkley visually expressed his feelings about Laimbeer. When Laimbeer questioned a call, Barkley pretended to cry. When Laimbeer later left the game, Barkley and Mahorn taunted him.

The Sixers taunts were played out on the court. Mahorn leveled Joe Dumars with an elbow to the head and Dumars angrily grabbed Mahorn's jersey. A foul wasn't called on Mahorn, but rather on Rodman for grabbing Barkley.

When the Pistons complained, Barkley and Mahorn gave each other a congratulatory headbutt for a job well done. (Sharp 1990).

I was seven when I played my first year of organized basketball. In one of Team Yellow's first games, an opposing player stole the ball and looked to break. This kid didn't conform to the fundamental rules of basketball. Dribbling was beneath him. He carried the ball under his arm like a halfback and sprinted down the floor. I looked incredulously at the ref (see: the opposing coach), who had swallowed his whistle. It was up to me, I figured. I watched a lot of Sixers basketball on Prism, and if I learned anything, it's that the smart play was to stop the break. "Smart foul," the announce team would say, or a "heads up decision by Johnny Dawkins" to commit the reach-in at half court. Imitation is the sincerest form of flattery, so I tracked the kid down and fouled him. I gave him a two-handed shove in the back and watched him face plant on the foul line. The ball rolled idly into a row of medal folding chairs as parents of both teams gasped.

I led the Pee Wee League in flagrant fouls that season with one. My mom was the assistant coach and pulled me out of the game. She asked me why I pushed the kid. I pleaded my case.

"Johnny Dawkins or Hersey Hawkins – when the other team has a fast –" I stammered.

"Dave, you can't just push someone."

"But Dr. Jack Ramsay says ..."

"Go apologize to him."

"But mom!"

"Go apologize to him, Dave."

I gave the kid a half-hearted apology and told him I had four more fouls left to dish out.

Rick Mahorn didn't take shit from anyone. A physical rebounder and enforcer, Mahorn lasted eighteen years in the NBA by being the closest thing to Dave Schultz. His highlight reel looks like a mashup of Kimbo Slice fight videos. If he was on your team, you loved him. If he wasn't, you loathed him. He was like Terrell Owens in that regard. Mahorn fought everyone on the Bulls, Celtics, Hawks, and Lakers. He fought Barkley while in Detroit. Then he came to Philly and fought the Pistons. Squaring off against Los Angeles in the '89 Finals, he got into altercations with AC Green twice, James Worthy twice, and Michael Cooper twice. Mark McNamara wisely didn't want to catch those hands.

Today's rules are much stricter - the league is way more protective of their players. But in the 80s? It was thunderdome. Mahorn didn't commit any cheapies. He didn't lead the league in reach-in fouls. If a player dared to attack the basket, they got a forearm to the thorax. He took offense to any opponent who had the audacity to attempt a lay-up. He was a member of Detroit's "Bad Boys," along with Bill Laimbeer and Dennis Rodman, and he may have been the toughest of the bunch. Opposing teams, opposing fans, they hated the Pistons. Their style of play was ugly and dirty, but they won. If Monopoly has taught us anything, it's that second prize in a beauty contest only gets you $10. There's no money in winning pretty.

Shortly after winning the '89 Championship, Mahorn was left unprotected and made available to the Minnesota Timberwolves and Orlando Magic for that year's expansion draft. Minnesota drafted Rick with their first pick at #2 overall. He was devastated at the thought of leaving Detroit. (Brown 1989).

Mahorn, the Timberwolves' first player chosen in the NBA expansion draft, has been unsuccessful so far in renegotiating his contract. He said Tuesday he wants to be traded and would rather retire than play for the Wolves.

"I really don't want to say much, but I am serious," he told the Detroit News after working out with some of his former Pistons teammates at the University of Michigan. "I don't want to play for them." (Associated Press 1989).

With both parties at an impasse, the Sixers swooped in and acquired Mahorn for a 1990 first round pick and two future seconds. A year later, Philly again traded their first rounder - this time for Manute Bol. The lack of draft capital, in addition to the poor Barkley return, left the cupboard bare after Charles' 1992 departure. The moves were short-sighted, but they also had a superstar with whom they were trying to win now.

There was excitement in Philly surrounding the Mahorn trade. If there ever was a Philly guy, gosh, Rick was it. Flashbacks of the Broad Street Bullies cross-checking opponents into oblivion danced through Philadelphians heads. Philly wants their teams to win, but, if they have their druthers, they also want to kick someone's ass in the process. Mahorn and Barkley together were known as the duo, Thump and Bump. Everyone who's anyone in the tri-state area had a Thump and Bump caricature t-shirt. It was a rite of passage in 1991, like booing Von Hayes.

"Get the bat off your shoulders, Von! You're getting paid to swing! Boooo! Boooo!"

Mahorn joined the Sixers right before their season opener. Aided by an ass the size of Montgomery County, he anchored a defense that improved in both opponents point per game and defensive rating from the season prior. He was named 2nd Team All-Defensive Team for his efforts. The Sixers clinched their first Atlantic Division title since 1983, finishing the regular season with 53 wins. Their division-clinching victory happened at the Palace of Auburn Hills against Detroit. Fittingly, the game ended in a brawl.

Isiah Thomas had been tossed moments earlier for taking two swings at Mahorn. Rick didn't even flinch. It was like a featherweight throwing a jab at Lennox Lewis. Mahorn laughed it off and flashed a look like, "Is this guy serious?" Moments later, in the waning seconds with the game well in hand, Rick took an inbound pass from Mike Gminski and dribbled the length of the court. He had a few options here. So let's play a game called, "Choose Your Own Mahorn Adventure?" Did he:

A) Reset up top

B) Dribble out the clock in the corner

C) Cross half-court and hand the ball off to a guard

D) Dunk it on Dennis Rodman for the And-1. Then stare daggers

If you chose "A," "B," or "C," please turn to page 232.

Kidding. Stay here. The answer was of course "D." Laimbeer took exception to the taunt and shoved the ball in Mahorn's face. Barkley then raced over and took a swing at Laimbeer. He caught Laimbeer with a left hook and gave the Detroit instigator a black eye. Both men then spilled over to the corner of the baseline near the first row of fans. The melee was on the side of the floor closest to the Pistons bench. The Detroit reserves rushed over to assist Laimbeer and/or break-up the fight, depending on the player. Mahorn was boxed out by the entire Detroit second unit. He yanked big James Edwards, a mountain of a man with a healthy Fu Manchu, pulling him off the scrum. Edwards and Mahorn then locked up. Pistons guard Vinnie Johnson moved between the two big men, attempting to play peacekeeper.

Things settled down for a few moments until Laimbeer, who had to walk past the Sixers bench to get to the Detroit locker room (a recipe for trouble), got into a heated exchange with Philly hero, Ron Anderson. Anderson said, and I'm paraphrasing here, "Here, someone hold these wristbands. Got some lightwork to take care of." While the players and coaches tried to break *this* confrontation up - and this next sequence was my favorite - Charles Barkley, who was also ejected with Laimbeer, walked off the court UNSUPERVISED. You don't take a field trip and let the bad kid in your class wander off without a chaperone.

Seconds later, the Sixers bench pointed towards the tunnel where Barkley was in a shouting match with some fans. The entire team rushed over to hold back Charles, and finally, finally managed to usher him back to the locker room.

Charles Barkley and Bill Laimbeer were suspended just one game. (Associated Press 1990).

Mahorn played two seasons with the Sixers, with both campaigns ending in playoff losses to Jordan and the Bulls. That first season with Mahorn, that team was the Sixers best opportunity at a Finals run. Trailing 2-1 in the Eastern Conference Semis to Chicago, Philly coughed up a double-digit lead in the second half at The Spectrum. The demoralizing loss effectively ended the series. Chicago won convincingly in Game 5.

Philly and Rick parted ways after the '91 season. His offensive numbers slipped, and he had a very disappointing series against the Bulls, averaging less than 3 points and 4 rebounds. Mahorn moved to the five spot after the Gminski trade mid-year, which could explain some of his struggles. Rick was a power forward, who was forced to play out of position for the first time in his career.

Eight years later, Mahorn signed with the Sixers for one final stint in February of '99. Rick was 40 years old during his final cup of coffee with Philly. He was the oldest player in the league at the time, and had teamed with guys like Elvin Hayes and Wes Unseld, who had played with guys like Pat Riley and Bob Ferry (father of Danny Ferry). Mahorn bridged these two enormous generational gaps, a crazy factoid or footnote, like the first time you heard that the 10th U.S. President John

Tyler, who was in office from 1841-1845, has two living grandchildren. Mahorn retired after the 1999 season, finishing a career that spanned across two full decades. His eighteen years were certainly eventful, highlighted by one championship and a laundry list of altercations. Mahorn was a character, a brawler, a great teammate. You wanted him next to you instead of across from you.

The Headband

Name: Brandon Davies

Height: 6'10"

College: Brigham Young

Sixers Tenure: 2013-2014

But the 6-10, 240-pound rookie is making quite an impression with the Sixers.

"He's got a real motor," Brown said of the forward. "He's got a tenacity that you are born with ... I love the way he plays." (Pompey 2013).

Everyone knows Brandon Davies' story. Davies played with a Jimmer Fredette-led Brigham Young team that raced out to a 27-2 record in 2011, before he gained national notoriety for reasons off the court. Davies was suspended in March of that year by the University for having sex with his girlfriend, which means that all of my friends would've graduated from BYU with a clean record. The Brigham Young Honor Code requests that one commits to a chaste and virtuous life. So, as a serious broadcast journalist - R.I.P. Bobby "The Brain" Heenan - I went back and immersed myself in this incident. I watched the coverage of the Davies suspension from *SportsCenter*, *PTI*, went down the Reddit rabbit hole, and - don't judge - even *Jim Rome*. That then led to the Jim Everett appearance on *Jim Rome*, then the 1989 L.A. Rams video yearbook (I fast-forwarded past their Wild Card Round win over the Birds naturally). Finally, after three hours of Flipper Anderson highlights, I caught an interview from CNN with a representative from BYU.

The Brigham Young rep suggested that Brandon Davies turned himself in - that he reported the violation to the school and his coach (CNN 2011). Which I call bullshit. I'm not surprised that a college kid wanted to tell someone that he just had sex. I just don't think the BYU Honor Code Office would be their first choice.

Davies probably did what every other college kid did. He told a few buddies while waiting in line for the waffle maker at the dining hall. What we have here is a nark. Was it a jaded ex? A teammate lobbying for more playing time? I'm not implying anything, but I am curious about Reno Mahe's whereabouts around that time.

Davies was reinstated to the team the following year and played two more fruitful seasons with BYU. He landed with the Clippers summer league team and joined the Sixers main roster days before the start of the 2013 season. He had some John McEnroe in him - both in effort and headwear. Brandon Davies' headbands created a fashion renaissance in Philly. It was a quick and easy way to identify the Real Hoopers on the playground. While a fashion icon, Brandon's playing time with the Sixers was sporadic. He seemingly took a three-month cruise in early January of that season. It's a bit clunky, but the name of the ship appears to have been, "Did Not Dress: Coach's Decision."

"Hey, you've seen Davies lately?"

"Hmm. Last I heard the cruise ship was spotted in Antigua in the West Indies. But that was like a month ago."

In one of Brandon's last few games with the team, Toronto's James Johnson dunked on Davies so violently that Johnson himself was cited for a violation of BYU's Honor Code. It was an unfortunate final memory for Brandon and his Sixers stint. Sam Hinkie traded him in December 2014, right in the *middle* of a game against Atlanta. Davies didn't play that night. The elusive 'DNP: Traded' is as rare as the 5-4-3 triple play. The trade involved a whole mess of players that would take three paragraphs to list out. But his departure had an effect on Brett Brown.

"When you start losing people that you are very fond of and have tremendous respect for ... there is a human side of it that bothers me because you are trying to grow chemistry, you are trying to grow a culture," Brown said after Thursday's practice.

"That takes a hit when teammates lose teammates. There is a respect, effort-wise, of how they go about their business. There is a reality to our job that is just

business in the NBA, but it doesn't mean it has to feel right." (Lynam 2014).

Davies developed a bit of cult following among the Process Trusters - like those who've seen special screenings of *The Room*. Davies' game was never the draw. It was the idea of Brandon Davies, what he represented. His shortcomings were never due to a lack of effort. He was a castoff, yeah, but he was our castoff.

The Contract

Name: Scott Williams

Height: 6'10"

College: North Carolina

Sixers Tenure: 1994-1999

Williams didn't blink when somebody wondered why a team would make a seven-season commitment to a 26-year-old forward-center with modest career averages of 4.7 points and 4.4 rebounds.

"I know what I can do," Williams said. "I've done it in practice. I've done it in games when Horace Grant and Bill Cartwright were out, when the opportunity was there. (Jasner 1994).

My mom broke the news to me.

I was in my room, surrounded by three ring binders and a Beckett's pricing guide. I was holding a '91 Skybox Hersey Hawkins. The edges were sharp, the picture, slightly off-center. It was summer.

"Dave, can you empty the dishwasher?"

"It's only worth 35 cents?" I asked, ignoring my chores. "Down a nickel from last month." I made a note in my notebook.

"Oh, the Sixers signed someone...a forward...Williams."

I perked up. "Buck? Walt? Was it Walt, mom?"

Scott Williams signed a seven-year (seven year!) contract with the Sixers back in 1994. When he finally left Philadelphia, sometime in the year 2015, Williams had a lower approval rating than every American not named Herbert Hoover - and even that's debatable, depending on which historian you ask. The most memorable note about Scott Williams' Sixers stint was its length. Basketball-Reference says that

Scott Williams played just five seasons for the Sixers. His tenure doubled both Jimmy Rollins and Éric Desjardins, so I'm not sure how that's possible. Sixers fans don't need to fact-check that. We lived through it.

After four years in Chapel Hill, Scott Williams went undrafted before signing with the Chicago Bulls. It was a soft landing for the big man. He stumbled into one of the greatest dynasties in NBA history. He played four seasons in Chicago, racking up as many rings as my basketball card binders. He had been hampered by injuries in previous seasons, which makes the length of the contract Katz handed out even more perplexing. Teams always get enchanted with role players on winning teams, like it's this sort of tangible quality that can be transferred city to city.

"Scott's flight lands at 4:00, but his winning pedigree should touch down around 6:45."

Williams played with Jordan and Pippen. Chicago could've rounded out their bench with the cast of *Family Matters* and still would've run through the league. But I don't fault Scott Williams. He capitalized on the opportunity. On his résumé, Williams just wrote, "RINGZZZ," like some Cowboys fan on the internet.

In his inaugural season in Philly, Scott provided 6 points and 6 boards in 77 games. If you applied some exponential growth theory to those numbers, Williams would turn into Wilt Chamberlain by year seven. As it stood, his first year as a Sixer was probably his best. His time in Philly was marred by various injuries. When he was on the court and healthy, the big man was booed, and booed loudly. Terry Francona and the boys were on the road for 81 games a year, so the fans needed someone to boo in the interim - like an emcee at a comedy show. Someone to rile up the crowd before the headliner took the stage.

"Good evening, everyone! Thanks for joining us at Helium. Who's excited to boo Francona and the bullpen later tonight? They're 25 games under .500! Let's hear your displeasure! Let's cup those hands together ..."

Even in wins, Williams was crapped on by the boo birds.

One of the few negatives of the night was the constant booing directed towards reserve center Scott Williams, who made about six pump fakes on a layup before missing a dunk in the first quarter. He was booed from that point on.

When asked if he would miss the home crowd since the euphoria seems to be growing, Brown responded by joking: "I don't think Scott Williams will." (Smith 1998).

Entering the '98-'99 season, the first year Larry Brown took the Sixers to the playoffs, there was Scott Williams, still there, still present, still getting booed. In the second game of the year, in a home opening win against Orlando, the Philly faithful were happy to have the team back after the lockout. The First Union Center was in good spirits, except for every time Scott Williams entered the contest. (Finocchiaro 1999).

It was the last game Scott Williams ever played for the Sixers. He found himself back on the injured list shortly thereafter. One month later, he was included in the Tim Thomas deal that brought Tyrone Hill to Philadelphia. Williams lasted four plus seasons as a Sixer. He got close but didn't see his contract finish in Philly. His teammate Lucious Harris also signed a seven-year deal, but he barely lasted one campaign. Harris never faced the same wrath, though. Lucious was jettisoned too quickly. Williams was an accessible and consistent target for the home faithful. With Scott now out of the picture, the fans had a chance to catch their collective breath, regroup. Focus their sights on another big man with a healthy contract.

More on Matt Geiger in another chapter.

The Jersey

Name: Greg Graham

Height: 6'4"

College: Indiana

Sixers Tenure: 1993-1995

That reality - completed at 2 p.m. - involved sending shooting guard Hersey Hawkins to Charlotte in return for a 1994 first round draft choice, guard Dana Barros, power forward Sidney Green, and the rights to guard Greg Graham, a first-round pick of the Hornets last June.

And, even though Sixers owner Harold Katz said, "I wouldn't have done it without Graham ... Graham makes the whole deal," the centerpiece coming to the Sixers is the pick. (Jasner 1993).

You become a creature of habit while writing these. I jot down personal memories, check YouTube for any clips/highlights/interviews, then Google the player's name. The search results are formulaic, the pattern obvious. Google spits out your subject's Wikipedia page, their Basketball-Reference page, and - HOLY SHIT - what's this?

Is that a Greg Graham jersey for sale!? A real, live Greg Graham Sixers jersey in the wild? Pinch me, I must be dreaming.

"#11 Greg Graham 76ers Sixers Champion Jersey Mens Indiana Hoosiers Rare"

Your cotdamn right that's rare, Mr. or Ms. eBay seller. For the uneducated, randomly finding a Greg Graham jersey, a reserve guard who started eighteen games in five years with four different teams, is like seeing a game-worn Danny Tartabull Phillies jersey on Antiques Roadshow.

The seller wanted $79.99, or 'make an offer,' for this absolutely stunning piece. That's what you call rare art, a 'piece.' Was $79.99 fair market value? Hell if I knew, but perhaps the name on the back doesn't dictate the price. The value was in its obscurity. For instance, the most expensive *Starting Lineup* action figure isn't a Michael Jordan, but actually the ultra-rare 1988 Karl Malone figure. Supply and demand, et al. The jersey, I figured, would fly off the eBay shelves. People just didn't know it existed – not yet anyway. How many people in 2020 Google "Greg Graham Sixers" on average per day? I don't have the analytics in front of me, but probably enough to make me nervous. I already missed out on that Hersey Hawkins jersey. Opportunity only knocks so many times. If you see Bigfoot in the forest, you snap a photo. You don't wait for a smile and better light.

I was deliberating a low-ball counteroffer, but then remembered an infuriating experience I had when selling my Wes Hopkins jersey. The buyer was asking strange questions with weird phrasing like, "How can you assure me that the jersey is the authentic color of the Philadelphia Eagles team we both know and love?" This back and forth went on for weeks. I think I became pen pals with a Russian bot.

I increased my initial offer to $40. I wasn't expecting to close the deal, but I threw some feelers out there. The seller responded quickly and counter-offered: $69.99. The dealer was playing hard ball. Who was going to blink first? I lobbed one more counter-offer and it worked. I am now the owner of a #11 Greg Graham jersey, maybe the only one of its kind. I was a proud papa. I was beaming. I sent a photo to my brother and some friends.

"Look at this beauty," I wrote. "A Greg Graham jersey."

"Wasn't Greg Graham #20?" one asked.

Come again? I rushed to the internet to confirm. Per Basketball-Reference, Greg Graham wore #20 for the Sixers (Basketball-Reference 2020). Fuck me. What an oversight. What have I done? I may as well have bought a Reggie White #47 jersey. I was suckered. Panicked, I then did an image search for Greg Graham. Most of his basketball cards have him wearing #11 – the fuck was going on here? Was I caught up in a giant conspiracy concocted by Fleer and Skybox? Was there a jersey number switch tied to Ron Anderson's departure? Why was anyone wearing Ron Anderson's #20 for that matter? Show some respect. For years, I dedicated my life to solving one great mystery: Why did Eric Matthews from *Boy Meets World* suddenly become a complete moron when he entered college? Now, I had another conundrum on my hands.

Why did Greg Graham switch jersey numbers?

I tried to track Graham down on Twitter, but he's off the grid. I slid into the DMs of some Indiana Basketball Historical Society, hoping they had a lead, or knew Graham's last known whereabouts. But like the reason behind Eric Matthews' sudden IQ drop, the truth eluded me. The best that I could conclude from my research was this:

Greg Graham wore #11 as a rookie in '93-'94. The Sixers signed Manute Bol in March '94. Manute used to wear #10 in Washington and Golden State, but #10 was set aside for Mo Cheeks' eventual jersey retirement. Bol wore #11 in his first stint as a Sixer, and then, upon his return to Philly, asked Graham for his #11 back. Greg obliged and switched to #20. I think anyway. I spent like two months trying to figure this out. Or maybe Graham switched numbers to increase jersey sales? If so, it was a successful marketing strategy since I'm now on the hunt for a #20 Graham jersey to complete the set.

On paper, and according to most accounts at the time, the Sixers won the Hersey Hawkins trade. The Graham selection by the Charlotte Hornets just two months prior had received high praise from pundits (Chandler 1993). So acquiring a first-round rookie as essentially a 'thrown-in' was a cherry on top of the Dana Barros sundae. It was a shrewd trade by a Sixers brass, who had stumbled over their own ineptitude time and time again. Graham played for Bobby Knight at Indiana, where he developed the reputation as a versatile guard who could play both positions. But stuck behind Barros and Hornacek (and later Jeff Malone), Greg struggled to carve out a role in his rookie campaign. Not showing much that first year, expectations were low for the young guard, but a strong training camp altered that perception. He was even tied to a trade rumor involving a straight-up deal with New Jersey for Rick Mahorn during this time, but John Lucas quickly dismissed that rumor. Maybe this was Graham's year after all.

For a long while, Greg Graham appeared to be nothing more than the fifth guard, a prospect who had to find his niche. But from the start of training camp, Graham's stock has risen consistently. (Jasner 1994).

What fans had here was a good ol' fashioned break-out candidate. "Buy all the shares of Greg Graham," wrote the random fantasy basketball expert in their 1994 newsletter.

"**Buy Low:** Greg Graham (Guard, Sixers. ADP: 237): Give me all the Greg Graham shares. The second-year guard should play a larger role in Lucas' system. Reports from camp are glowing. He's a bargain bin find that you can get in the final round or even on waivers. Has potential to stuff the stat sheet, and that's a lottery ticket worth buying late in drafts. I'm all in on G-Squared.

Sell High: Dominique Wilkins (Forward, Celtics. ADP: 22): People are falling in love with the name, but the new Celtic now has to compete for opportunities with Dino Radja, Dee Brown, and Sherman Douglas. Not sure if there are enough basketballs to go around. 'Nique will be taken early, but it won't be by me."

The Greg Graham Hype Train left the station, but it never got on track. There was a saturated market at the two-guard spot with Willie Burton (when Lucas went big), Jeff Malone, Jeff Grayer, Alphonso Ford, and every other shooting guard within a hundred-mile radius of the Spectrum. Graham hit three triples and scored 20 points in a December '94 road loss to the Jazz, but those minutes were a result of Jeff Malone's absence.

He spent the remainder of the season as a backcourt casualty, the fourth outfielder to Barros and whichever other guard John Lucas was smitten with that particular week. Graham's future in Philly was tenuous. Not even a month into the '95-'96 campaign, Greg was included in the Shawn Bradley deal to New Jersey. I think Graham wore #20 for the Nets, but who knows anymore.

The Hammer

Name: Armen Gilliam

Height: 6'9"

College: UNLV

Sixers Tenure: 1991-1993

I may be in the minority here, but I loved Armen Gilliam. He scored points. When you're a kid and trying to select your favorite players from your favorite team, you have a pretty short checklist.

Does this person score points? Check one.

Yes ___

No ___

I didn't open up a pack of cards (Definitely not Stadium Club. I'm not a trust fund baby), and cross my fingers hoping for a Johnny Dawkins or an Eric Murdock. Passing wasn't a concern of mine. Neither was defense. It's why I obsessed over Dana Barros' point total night after night and named my pet hamster Willie Burton. Armen Gilliam's only concern was scoring. I could get behind that.

Armen Gilliam was also doomed on arrival. When the best player on the team and one of the most popular figures in the city turns on you, the fans will inevitably follow suit. Gilliam was a square peg in a round hole, an awkward fit that stunted the team's trajectory. He was brought in to complement Charles Barkley, yet they played the same position. Their games clashed, because their styles were so similar. Hell, even their personalities clashed. Charles was outspoken and a notorious partyer. Armen was more reserved. He never drank or smoked. Out from under Barkley's shadow or criticism, the Hammer may have thrived. But that's not the story we have to tell.

Dubbed "The Hammer" by a UNLV teammate because of his stout frame, the moniker has survived the test of time (Downey 1987). 'The Hammer' stuck. Centuries from now, a parent will ask their son or daughter to hand them the hammer, and the child will perk up and ask, "You mean Gilliam or Greg Valentine?" The parent and child will share a laugh, before putting a nail in the wall for their Philadelphia 76ers 3088 NBA Champions framed poster.

Armen Gilliam had a second, lesser-known nickname, like how "Old School Chevy" Elton Brand was also, "Chief Beef." Gilliam was also dubbed the "Black Hole." Once that ball went into the low block, it never came out. But was that an indictment? The Hammer was a point getter. His job wasn't to get others involved. He was a low-post scorer, not a volunteer sign-up sheet.

After a loss to Indiana in the Final Four of the 1987 NCAA Tournament, Gilliam was selected #2 overall by the Phoenix Suns. His knack for scoring followed him to the NBA, where he averaged double figures his first nine seasons. He was the epitome of low-block consistency. If Gilliam's game was rock, paper, scissors, the Hammer just threw rock over and over again. Armen also had some George McGinnis in him. His left hand slid off the ball early - his jump shot and free throw was essentially one-handed. It was like his opposite hand was a tourist who just stopped to ask the ball for directions before going about its way. But in the post was where Armen did his handy work. You don't get dubbed, "The Hammer," and spend your career shooting elbow jumpers.

Gilliam moved from Phoenix to Charlotte, before coming over to the Sixers mid-season in early January '91 for Mike Gminski. The timing of the acquisition was interesting. Did the Sixers think the potential of the Barkley, Gminski, and Mahorn frontcourt was capped? Gminski was struggling that season, shooting a career-low 38% from the floor at the time. Maybe it was a panic move. The Sixers were in the midst of their annual Christmas west coast road swing, and had lost handedly at the Suns, Lakers, and the Sonics. Perhaps it was a combination of multiple factors. Gilliam provided a more consistent scoring punch than the G-Man, was also much younger, but was not nearly as capable a defender. The Sixers went just 25-27 (albeit it with Barkley missing some time) after the Gilliam acquisition, never seemingly able to gel. Barkley openly criticized Armen, both in public and behind closed doors. The Hammer's rebounding, or lack thereof, was a consistent source of contention.

"He can play, and he plays hard," Barkley said. "People think Armon and I have problems, but we've never had cross words. I criticized his rebounding once, but that's because I made the mistake of reading the paper. The paper said Armon Gilliam had one defensive rebound in two games. If he has one defensive rebound in two games and we're getting killed on the offensive boards, then he's not doing his job." (Ford 1991).

After getting ousted by the Bulls in the second round, the Sixers had a myriad of issues entering the '91-'92 season. Barkley was unhappy, and openly wondered if a trade was the best thing for him. Playing Charles and Armen together, after a half-season case study, was an experiment that produced disappointing results. It wasn't quite Nerlens Noel and Jahil Okafor together, but it was a glaring issue. Unless Armen Gilliam suddenly developed an outside jumper, or grew three inches, it was a problem without a viable resolution. Also, Barkley's buddy, Rick Mahorn, was now gone - replaced with Charles Shackleford who served only to take some of the brunt of Barkley's ire away from Gilliam. Then there was the autobiography.

Barkley, along with co-writer, Roy S. Johnson, had co-authored, *Outrageous!: The Fine Life and Flagrant Good Times of Basketball's Irresistible Force*, which got published in early '92. By the end of '91, excerpts from the book got leaked to the media. Barkley criticized some of his current teammates - Gilliam and Shackleford being the most notable. When confronted about the negative comments, Barkley pivoted and said he was misquoted - a dubious explanation when it's your autobiography.

"I can't believe anybody that has a brain would believe he was misquoted in his own book," Gilliam said. "He apologized and said things in the book were mistakes.

But Simon & Schuster is a reputable company. They don't make those kinds of mistakes. (Ford 1991).

Gilliam started 81 games that season, putting up just under 17 points and 8 rebounds per contest. But the team's seven-game losing streak in November and a disastrous March cemented the Sixers' first losing record in a number of years. Barkley was then moved to the Suns in the offseason. Armen averaged double figures again during the '92-'93 campaign, but his playing time took a huge hit, a casualty of Doug Moe's system. "Dump it into the Hammer" wasn't exactly an option in Moe's playbook. Gilliam for the most part, and to his credit, had taken the high road after Barkley's public criticisms. His frustrations boiled to the surface though, when Barkley and the Suns came to the Spectrum in March of '93.

Philly's Prodigal Son received a hero's welcome and a standing ovation when introduced by the PA announcer. Charles really was the precursor to "Stone Cold" Steve Austin. An unapologetic anti-hero who hated his boss and spoke his mind. Philadelphians ate it up. Barkley had flaws fans conceded, but the finger should be rightfully pointed at everyone else. On this night, and in an interesting sub-plot, the fans saved their booing for the home team and Gilliam himself. The Hammer did get to exact a bit of revenge on Barkley. Armen took a long rebound the length of the court and dunked over a waiting Charles, who was preparing for the rejection. The crowd erupted. Gilliam even flashed Barkley a post-dunk stare. But the Hammer's postgame comments made it clear that the negative reaction from the Spectrum faithful bothered him.

"I think it was Charles' comments and some of the things said by Doug Moe, who never really liked me, that have painted a negative perception of me in this town. It became a thing where today, the people rooting for Charles Barkley were rooting against Armon Gilliam and vice versa. Being the megastar he is, obviously more people were rooting for him. I'm the bad guy." (Groller 1993).

For one season, Armen Gilliam was my favorite player in the NBA. I didn't follow superstars around and collect jerseys from other teams. My favorite player was always a Sixer. That was a hard rule (My only transgression was once asking my mom for a Tim Hardaway jersey. I still feel guilty about it). Barkley left Philly so I adopted a next man up policy. My guys were now the Hammer and the Hawk. A year later it would be Clarence Weatherspoon. The Gilliam Experiment was a failed one, but at 8, 9 years old, I didn't care about fit or spacing or defense (as if). The Hammer checked all the boxes. He scored points. What was more important than that?

The Yeoman

Names: Tony Massenburg

Height: 6'9"

College: Maryland

Sixers Tenure: 1996

"The Sixers thank Tony Massenburg for his contributions last season and wish him well as he pursues his basketball career elsewhere," 76ers general manager, Brad Greenberg said. "He has carved out a niche for himself in this league as a result of his hard work and rugged style." (Associated Press 1996).

Does Brad Greenberg just thank Massenburg publicly for his contributions, or does he also sign Tony's 1995-1996 Sixers Yearbook or something? Maybe write something a bit more personal.

Yo Tony!

I can't believe the year is over already. It went by so fast!

You've carved out a niche for yourself in this league as a result of your hard work and rugged style. Stay cool this summer. K.I.T.

Thanks for your contributions,

Brad (aka "Greeny")

It would've been a nice touch by Greeny is all I'm saying. Tony Massenburg came over with Ed Pinckney in a trade with Toronto for Sharone Wright. Hindsight is of course 20/20, but it sure seems like there were a bunch of trades in the 1990s that ultimately didn't move the needle one way or the other. It's like when I agonized over trading my Kevin Maas rookie card for weeks, before ultimately pulling the trigger on a 1990 Bowman Andres Galarraga. What was the thought-process of these general managers? Sharone Wright obviously didn't pan out, but what was the end goal? Wright butted heads with John Lucas, but it was a 'sell low' move - spats with the coach or not.

@NBAInsideStuff

See Ahmad Rashad and his exclusive interview with the newest member of the #Raptors #SharoneWright! And we'll have bloopers and more! Tune in Saturday morning on @NBC!

10:07 AM · Feb 23, 1996

18K Retweets 47K Likes

The Sixers would've gotten *killed* for making a trade like this in today's world. I would've disabled Twitter and immersed myself in a book or burned mixed CDs for the next six days. It's the same thing I do after an Eagles loss. There may have been some logic to the Wright move, though.

"Sharone showed tremendous progress at the end of last year and the beginning and middle of this year. Then he began to fade," said John Lucas, the Sixers' fourth head coach since 1992. "He lacked aggressiveness. I thought he'd improve quicker than he did. We were not willing to wait for him to make progress. When we traded to get D.C. (Derrick Coleman), we had to move a little quicker." (Long 1996).

Now before you bash John Lucas for "having to move a little quicker" and finding a correlation between 'a quicker upward trajectory' with two journeymen who played the same position, it should be noted that Pinckney and Massenburg's contracts expired after the end of the '96 season. This trade was nothing more than a salary dump. But the idea of making these moves to build around Derrick Coleman of all people? DC was in his late 20s at this point. He didn't want to be in Philly and had never reached the second round of the playoffs. It was a flimsy strategy at best. Spoiler alert: The '96-'97 Sixers did not qualify for the postseason.

Tony Massenburg played for everyone. That's not hyperbole. Massenburg really played for everyone. The only teams he didn't suit up for were the Lakers and the Spirits of St. Louis. His seventh NBA stop was with the Sixers and he knew his time in Philly was temporary.

"The 76ers were the worst team in the league," says Massenburg. "Horrible top-to-bottom. Knowing I wouldn't be there long, I spent a lot of time on South Street and at King of Prussia Mall shopping." (SI 2005).

Massenburg was also attached to one of my favorite - and one of the more underrated catchphrases, or 'Zoo-isms' of Marc Zumoff: "yeoman-like." This catchphrase was a B-side track. It never got the radio play or received the fanfare of "locking all windows and doors" or "we're on the seesaw," but the diehards know. They know. "Yeoman-like" work on the glass or "yeoman-like" effort on the defensive end are all appropriate and acceptable examples of this deep cut. And nobody had a better "yeoman-like" reference to play ratio than Tony Massenburg. Now, I had no idea what, or who the Yeomans were, but I was determined to find out.

So, this was 1996 mind you, I pulled out our family's Encyclopedia Britannica and researched. There was one small problem: I didn't have the slightest idea on how to spell 'yeoman.' It's not like Zumoff spelled it out during a Sixers/Nets telecast.

"Another floorboard by Massenburg – yeoman-like effort tracking down that loose ball. And hey, Sixers fans, don't forget. There's an 'e' in 'Yeoman.' Coach Lucas is gonna take a quick twenty second timeout. Set something up out of the break. We'll keep it right here."

I skipped right to the 'Yo-" entries in the encyclopedia and read up on yo-yos, York, and Yonkers. The search proved futile. Much later in life, I discovered that "yeoman-like" just means honest, hard work. Looking back, the context clues were already there. You don't play for 462 different teams by being lazy. That's what Zoo was telling the viewer. But on the shoulders of Tony Massenburg's rebounding prowess, I now know the fourth largest city in New York State.

The Double Zero

Name: Benoit Benjamin

Height: 7'0"

College: Creighton

Sixers Tenure: 1998; 1999

I was in Las Vegas in 2012. There was a Ross Dress for Less on the Strip that I planned on hitting up, but name brands at discount prices would have to wait. I had a date with the roulette wheel. I was in Vegas for barely an hour when I handed the dealer $50 and put all of my chips on "00."

"For Spencer Hawes," I said. "I've never been more confident of anything in my life."

I was quickly down $50. Three days later, I traveled back home with nothing but a 3-pack of dress socks that were on clearance. There have been more players than I thought who wore jersey number "00." But outside of Robert Parish, and maybe Kevin Duckworth or the aforementioned Hawes depending on your age, there was no "00" more notorious than Benoit Benjamin. I dig the double zero. It's a fresh, clean look. My mom used to officiate basketball games, and she was vehemently opposed to jersey numbers that contained the digits, six through nine. You had to use at least three hand signals to relay the call to the scorer's table. It was cumbersome. Former Sixer Alexey Shved wore #88. Only a 3rd base coach could report a reach-in foul on him (be sure to look for the belt indicator). But is "00" even a real number, or, flexing my 9th grade Algebra, even an integer? 5-5=0, not 00. And if "00" isn't a real number, what's stopping NBA players from putting fractions or long division problems on the back of their jersey. Double zero is a slippery slope.

Benoit Benjamin was part of that cesspool in the 1980s, known as the Los Angeles Clippers. Everything that franchise touched back then turned to shit. The 80's Clippers weren't void of talent, though. A lot of great players rolled through Los Angeles, but they were included in lopsided trades or suffered enough horrific injuries that it made you wonder if there was a Papa Shango-like hex placed on the team. Benoit played under New York Knick great Willis Reed at Creighton, before being selected #3 overall in the '85 Draft. Benjamin was picked by Los Angeles, ahead of guys like Chris Mullin, Karl Malone, and Joe Dumars. But Benoit wasn't a bust in the traditional sense. He wasn't Michael Olowokandi. He had a healthy fifteen-year career, but never reached the lofty expectations bestowed upon him. In the fall of 1987, the *LA Times* wrote an article harshly titled, "Growing Pains: A Failure at Age 22, Benoit Benjamin Vows Clippers Will See a Change in Their Center of Controversy."

"He has the potential to be a great player," Chaney said, speaking from his home in Atlanta, where he's now an assistant coach with the Hawks. "But he's his own worst enemy. If he doesn't reach that level, he has only himself to blame. In order for him to reach that full potential, he has to put in time in the off-season. And I don't think he's that dedicated." (Baker 1987).

Benjamin had two different stints in Philly - joining the organization each spring like a September call-up in baseball. Property records gave no indication, however, that he owned a timeshare with Eric Valent and Jon Zuber. The Sixers signed Benjamin to a 10-day contract in March of 1998 and eventually inked the big man through the rest of the season. Benoit was previously playing for the Continental Basketball Association's Yakima Sun Kings, proving that the Sun Kings/Sixers pipeline was indeed strong.

I asked my mom if we had any relatives or family friends in Yakima. I wanted to connect with a Sun Kings die hard, get the inside scoop on Benjamin. See how his conditioning was holding up. Mom told me no but said my great aunt had just moved to Carson City. Close enough, I figured. I gave her a call. Aunt Joan didn't know anything about Benjamin or the Sun Kings, but she was excited about the new sectional that was getting delivered on Tuesday.

Benoit played initially, backing up Theo Ratliff and Scott Williams, but quickly ceded minutes to Joe Smith, who was playing for his second of eventual 43 NBA teams. He latched on with the Sixers once more, this time in '99, but the Benoit Benjamin sequel went straight to video (like *Kindergarten Cop 2,* starring Dolph Lundgren). He only appeared in six games and was released in favor of 40-year-old Rick Mahorn in February. In October of that same year, the Sixers *again* contacted Benjamin.

"Benoit u up?"

Needing a frontcourt player, the Sixers were considering Benjamin, John Salley, and even old friend, Armen Gilliam. But they spurned all three big men in favor of Stanley Roberts, who signed later that month (Whittaker 1999). Benoit played a couple of games with the Cavs before retiring that same year. Benjamin's story was one full of promise. His time in Philly, though, was a chapter that most have long forgotten.

The #1 Pick

Name: Kwame Brown

Height: 6'11"

School: Glynn Academy - Brunswick, GA

Sixers Tenure: 2012-2013

Said Brett Brown yesterday: "He was slowly trying to get back to some level of shape. He's putting in the time. He's on the treadmill all the time and we haven't gotten to any timeline. He's still a ways away." (Murrow 2013).

Kwame Brown never could shed the 'bust' label. The first #1 overall pick to be selected straight from high school, Brown evolved into nothing more than a guy off the bench - a role player and a journeyman who bounced from team to team during his twelve seasons in the league. Like an older sibling's David Bell t-shirt, the Sixers were given #1 overall pick hand-me-downs. Brown and the Sixers was a mediocre match made in heaven. Joe Smith? Sure. An aging Chris Webber? Why not? Kwame Brown? Now it's a party. Remember when JaMarcus Russell spelled Gordan Giricek for a few minutes on that three-game Texas trip? Legendary. Brown became a punchline, a cautionary tale of a "workout warrior" without the track record, without the substance. He dominated fellow draftee Tyson Chandler during a workout with the Wizards, and afterwards, infamously told team executive Michael Jordan that, "If you draft me, you'll never regret it." (Abrams 2016).

"Hear the Sixers signed Kwame Brown today?"

"It's too early for this shit, Pat."

"It's four in the afternoon."

The details surrounding Brown's signing were foggy. At Doug Collins' behest - Kwame Brown's first NBA coach in Washington - the Sixers signed Brown before the '12-'13 season to a two-year, $6 million deal with a player option. Kwame, of course, exercised that option the following year. The contract was a hefty price tag - even the length of the deal, the player option, was a gamble. Brown was coming off a season-ending chest injury in Golden State and had played for six other organizations previously. Despite an earned reputation as being stout defensively, his career production at his age warranted nothing more than a low-risk, one-year deal. No other team was offering Kwame Brown multiple years. Were the Sixers worried that Billy King was going to swoop in and offer him a 22-year contract with a player option in 2034? Incredibly though, the Sixers dodged a bullet with only the two years. It could've been much worse.

"According to sources with intimate knowledge of the situation, Collins wanted to sign center Kwame Brown to a guaranteed five-year, $30 million deal before the lockout-shortened 2011-12 season.

Harris, on Thorn's advice, vetoed the signing. Unfortunately for the Sixers, it was revisited." (Mitchell 2013).

Pardon? Five years for Brown? Doug meant Dee Brown, right? Or was it P.J.? Sixers supporters trashed the reports. The news made the national cycle. Fans bombarded the Twitter feed of former Sixers CEO, Adam Aron, who at that moment probably regretted the fan interaction he once cherished. This original offer was Scott Williams reincarnated. After Kwame's deal with the Sixers became official in the summer of 2012, things escalated quickly. Brown wasn't just brought here to provide minutes off the bench as most anticipated. Doug Collins declared Kwame Brown the TEAM'S STARTING CENTER. The hubris of Doug. This was like when Bobby "The Brain" Heenan claimed he could make anyone a star and took the Brooklyn Brawler under his tutelage. And I admit that's an obscure joke, but I need you to understand the gravity of the situation.

Collins' plan was to start Brown and Spencer Hawes in the frontcourt, together, on purpose, at the same time. The tandem wasn't exactly Olajuwon and Ralph Sampson, or even Tim Perry and Andrew Lang for that matter. The Brown signing, and the intended starting line-up, seemed to stunt any momentum the fanbase carried from the previous season when they upset Chicago.

Then the Sixers acquired Andrew Bynum. Whew. Finally, we did it. Philly landed their superstar, the new cornerstone of their franchise. Kwame would be relegated back to the bench, and the Sixers would enter a new chapter on the back of their young, 7'0" dominant center. All was right in the world.

It sounded good on paper anyway. Despite Bynum's absence, Kwame Brown was a ghost. When he did play, the fans showered him with boos. Doug Collins pleaded with the fans to remain positive and supportive of Brown. Philly fans don't like to be told what to do, so they booed Kwame even more. He ended the season with a streak of thirty DNPs (Did Not Play). It wasn't quite Joe DiMaggio's 56 games, but it was noteworthy, nonetheless. A few years later, Brown publicly blamed the Sixers medical staff for their handling of a hamstring injury he suffered back in 2013 (Kilinski 2017). Which knowing the track record of the Sixers medical staff, that mishandling is entirely possible. They reportedly called Joe Theismann 'day-to-day' when Lawrence Taylor broke his leg on *Monday Night Football*. The misdiagnosis, Brown claimed, ended his career prematurely. The controversy was another footnote in a disastrous tenure that lasted just 22 games. Dealing with that hamstring injury entering the '13-'14 season, the Sixers elected to release Brown - leaving the organization on the hook for his remaining salary.

Doug Collins said in a presser after the signing that Kwame Brown was no longer the #1 pick in the draft. He was just Kwame Brown.

You won't get any argument from us, Doug.

The Flight Brother

Name: Larry Hughes

Height: 6'5"

College: Saint Louis

Sixers Tenure: 1998-2000

Contributions to an incredibly exciting win came from everywhere. Larry Hughes drained a three pointer with seven-tenths of a second remaining in regulation to force the extra period. (Jasner 1999).

The December 20th, 1999 battle with the Pistons was a nutty game the Sixers had no business first losing, and then eventually winning. Philly was up four with two minutes left when the Pistons went on a 7-0 run. The Sixers took a timeout with 3.8 seconds left, preparing to inbound the ball from midcourt. With all the attention focused on Allen, it was second-year man, Larry Hughes, a 17% three-point shooter coming into the night, who rose up and buried the triple to force overtime. In the extra frame, trailing by one with one second remaining, Eric Snow knocked down a game-winning fifteen-footer as time expired to clinch a 122-121 Sixers victory.

Forty-eight hours earlier, Iverson and Larry Brown's relationship came to a boiling point after Brown benched Allen for the final twenty minutes in a convincing loss at Detroit. After the Hughes triple to force OT, Iverson embraced Larry with a gigantic bear hug, a genuine moment of elation. One win didn't solve the internal issues of the team, but another loss certainly wouldn't have helped either.

Larry Hughes was a Flight Brother. Coined by Marc Zumoff, Hughes, the dynamic and athletic guard from Saint Louis, earned his moniker by often being on the receiving end of an Iverson alley-oop. In today's world, some Sixers fan would've photoshopped Hughes and Iverson onto the *Top Gun* movie poster on a Monday, and it would've been a t-shirt for sale on TeePublic by Wednesday. I would've bought two; one to wear immediately and one to bequeath in my will to my favorite grandchild with the special message, "Always reach for the stars. Love, Pop Pop."

There have been plenty of tandems in Philly sports history - Schmidt and Carlton, Dr. J and Moses, Utley and Rollins - but there were no real nicknames attached to them. Outside of "Thunder and Lightning" (Ricky Watters and Charlie Garner) and "Thump and Bump" (Mahorn and Barkley), the Philly tandem nickname scene is lacking. AI and Hughes were an incredibly popular duo that fans assumed would have a long shelf life. But the Flight Brothers barely got off the runway. A year and a half into his NBA career, the Sixers traded Hughes. What would Zumoff have hypothetically dubbed Iverson and Paul Pierce?

"I always used to always tell our staff, 'We gotta go for the best player period.' Let's not even think about our needs unless they were very, very close. When we lost Paul Pierce at 10, we had him rated at two. We took Larry Hughes because we thought we had a need, but the reason we took Larry is I promised when we interviewed him, we knew we were getting the eighth pick, I promised him if he were there at eight we would take him. And I would never do that again." (Pavorsky 2015).

So now Larry Brown gets a conscience. Guy was the Zsa Zsa Gabor of NBA coaches. He left the Sixers in a Mayflower truck in the middle of the night. Larry packed up everything but Greg Buckner's contract. Hughes had a decent NBA career, but he wasn't Pierce or Nowitzki. Pierce can be annoying, and he'd probably wheel into the arena every night like Professor X claiming this injury or that, but still. I'd have found a spot for him. Hughes was a strong defender, had athleticism for days, but was also just a career 40% shooter from the field.

His poor shot selection was so notorious that a Cavs fan went to the trouble of creating a website called, HeyLarryHughesPleaseStopTakingSoManyBadShots.com. That's dedication to your scorn. If my family had the internet in '97, I would've created a website called, HeyChrisBoniolPleaseKickItStraight.com, but instead I just yelled at the TV and called for Ruger Ruzek.

Hughes had a nice rookie campaign. Coming off the bench, he averaged double digits, highlighted by a 22-point effort against the Raptors in April. His second and last season in Philly, however, was ripe with discontent. It's not so much that Hughes regressed, but rather the team felt that Larry didn't progress as they had expected. Turnovers were an issue, but not unexpected for a young guard. As the calendar moved to January, Brown played Larry less and less, shortening up his rotation. Trade rumors began to swirl as Hughes openly questioned his playing time. When he wasn't getting game-winning buckets anyway.

Only three days ago, Larry Hughes sprinted down court in the waiting arms of 76ers teammates, who suffocated him with praise after he tipped in a miss for a buzzer-beating win over the New Jersey Nets.

Last night, the second-year guard said it may be time for him to leave town. (Smith 2000).

Sandwiched between game-winners and public gripes about playing time, Hughes participated in the 2000 NBA Slam Dunk Contest. I didn't watch, still serving a self-imposed ten-year ban from dunk contests as a result of Tim Perry's efforts. The saga snowballed. A year and a half prior, Brown and his staff selected Larry #8 overall. Now, it was a question of when, not if, Hughes was going to be moved. Just one week after his game winner against New Jersey, Hughes was traded. As part of a three-team deal, the Sixers shipped the young guard to Golden State and received Toni Kukoc in the exchange. Larry Brown and the Sixers weren't willing to wait for Hughes' maturation on the court. Brown was known for deferring to veterans at most opportunities. But the mistake in this story wasn't the trade, or the moving on from Larry Hughes prematurely. It was the 1999 Draft itself.

The (Pending) Physical

Name: Steven Hunter

Height: 7'0"

College: DePaul

Sixers Tenure: 2005-2007

"I really don't know why," King said Wednesday, when asked why things didn't work out. "Sometimes you sign guys and hope that things work. But this one just didn't, and it gave us a great chance to add some picks and get some flexibility within the (salary) cap." (Juliano 2006).

Steven Hunter dunked a lot. An athletic big man, Hunter's game was best tailored for a three-minute highlight reel rather than reliable starter's minutes. He played for four teams in eight seasons, never quite able to maintain a steady role at any location. His rebounding numbers (7.6 per 36 min) were a concern for a player his size. The Sixers *tried* to trade Hunter in 2006 - more on that in a moment - but, geez, did he dunk a lot. I think there may have been one jump hook back in '04, but I couldn't get visual confirmation. YouTube is littered with Steven Hunter dunk montages. I spent one long weekend watching nothing but Hunter dunk on Brian Cardinal's receding hairline.

He signed with the Sixers in 2005 on, what else, a five-year deal. He proved to be a useful insurance policy, starting in the place of Samuel Dalembert who missed some time early on with a leg injury (Narducci 2005). Hunter showed some promise, flashing that athleticism that teams salivated over, but he moved back to the bench once Dalembert returned. He saw his playing time drastically diminish. Sammy D was a fixture in the rotation, and Hunter joined Villanova star Michael Bradley behind Sammy in the frontcourt pecking order.

In February of that season – year one of the five-year deal – the Sixers moved on from the young big man. Billy King traded Hunter to the Hornets for two second round picks. After the trade, pending a physical mind you (just a formality), the Sixers used that open roster spot to sign Zendon Hamilton.

Oh, about that physical.

In his brief time with the Sixers, Steven Hunter didn't pass the muster. Traded Wednesday to the New Orleans/Oklahoma City Hornets, the 7-foot center apparently didn't pass his physical.

"We're in discussions," Sixers president/general manager Billy King said. "Our doctors are talking with their doctors." (Jasner 2006).

The Hornets medical staff wouldn't clear Hunter, leaving his status with either team in limbo. Meanwhile, Zendon Hamilton was chilling in the Sixers locker room, angling for *his* five-year contract. Zendon already moved his stuff in. He brought his PS2 and everything. It was a tense few days. I skipped a few classes that week to monitor the situation. Wanted to show my support for both organizations and the medical process in general. I penned an email to my friends and family – just to keep them abreast of the latest developments.

From: SixxxersFan1983@hotmail.com (Feb 6, 2006, 9:47 AM)

To: Mom, Dad, Bill, Mike, Amy, AJ, Lou, Jen, Blair

Subject: Let's Get Physical (The Steven Hunter Situation)

Hi all:

I know it's been a trying time this week, so I figured I would send one email to use as a constant stream of communication.

Here's what we know:

The Sixers traded Steven Hunter to New Orleans for two second round picks. It was a fair return, and I've already begun my homework on some potential sleepers. I'll send another email with my thoughts/research. Look for that later this week.

Reports from New Orleans suggest there is or may be an issue with the results of Hunter's physical. I'm one step ahead of you. I don't know if the pass/fail requirements for these physicals vary state to state. There's a girl in my Econ class whose uncle is a doctor – I'm curious to see what he may know – but thus far, she has not responded to my AOL IMs. I'll try again later this afternoon.

I guess I should also address the elephant in the room. What about Zendon Hamilton? The short answer is that we just don't know. I think we need to let this play out and not jump to any conclusions. There has been and will continue to be a lot of information coming and going.

Let's remain diligent throughout this process.

I'll provide more updates once they are confirmed.

Everyone hang in there,

-Dave

On February 8th, one week after the initial trade was agreed upon, the deal was rescinded. Steven Hunter: Dino Radja 2.0. The Hornets medical staff pointed to a right knee injury from a few years prior. Management on both sides seemed surprised by the diagnosis, which led to Steven Hunter, former Sixer, to now once again present Sixer, with four years still remaining on his deal.

"None whatsoever," King said. "I was shocked when they told me there was a problem."

The Sixers were in Charlotte for a game Wednesday night, and Hunter wasn't expected to rejoin the team until Thursday.

"The initial stages will be odd, but his teammates and coaches will welcome him back with open arms like everyone else," King said.

"We were doing the deal because it gave us [salary] flexibility, but at this point in time, we're just trying to get him back on the court," King said. (ESPN 2006).

This is awkward. Steven, have you met Zendon? Zendon, this is Steven. King obviously had to backtrack. First it was, 'Not sure why things didn't work out.' Then, post physical, it was, 'We just needed the cap flexibility.' It couldn't have been a great few weeks for Hunter, who was now back with the same club who tried to trade him. Hamilton remained on the roster for a couple of weeks, appearing in one game, before he was released.

Hunter played one more season in Philly. In a 50-point loss to the Rockets, the big man registered a whopping -48 +/-. In Hunter's defense, the Rockets were on a 5 on 3 Peco Power Play for most of the night. The '06-'07 Sixers had trouble staying out of the penalty box. In the off-season, Hunter was again traded - this time for good - ending one of the more bizarre tenures in Sixers history.

The Collector

Name: Reggie Evans

Height: 6'8"

College: Iowa

Sixers Tenure: 2007-2009

I played in a 3-on-3 Hoop It Up tournament one year. I think it was held at the Franklin Mills Mall parking lot. Every team was named, "Hoop Stars" or "Hoop Stars II" or "The Hoopers." Before the tournament, they mailed you a schedule and a sheet with the teams in your age bracket, listing each player's name and height. I quickly looked to see if I was the shortest kid in the bracket. I was. Did my mom *have* to write 4'7" on the sign-up sheet? We could've rounded up. It was a registration form, not a polygraph.

Our team was lousy. I left my two friends for dead. I watched idly while the other teams just devoured us on the glass. I think at one point I was biting my nails at the top of the key, eyeing up the Gatorade stand (they had free samples), while our opponents did the Mikan Drill over and over. Looking back, I could've boxed out more, tried to put a body on someone. The lemon-lime Gatorade was ice cold, though. I got my money's worth.

It's strange to have such fond memories of a player who averaged just four plus points and six rebounds a game in his two seasons in Philly, but here we are. Reggie Evans, the Patron Saint of Rebounding and Second Chances (based on his career 15% Offensive Rebound Percentage). People in the Delaware Valley didn't count sheep to fall asleep. Just Reggie Evans boards. He had one elite skill, and he did it really, really well. From a rebounding perspective, he was the closest thing to God and Dennis Rodman. While playing for the Nuggets, he recorded a mind-blowing

0-point, 20-rebound performance. By accident, you'd think he would've had a put back or a single free throw somewhere in there. But nope, not Reggie Evans. Reggie Evans was a giver. He wasn't selfish. Evans' only vice was rebounds, and he hoarded those like soy sauce packets from your favorite Chinese restaurant.

Drug-tested once in-game, Evans told reporters afterwards that he was, "just cleaner than clean. I'm cleaner than Pine-Sol." While in Denver, he infamously grabbed the Clippers' Chris Kaman's junk and paid a $10,000 fine for "unnecessary and excessive contact" (Associated Press 2005). As an opponent, Evans was infuriating - an active, blue-collar nuisance who seemingly tracked down every loose ball. He antagonized your favorite team, and if you can't beat 'em, acquire 'em. In 2007, Denver packaged Reggie Evans and folk hero, Ricky Sanchez, to Philly for Steven Hunter and Bobby Jones. On the surface, it was a relatively small move, but considering Evans' eventual contributions and the subsequent Sixers podcast that followed, it was a clear win for Philly.

Outside of his rebounding prowess, Reggie Evans had some, how do you say, offensive challenges. His range was limited to a six-foot radius, maybe five depending on the wind pattern that day. His numbers say he was a 53% free throw shooter, but I can't vouch for that. I never saw Evans get to the foul line. In fact, I only remember Reggie attempting one shot in two seasons. And he buried it.

Game 1 of the 2008 Playoffs against Detroit. The Sixers clung to a one-point lead on the road, with less than five minutes remaining. The shot clock was winding down. A desperate Iguodala passed to Reggie Evans who was WIDE OPEN at the top of the key. Of course, he was open. No defense even acknowledged Evans until he stepped into the paint. It was like giving your toddler some Tupperware and measuring cups to play with while you cooked dinner. You weren't concerned with their whereabouts until they got too close to the stove. A Reggie Evans jump shot would've been listed just ahead of a Jason Smith skyhook in terms of shot selection preference, but, hey, beggars can't be choosers. Evans delivered. He drilled a 17-footer, pushed the Sixers lead to three, and the Black Shirts never looked back.

With Thaddeus Young's emergence, and the Sixers searching for more punch on offense, Evans played considerably less his second season. A team eventually has to ask themselves if the one, unique skill Evans brings to the table outweighs the liability he carries on the other end of the court. The Sixers made their decision. Following the '09 season, Philly moved Reggie to Toronto for his polar opposite, the three-point specialist, Jason Kapono. His work ethic and style of play garnered a lot of support from Sixers fans. If you needed a rebound, you called Reggie Evans. If you needed a second chance, you called Reggie Evans. If you need a basket, then go ask one of the other guys.

The One-Year Deal

Name: K.J. McDaniels

Height: 6'6"

College: Clemson

Sixers Tenure: 2014-2015

The term, "3 and D," entered the basketball lexicon about fifteen years ago. A '3 and D' player is designated for anyone who's between 6'4" and 6'9," who can maybe play defense and maybe has a jumper. But all of those factors are negotiable. There was always one kid on your hoops team whose best sport was soccer. Every team had one. They wore the classic black Adidas Sambas and could run like a deer. They would play in Umbro shorts, because they had to leave in the 3rd quarter for their indoor soccer game. They never scored a point and they never got tired. Those kids were '3 and D's, more or less.

"Player X could develop into a '3 and D' guy" just means that their jumper, in its current state, is broken. It's the potential of it all - that's the appeal. An ideal NBA roster has two or three superstars, someone else who can dribble (maybe), and then a bunch of guys who do nothing else except play defense and park out in the corner. '3 and D' players are exclusive to the NBA. If there was a player in your high school who could lockdown defensively and shoot, then he or she wasn't a '3 and D.' They were just your team's best player.

K.J. McDaniels, along with thirty-seven other guys, entered the 2014 NBA Draft with that potential '3 and D' designation. Riding a successful career at Clemson, it wasn't a question if McDaniels' athleticism would translate, but whether any other part of his game would. Despite the question marks, many draft pundits assigned him a first-round grade. K.J. slipped to the early second, though, where Sam Hinkie and the Sixers happily scooped him up at #32 overall. Philly had struck gold at #32 overall in past drafts having selected Brain Oliver, Alphonso Ford, and Ryan Minor. K.J. had big shoes to fill. The athletic McDaniels was great value for the Sixers, but this second round landing spot is where this story took an interesting turn.

Contracts for first round picks are more regimented - on a pay scale depending on draft order, etc - but K.J. was drafted just outside the first round. Using a contract strategy popularized by Sam Hinkie's old organization, the Houston Rockets (among others), the Sixers offered McDaniels a four-year deal, the maximum length a team can offer a second-round draftee. The latter two seasons of these deals were non-guaranteed. The thought-process makes sense. If the team hits on one of these lottery tickets, they'll have a rotational player at a bargain bin price for an extended timeframe. The rub is that both parties need to agree. K.J. McDaniels and his agent had zero interest in being locked into a contract at minimal value for that length. They balked. Tense negotiations dragged on into October, causing McDaniels to miss the first day of training camp. He eventually signed a one-year deal with the Sixers, a rarity for any draftee entering the league. K.J. simply bet on himself. (Cooney 2014).

All parties can toe the company line and say, "it's just business," but that's a rocky start to a marriage. K.J. McDaniels may not have had an issue with the team - he certainly got playing time - but you couldn't blame him for feeling like a prop or cheap labor above all else. On the court, however, McDaniels electrified. YouTube has a 9 minute 33 second video of K.J. Sixers highlights just dunking on people (1677091 Productions 2015). I needed a cold shower by the three-minute mark. A cigarette halfway through. One clip was Tony Wroten throwing an alley-oop OFF THE BACKBOARD to K.J., and my sincerest apologies to my next-door neighbor for running through their dining room window. He had five multiple block games in his first nine contests and the jump shot - the biggest unknown entering the draft - held up ok. McDaniels wasn't Kyle Korver from behind the arc, but the Sixers didn't need him to be. K.J.'s play tapered off as the calendar moved from

December into the New Year. It was an understandable and expected regression for a rookie adjusting to his first taste of the NBA.

Then he was traded. Just like that. In February, the Sixers moved the young rookie to the Rockets for Isaiah Canaan and a second-round pick. You could argue that it was a short-sighted decision. The Sixers traded a rookie who had shown flashes of potential. But the reality was Sam Hinkie traded a player who was set to be a restricted free agent; a player that was looking at a healthy pay raise the following year. If the organization had no intention of re-signing McDaniels, or matching any substantial offer sheet anyway, then Philly had an obligation to maximize his return. The McDaniels saga and eventual trade accentuated the dirtier side of the business. K.J.'s value was tied to a long-term, team-friendly contract that he ultimately chose not to sign.

Everything on the court was secondary.

The Trade Kicker

Name: Matt Geiger

Height: 7'0"

College: Auburn; Georgia Tech

Sixers Tenure: 1999-2002

After being booed mercilessly almost the entire night, Matt Geiger had a final minute that put Philadelphia back on his side.

Geiger kept the ball in the Sixers' hands for most of the final minute by tipping two missed shots to teammates and grabbing an offensive rebound.

The latter play brought a half-hug, half-back slap from Allen Iverson that was an emotional high for the 76ers in a 93-91 victory Wednesday night over the Toronto Raptors.

"You have to be deaf not to, so yeah, I heard them," Geiger said of the boos. "That's just Philly. When I play bad, they boo." (ESPN 1999).

Matt Geiger only played three seasons and change with the Sixers, but it certainly felt like a lot longer. One of the premier free agent signings brought in to complement Allen Iverson, Geiger had a frustrating, injury-riddled tenure that was highlighted by a trade kicker. Or, more specifically, a trade kicker that was never waived. Mistakes by Geiger were easily identifiable. 7'0" bald guys tend to stick out. Just ask Pennsylvania's Lieutenant Governor. Matt shaved his head for a very noble and admirable reason - a sign of solidarity when his twin brother was going through chemotherapy - but that also meant fans always knew his exact latitude and longitude on the court. Kareem Rush went an entire season undetected. Matt Geiger could sneeze once and get cited for a noise complaint. I actually had a friend with the last name of Geiger. He stopped going to Sixers games until Matt left. He was traumatized. He was tired of hearing, "Hey, Geiger! You suck! You suck Geiger!" over and over and over. Even though the insults weren't directed at him, it still hurt.

In the 1988 NBA Expansion Draft, the Lakers conspired with the newborn Heat and Hornets. Los Angeles designated legendary Kareem Abdul-Jabbar for the draft but brokered a deal with both clubs - an offer of a second-round pick - to *not* select Abdul-Jabbar (Laye 1988). It reminds me of the *Saved by the Bell* episode, "The Date Auction," when Jesse threatened any girl who dared to bid on Slater. This type of deal is apparently legal and also fascinating. What if the Hornets were like, "Eh, screw it. We're new here. Let's ruffle some feathers. What the hell are we supposed to do with Dave Hoppen anyway? Let's take Kareem at #4. Call it in, Ed."

"But we made a deal –"

"I said call it in, Ed, god damnit!"

All publicity is good publicity after all, and to date, I've never seen anyone in a Hoppen Hornets jersey. The Heat used that second-round pick in '92 from the Lakers to select Matt Geiger. So in a weird way, Geiger was traded for Kareem. Kinda? Matt developed into a competent frontcourt player and entered free agency in 1998 seeking a big pay day.

After the brief NBA lockout, the Sixers inked Geiger to a massive six-year deal before the start of the '99 season. He played pretty well his first year. He averaged double figures and played all 50 games of the shortened campaign. In the Sixers convincing Game 1 win at Orlando in the first round, Geiger rose to the occasion, collecting 23 points and 10 boards. Then Matt laid an egg. A 3-15 performance from a 7'0" guy was both alarming and impressive. That two-game swing was a microcosm of the inconsistency fans would see from Geiger in year two and beyond. He labored through an injury-plagued '99-'00 season, missing 17 games and ceding playing time to Theo Ratliff. The fans turned on Geiger, pelting him with boos at the first missed shot or defensive lapse.

Maybe I've gone soft, but did Geiger really deserve all the booing? Yes, he was overpaid, but if Philly fans relentlessly booed every player who didn't perform to his expectations, then we would've lost our collective voices during the Lance Parrish Era. Geiger's season ended with a fight - not with Sixers fans - but with Reggie Miller. He was suspended for two games after an altercation in Game 4 (McGreachy 2000). The incident got Miller suspended for Game 5 - a crafty move by the veteran Geiger. It was a good trade-off for the Sixers, like sending Donald Brashear after Martin St. Louis and watching them both go to the box. The Sixers smoked the Miller-less Pacers in Game 5 but fell to Indiana and a returning Reggie in six games. Actually, it would've been useful if Geiger lured Jalen Rose and Rik Smiths into the melee, too. Got them suspended as well. It was a job only half-complete. So, on second thought, Geiger, boo! Boo!

This seems like a good spot to pause, collect our breath, and discuss the Sixers Promotional Giveaway, the Matt Geiger Tiger. Geiger Tiger is a member of an exclusive club of promotional giveaways that is stored in Sixers fans' memory banks, or, at the very least, stored in a box in people's garages. The fraternity includes the Sixers old school painter hat, any Manute Bol or Shawn Bradley life-size poster, the Allen Iverson rubber ducky, and of course, the Eric Snow Globe, which is used as a paperweight by most office workers in the region. The Geiger Tiger was a Beanie Baby, and this beauty fetched quite a price on the secondary market. You could purchase one on eBay, but bidding started at $100 and did not include shipping & handling. For his birthday, my son asked me for a Geiger Tiger, but I was only able to deliver four Sixers car flags stuffed inside a shoe box.

That offseason, the Sixers concluded that Iverson and Larry Brown could not coexist. They were involved in an elaborate four-team deal to move their superstar. Half the league was set to be traded as part of this deal - including Iverson and Matt Geiger (Joe Smith and Jimmy Jackson just assumed they were on the move). Philly, as it was reported by Marc Stein from ESPN.com, would have received Temple standout, Eddie Jones, Glen Rice, Jerome Williams, and Dale Ellis (ESPN 2001).

I love me some Dale Ellis, but let's be honest: that's a light return. Jones would've been good, Larry Brown would've benched Glen Rice in favor of George Lynch, Greg Buckner, Bruce Bowen, or someone else who couldn't score, and Billy King would've given Jerome Williams a ten-year contract. The deal, of course, never happened. Matt Geiger had a 15% trade kicker, which turned out to be a touch more than $1.2 million per season. Detroit, Iverson and Geiger's intended destination, couldn't absorb the extra cash. Matt could've waived the kicker but thought better of it. Geiger squashed the entire deal. (Jasner 2000).

Matt Geiger, hero. Save your boos for Bobby Abreu and his .416 career OB% with the Phillies, if you must. The magical '01 Sixers run would never have happened. Iverson's jersey never would've been raised to the rafters. Allen wouldn't be seen at the Wells Fargo Center today as an icon, and a genuine fan of the team, a guy who loves this franchise and this city. That proposed deal wouldn't have moved the needle for the Sixers. It was an out for Brown and ownership, not a solution. (Although Dale Ellis would've featured prominently in this book).

Geiger's on the court tenure with the Sixers, however, remained a tumultuous one. In one of the first days of camp at the start of the '00-'01 season, he landed on Toni Kukoc's foot and required knee surgery (Whittaker 2000). He saw action in just 35 games with the Sixers that season, buried on the bench behind newly acquired Dikembe Mutombo. He played sparingly in the Finals run, used primarily as a Hack-a-Shaq mercenary. Geiger's career came to an end after just a handful of games in '01-'02. Knee injuries left him unable to compete, and he hung up the sneakers with three years still left on his contract. Matt Geiger's tenure was never dull. He was booed relentlessly. But despite the abuse, he decided there was no place he'd rather be.

The Founding Father

Name: Tony Wroten

Height: 6'5"

College: Washington

Sixers Tenure: 2013-2016

Tony Wroten was good. Actually, I think Tony Wroten was really good, and if that's considered controversial, or considered a hot take, then wrap me in a Jason Whitten jersey and call me Skip Bayless. The Process Era was defined by a sacrifice in the short-term for a prosperous future, for a brighter long-term outlook. I trusted the Process - where was 41-41 season after season getting the Sixers - but the only heroes that seemed to rise from these years were GM Sam Hinkie, a cult hero to many, and we, the fans. Like the fans did anything of note. I've watched bad basketball for 90% of my life, but only in 2013 did I start getting credit for it.

The Sixers had a carousel of players during these years, rotating in and out like Phillies relievers after a Vince Velasquez 2 ⅓ inning outing. TJ McConnell is widely considered the Face of the Process, but Tony Wroten is actually credited with the term, "Trust the Process." Wroten is the Founding Father of this Era. Without him, without his ingenuity, the city, the media, would be calling this era something lame like "Tears for Years." "Trust the Process," though, man, what a euphemism, what a positive spin. I hope Wroten knows he has a career in PR awaiting him whenever he wants it.

A former first-round pick of the Grizzlies in the 2012 Draft, the Sixers acquired Wroten in '13 for virtually nothing. They gave up a protected second-round pick for him. It was as low risk as you can get, like opting for a multigrain bagel instead of your usual sesame. Wroten was also the founder of the Sixers hip-hop group,

Team WHOP, featuring teammates, Michael-Carter Williams, Khalif Wyatt, and the wonderfully named, Vander Blue. 'WHOP' stood for "We Handle Our Problems," which was good because the Sixers had quite a number of them.

Tony Wroten could go. A lefty point guard who relentlessly attacked the rim, Wroten knew that the quickest way from point A to point B was with a left-handed dribble straight through the opposing point guard's chest. Tony would've been a nightmare to defend in pick-up games. Your buddies left you on an island while Wroten keeps barreling into you every possession. Your feet are set, but if you call a charge in pick-up then you're telling the other nine players on the court that you're a complete shithead.

I won't recklessly throw out Iverson comps, but if you squint hard enough, and maybe in a certain light? At the tender age of 21, Wroten averaged almost 17 points and 5 assists on a really, really bad Sixers team. So maybe Iverson is the wrong comp. Maybe it's Shareef Abdur-Rahim, who was synonymous with putting up big numbers on a bad team. What could've Wroten accomplished on a good team? A Jamal Crawford-type, who came off the bench for twenty minutes a game and terrorized second units. Sure, Wroten didn't have a jump shot, but neither did Ben Franklin, and look what he accomplished.

The '14-'15 Sixers had a rough go of it. A few bad breaks and unlucky bounces snowballed into an 0-17 start. Hey, we've all been there. This losing streak triggered a series of "Could the University of Kentucky beat the Sixers" nonsense. Eric Bledsoe piled on and said, "I would take Kentucky." (Kaskey-Blomain 2014). All of this talk was trash by the way. The Sixers would've waltzed into Rupp Arena and hung a 130 spot on Calipari. Tony Wroten wasn't having any of that noise. He rightfully called Bledsoe out. No one in the SEC was locking down Wroten. No college team was beating the Sixers and Nick Saban and Alabama are never beating an NFL team. Not even that lousy Ray Rhodes team from 1998 who went 3-13. Bobby Hoying would've lit up the Crimson Tide secondary.

Associated Press

TUSCALOOSA, AL – After giving up an opening drive field goal, the '98 Eagles soared past the Crimson Tide of Alabama at Bryant-Denny Stadium, 45-3. It was an impressive win for the '98 Birds, who, for the large majority of them, hadn't played an organized football game in over two decades.

46-year-old tight end Jason Dunn hauled in four catches for 72 yards and a score in the victory.

In a January 13th game against the Hawks, Wroten went down with a partially torn ACL. The injury ended his season, and effectively, his Sixers run. He returned to the team about eleven months later but appeared in just 8 more games. One of those games, a 10-point home loss to the Knicks, was a glimpse of The Wroten Joyride. He scored 15 points in not even a half of basketball but coupled that with 7 turnovers. It was Good Tony and Bad Tony rolled up into one stat-stuffing rollercoaster.

On Christmas Eve 2015, the Sixers released Wroten to make room for their newest acquisition, Ish Smith. I was devastated. I called my wife and dog into the living room for an emergency family meeting. I told them Christmas was canceled. I told them that Christmas 2016 wasn't looking good either. My wife balked; said we were hosting Christmas Eve dinner tonight and shipped me off to Fine Wine & Good Spirits. I was anything but in good spirits. Wroten was my Process Guy. We all had one – Hollis, Davies, Cov, TJ, JaKarr, etc. Tony was mine. Ish Smith provided a steadier hand at the point guard position, and for a young team trying to find an identity, the move made sense. But I prefer a little more danger in my backcourt, someone a bit more unpredictable. Wroten never let you get too comfortable. I appreciated that.

The Resurgence

Name: Damien Wilkins

Height: 6'6"

College: North Carolina State; Georgia

Sixers Tenure: 2012-2013

By playing hard down the stretch rather than dogging it - he scored in double figures in 17 of the last 28 games - Wilkins probably earned a ticket out. Some playoff contender will probably rescue the classy vet from the Titanic. (Mitchell 2013).

I always confused Damien with his father and former Knicks guard, Gerald Wilkins. When the Sixers inked Wilkins to a deal, I was taken aback. "Isn't Gerald like 50?" I thought. Will he have fresh legs on the second night of back-to-backs? Is Doug Collins planning on hiding Wilkins in a 2-3 zone? It was just mistaken identity. In September of 2012, the Sixers signed the younger Wilkins, albeit the 33-year-old version, who was playing for his fifth team in five years. He was someone you could be convinced was on the end of any team's bench. You call him a modern-day Chucky Brown. I say Damien Wilkins was just well-traveled.

The NBA Draft offers an immediate reprieve, a quick fix to a team's woes. In the NFL, a team can bounce back from a disappointing season with some injury luck and the benefits of a last-place schedule. In Major League Baseball, the draft won't provide instant dividends, but with no salary cap, just open your checkbook. In the NBA, though, the draft is a team's salvation. Optimism in October - "Hey, I hear Spencer Hawes has been in the weight room" - is replaced with tanking aspirations at the drop of a dime. If a team starts the year 1-5, half the fan base calls for the season to be shut down, like Jon Taffer at the first sight of mice droppings in a kitchen. It's strange to think that a journeyman guard who had bounced around the league for close to a decade could play such a pivotal role in the Tanking Movement, or should I say, the Anti-Tanking Movement, but such was life in the spring of 2013.

On March 8th, the Sixers lost a road game to LeBron James, Dwyane Wade, and the Miami Heat. There was no shame in losing to LeBron and co., but that defeat was the Sixers' eleventh loss in their past twelve games. Any chance of a playoff berth, surprising some high seed in the first round via another smorgasbord of torn ACLs disappeared as the calendar approached St. Patrick's Day. That night in Miami was the last time Damien Wilkins came off the pine.

The Sixers lost their next contest in Orlando. Wilkins just needed a game to find his sea legs. He then captained the Sixers to an 11-10 record in their final twenty-one games. Those win/losses may seem blasé on the surface, but aggregated over the course of 82 games? Damien Wilkins carried this merry band of misfits to the brink of a #6 seed.

The team had specific instructions to roll over, but Wilkins defied orders. Damien went into business for himself, like Shawn Michaels at the 2005 SummerSlam. I was caught flat-footed. I turned my head for one second, just a moment, just trying to see what the Phils had in Laynce Nix. I watched one, maybe two Victor Oladipo YouTube highlight packages? It was an innocent mistake. It could've happened to anyone. Next thing you know, I'm reading things like, "Wilkins and Sixers committed to finishing the year strong." How long were those Nix plate appearances? Finish the year *weak*, guys, with barely a whimper. That's what we want. Damien Wilkins was putting up double-digits every night. He was consistent and reliable and a leader and all those annoying things. He became the face of the Anti-Tanking Crowd, a hard-working guy who was finally getting his just due. For the other half of Sixers fans, Wilkins was public enemy #1.

Damien was a professional. The Sixers future, their draft odds, was - rightly - no concern of his. Rolling over was not going to secure him another contract and hell hath no fury like a veteran off-guard scorned. Wilkins, though, didn't secure another NBA contract until five years after his late-season surge in Philly. He played one year in Indiana before retiring from the NBA. As for the Sixers, their draft position fell to #11, where they still passed on Giannis Antetokounmpo. So, looking back, go nuts, Damien. Play your little heart out. Don't let the tanking crowd stand in your way.

The G-Man

Name: Mike Gminski

Height: 6'11"

College: Duke

Sixers Tenure: 1988-1991

1990 All-Star Voting

Eastern Conference

Centers

1. *Patrick Ewing, New York* *50,142*
2. *Bill Laimbeer, Detroit* *40,786*
3. *Moses Malone, Atlanta* *19,863*
4. *Robert Parish, Boston* *15,614*
5. *Bill Cartwright, Chicago* *9,994*
6. *Rik Smits, Indiana* *8,888*
7. *Brad Daugherty, Cleveland* *7,618*
8. *Joe Barry Carroll, New Jersey* *5,431*
9. *Jack Sikma, Milwaukee* *5,354*
10. *Mike Gminski* *4,063*

(Philadelphia Daily News 1990)

There's this magazine cover of Mike Gminski from back in the day where his mullet is nice and feathered and he's looking like George Michael in a Sixers tank top. I thought it was *Philly Magazine*, but after some research, the cover was actually from the November 1989 edition of *Philly Sport*. Someone was selling the exact edition on eBay, so of course I bought it. (This book is costing me a fortune). In the middle of a pandemic I'm reading a magazine from 1989, like Will Smith in *I Am Legend* watching old episodes of *The Today Show*. There were profiles on Gminski, Luis Zendejas, Penn State's Blair Thomas, and a former Sixer named Raymond Lewis.

Lewis was drafted the same year as Doug Collins and apparently lit Doug up in preseason camp. As a result, Lewis wanted to redo his contract right then and there – get paid more like the #1 overall pick Collins. Lewis ended up walking out on the team twice and never played an NBA game (Buschel 1989, 26). Though I didn't get to read the entire article because pages 30 and 31 were missing from the magazine. If anyone has the missing pages, please return them.

The 1990 All-Star fan voting notwithstanding, Mike Gminski was a popular player around these parts. For years, I wanted to spell Mike's last name 'Giminski," but he taught me that less is more. Women all over the Delaware Valley had his 6'11" poster (to scale) thumbtacked on their ceiling, because G-Man's picture could melt most load-bearing walls. They tucked the November 1989 edition of *Philly Sport* underneath their mattress. For the articles of course. G-Man sported a trademark beard, a full-bodied, luscious beard that said, "I took a cab to the Spectrum straight from the set of *The Young and the Restless.*"

Gminski started growing his beard during a win streak while a member of the Nets. New Jersey coach Stan Albeck had a theory that back-up white centers didn't get foul calls from officials. So even after the Nets' win streak ended, Albeck encouraged G-Man to put away the razor. The idea being if Gminski appeared tougher and more rugged, the big man may be the beneficiary of a few more whistles (Yagoda 1989, 48).

Just gonna leave that one there.

Clean-shaven or not, Gminski could play. He was a jack of all trades whose weapon of choice was the patented 'G-Man Jumper.' The dictionary defines a 'G-Man Jumper' (*noun*) as a sixteen-footer so silky smooth you could spread it over a piece of toast. The jumper was art in motion, more lethal than Randall Cunningham outside the pocket. The G-Man Jumper craze swept throughout the city, nay, the nation. The infatuation with the G-Man Jumper was so strong that thousands of kids born in 1990 and early '91 are named Gary or Gabe or George. Mike Gminski was everything we wanted Spencer Hawes to be.

Trying to mask the mistake of the 1986 Moses Malone trade and fill the crater-sized hole at the center position, the Sixers acquired Gminski and Ben Coleman from the Nets for Roy Hinson, Tim McCormick, and a second rounder.

"Gminski conceded that he was originally disturbed by the rumors of the trade because he was so firmly entrenched in the North Jersey area. But remembering what life with the woeful Nets had been like - and with the team's current record (7-27) staring him in the face - he reversed his thinking quickly." (Bruton 1988).

The Sixers committed to Gminski. In March of '88, they inked the big man to a 5-year, $8.75 million dollar contract. The deal made G-Man the second highest-paid player in Sixers team history behind Moses (Yagoda 1989, 36). The durable G-Man started 239 of 240 career games in Philly. He provided a toughness at the five spot that the Sixers had been lacking. He was solid in most phases of the game. The '89-'90 Sixers won't win a popularity contest with those Buddy Ryan Eagles teams, but this Sixers rendition was an incredibly likeable bunch. And, unlike those Birds teams, they at least managed to advance a round in the playoffs. (Now if you'll excuse me, I'm going to pour myself a glass of wine and watch 'The Bodybag Game').

Gminski took on a leadership role, even orchestrating a road trip to get guys their ears pierced to celebrate a string of wins. This article gave me all sorts of *Parent Trap* flashbacks.

Mike Gminski and Rick Mahorn showed up at the 76ers' practice yesterday wearing diamond-studded earrings.

They seem determined to take teammate Charles Barkley with them to jewelers' row.

Two weeks ago, after the Sixers won their 10th consecutive game, Barkley announced that he, Gminski, Mahorn, Derek Smith and rookie Lanard Copeland had made a pact to get their ears pierced.

"I guess Rick and I have to take Charles by the hand," Gminski said. "I just want to make it clear this isn't a lifestyle commitment. This is more a reminder of what we accomplished." (Weiss 1990).

Let the record show that the ear piercing is NOT a lifestyle commitment. My client has no further comment at this time. But how adorable. A team bonding ear piercing? Did they make a day of it? Grab lunch afterwards, squeeze in a tour of Independence Hall? Maybe the rookie Copeland tried on some new digs at a high-end boutique while Gminski and Mahorn looked on – like a scene from every 80's movie ever.

Despite the team camaraderie, Gminski's tenure ended abruptly in '91 with the mid-season exchange for Gilliam. G-Man was involved in trade rumors a month prior. He and his agent supposedly told the Hornets that Gminski had no interest in uprooting his family to Charlotte. But a month later, the rumors resurfaced and this time a deal was finalized. After learning of the trade, reports mentioned a visibly shaken Gminski fighting back a lot of emotion.

"He was devastated," Sixers captain Charles Barkley said. "I know Mike. He had to be." (Jasner 1991).

The trade didn't pan out and in hindsight, probably accelerated Barkley's departure. Armen Gilliam and Barkley had similar offensive games. Sprinkle in Mahorn and that was three guys trying to get to the same spot on the court. Chuck operated almost exclusively on the low block. Gminski, on the other hand, complemented Charles' game well. Choose to double Barkley and face the consequences.

You're staring down the barrel of a G-Man Jumper.

The Injury

Name: Shavlik Randolph

Height: 6'10"

College: Duke

Sixers Tenure: 2005-2008

Overheard at the bar at Bennigan's:

Date: November 18, 2006

Time: Approximately 9:49 P.M.

"Excuse me, can you switch the TV over to UCLA/Arizona State? Got a four-team parlay and -"

"Sorry, man, no can do. I made a promise to the guy in the Shav Randolph jersey. He'd kill me. Randolph is starting tonight."

"He bought a Shavlik Randolph jersey?"

"A home and road."

I lived in Manayunk in my early 20s. Everyone lived in Manayunk at some point in their 20s. Living there created its own set of challenges. There was this amazing breakfast sandwich place that only served breakfast until noon. The night before, I'd set my money aside like a kid planning my school clothes for the following morning - $10 for a Gatorade and a scrapple, egg, and cheese on a long roll. One Saturday morning, the day had gotten away from me (see: *NBA2K*) when I glanced at the clock: 11:58 AM. It became a race against time, *Run, Lola, Run* in live form. I sprinted barefoot out of my house, waving my money and shouting, trying to order a sandwich from eight blocks away.

"Scrapple, egg, and cheese on a long roll!" I screamed. I startled a couple walking their dog. They quickly shuffled to the other side of the street.

"And a red Gatorade!"

I was a regular. The owner knew me. But he also had a very strict 12:00 policy. I arrived at 12:04 PM, not egregiously late, but rules are rules. The stove was already off. Heartbroken, I walked away with a Gatorade, two soft pretzels, and a *Daily News.* What does this story have to do with Shavlik Randolph? Nothing, but his Sixers tenure intersected with my time in Manayunk. My memory works in a unique way. When I'm trying to recall a past event in Philly sports, I first put myself in that time period.

"Who led the Sixers in rebounding in the '95-'96 season, Dave?"

"Well, I was in 5th grade then. My first girlfriend dumped me at a roller skating party at The Palace. So it had to be Weatherspoon."

The '01 Finals Team is my baseline. I was a junior in high school then. I then add or subtract years as needed. The post-Barkley Dark Ages are my grade school years. Iverson was junior high through college, and so on and so forth. The Manayunk Years bridged the Iverson swan song to whatever went wrong in Eddie Jordan's one season.

Randolph joined the Sixers as an undrafted free agent in 2005. He played in the Rocky Mountain Revue, the bizarro anti-Vegas Summer League. The Revue is like playing college hoops, thinking you made 'the tournament,' then discovering it's actually the CollegeInsider.com Tournament (CIT) and you're hosting the University of Hartford in the first round. Randolph didn't have much of an impact his rookie season outside of a handful of big rebounding performances. During the '06-'07 season, however, Shavlik found himself in the starting line-up due to a Chris Webber injury. Which brings us back to Manayunk.

Saturday, November 25th, 2006. My friends and I didn't go out on Main St. that night. The walk down Green Lane wasn't a bad one. It was the walk back up hill. This was pre-Uber and Lyft, mind you. Cabs were scarce. You're left with a decision. Wear a coat to the bars and awkwardly lug it around with you because the inside of these places was hotter than Death Valley. Then you make the walk back, and let the cold, crisp Northwest Philly air roll off the jacket you got at Boscov's. Or, don't wear a coat. Enjoy a stress free, hands-free night out and wait for bronchitis to nab you three days later. Decisions, decisions. My buddies and I sat this one out and took in some Sixers/Cavs November basketball. Hard to believe I was single at the time.

Between solving the puzzles on the caps of a Lionshead bottle and listening to Incubus, we watched a pique Shavlik Randolph performance. He was active that night, recording 12 points and 6 boards in just over 22 minutes of action. He jumped off the screen, seemingly always in the right place that night. He wasn't an all-star, no, but he was a piece. Then I said those fateful words that foreshadowed his pending doom, the same words I texted out after Jahil Okafor's first pro game against the Celtics.

"I think we have something here."

Five days later, Randolph broke his ankle.

Philadelphia 76ers forward Shavlik Randolph broke his left ankle during practice Thursday and will undergo surgery.

"It is unfortunate Shav got hurt today," 76ers President Billy King said. "He will be missed as he is an integral part of this team, but I am confident that the rest of the guys will step up in his absence." (ESPN 2006).

While rehabbing, Randolph managed to get himself in the news for all the wrong reasons. In February of '07, former Penn State product, John Amaechi, wrote an autobiography where he was coming out as a gay man. NBA players were asked about Amaechi, and the idea of playing with a gay teammate in general. Randolph's response made headlines for its ignorance, saying, *"As long as you don't bring your gayness on me, I'm fine."* (Daily News Wire Services 2007). It was his final attention-grabbing moment for the Sixers. Randolph played just nine more games in Philly the following season. He bounced around the league for a few more years, but he and Philadelphia's paths never again crossed.

The Consolation Prize

Name: Jeff Hornacek

Height: 6'3"

College: Iowa St

Sixers Tenure: 1992-1994

"This, by far, was the best deal offered," said Katz yesterday.

The Suns dickered for more than a week before putting Lang, Hornacek, and Perry on the table. The Sixers had attempted to get either point guard Kevin Johnson or swing man Dan Majerle. (Ford 1992).

Jeff Hornacek's Sixers tenure will forever be linked to the Barkley trade, and that probably isn't fair. Hornacek didn't pull the trigger on one of the most lopsided deals in NBA history. That honor is bestowed upon Jim Lynam and Harold Katz, who personally set out to ruin an eight-year-old boy's childhood. Seems a bit vindictive, but whatever.

"Dave, honey. Are you sitting down? We have to talk. Your dad and I have something to tell you."

"What is it, mom? Is everything alright? Are you getting divorced? Is it grandma?"

"No, no. Grandma's fine. But – well, there's no easy way to say this." Mom exhaled. "The Sixers just traded Charles Barkley for Jeff Hornacek, Andrew Lang, and Tim Perry."

That couldn't be right, I thought. She must've misheard.

"What about Kevin Johnson? Or Thunder Dan? And the picks? How many picks, mom?"

She shook her head, like she couldn't even believe the words that were about to come out of her mouth.

"No KJ or Majerle. No picks, sweetie."

"But Barkley's a top-five player in –"

"Why don't we have some ice cream for dinner? Would you like that?"

Katz said that this package from Phoenix was the best offer the Sixers received. But was it? Of all the phone calls Katz and Jim Lynam fielded for the disgruntled superstar, was the Phoenix pu pu platter the most enticing? Buckle your seatbelts. It's time to step inside The Trade Rumor Time Machine. Let's go back to 1992.

Sixers Give: Charles Barkley and Hersey Hawkins
Warriors Give: Tim Hardaway and Billy Owens

Hardaway was legit - a 25-year-old stud, a two-time all-star, and fresh off a campaign where he Texas Two-Stepped his way to a 23-point and ten-assist season. Billy Owens was just named to the All-Rookie Team. Giving up both the Hawk and Barkley would've broken my little eight-year-old soul, but Hardaway and Owens would've been a calculated gamble and a sufficient return. I would've gotten over it. (Missanelli 1992).

Sixers Give: Charles Barkley
Bullets Give: Pervis Ellison and considerations

What were the other considerations? Peter Bondra and the Lincoln Monument? Pervis Ellison just had a career year, compiling a 20 and 11 season, but that package is lighter than the attendance for a David Buchanan start in September. "Considerations" is clearly a loaded word here, but unless there are multiple picks traveling up the Northeast Corridor to Philly, yama hama. Hard pass. (Jasner 1992).

Sixers Give: Charles Barkley

Trail Blazers Give: Kevin Duckworth, Jerome Kersey, Danny Ainge, two unspecified Blazers, and two draft picks

Those are a lot of players not named Clyde Drexler. And what does 'two unspecified Blazers' mean? Portland planning on sneaking two walk-ons from the University of Alabama-Birmingham's hoops team into the deal on a technicality? Two defensemen from the Philadelphia Blazers of the World Hockey Association? Can we be a bit more specific here? (Jasner 1992).

"We never said anything about Blazers from *Portland*, Harold."

Sixers Give: Charles Barkley and Ron Anderson

Lakers Give: Elden Campbell and James Worthy

This trade rumor actually floated around in January of '92. According to an interview Barkley gave *Sports Illustrated* in 2015, his agent actually had called Charles to say he had been traded to LA. Excited about the news, Barkley did a little day drinking at lunch to celebrate. Can't blame 'em. His agent then again called up and said the trade was a no-go, so Barkley suited up for the Sixers that night a few drinks deep. (Deitsch 2015).

On the surface, the trade was a one-sided deal for Los Angeles. Worthy's best days were behind him, and Campbell, albeit a young big with potential, wasn't on the same planet as Barkley. There were reports of a three-team deal involving the Lakers, Sixers, and the Hornets around the All-Star Break. The Lakers would send James Worthy to the Hornets. Charlotte would have sent Philly Kendall Gill and Rex Chapman who, paired with Hawkins, may have battled for a playoff spot. The proposed return presented a much greater ceiling than the eventual Suns package. Better than 'two unspecified Blazers' anyway (Goldstein 1992). Although the greatest gift the Phoenix haul provided Philly was that it was so shitty, that it forced the Sixers to bottom out. They then landed Iverson #1 overall in 1996.

"If you want to discuss this seriously, is Charles physically the same guy he was when he was 21 years old?" said Lynam. "No. He's subjected to a savage beating every night. When you see his numbers are down, figure it out. He's not a machine."

Trading Barkley a year too early rather than a year too late was important to the Sixers. Tack on another season of nagging injuries -- perhaps a major one -- and toss in another season of demoralizing controversy, and Barkley might have been untradeable. (Ford 1992).

If Philly could only land Hornacek, Perry, and Lang in the summer of '92, what did the Sixers brass think would be out there a year later? Barkley and a couple of first rounders for Andrew Lang? Greg Dreiling? It was an acknowledgement that they sold low but could've sold even lower. Thanks for thinking of us, Jim?

Hornacek was the prize acquisition from Phoenix. The Iowa State product was a sharp-shooting two-guard and creative scorer whose arsenal was full of off-balance learners and floaters and scoop lay-ups. Horny could get buckets, which was all the more impressive because he looked like the guy who wore a sweater vest to a July 4th cookout. He'd bring over a bottle of Rosé when all you really needed was a twelve of Miller and some hot dog buns.

Jeff was fresh off a 20-point per night season. His numbers improved each year. He turned himself from roster filler in Phoenix to a starter, and then eventually an All-Star. But by the time Hornacek's evolution was complete, he was already 28 years old. The '92-'93 Sixers faced a rebuild so daunting that they were better off trading Barkley for some junior high kids whose parents were tall. Figure in ten years, when the Sixers were good again, these kids would be in their early twenties and ready to roll.

Hornacek was lukewarm to the idea of coming to Philly to say the least. He even hinted at hanging up the sneakers upon hearing the news.

Hornacek was hit hardest by the trade and has suggested he might retire.

"I have enough money saved up to do it," Hornacek said. "Money isn't everything. My family is more important to me. If we get back there and don't like it, I'd actually consider retiring." (Obert 1992).

Whoa, whoa, whoa, don't do anything hasty, Jeff. Should we remind you that Doug Moe is now in charge, and he's bringing his fast-paced attack and polyester suits to Philly? Before you cash in your 401(k), have you envisioned yourself running the pick and pop with Armen Gilliam? Hornacek had a nice initial campaign for the Sixers, putting up 19 points and 7 assists a contest. When your team gives up 185 points per game, though, the 19 and 7 doesn't hold much water. He entered the next season by holding out - whether for a new contract, or a ticket out of Philly, or possibly both. He still had four years on his deal, but at about $1.7 million per year, he was certainly underpaid for a player with his production. He suggested that the Sixers trade either he or Hersey Hawkins before the season, and if Hawk was the one to go - Hersey was - that renegotiating his contract would be paramount. Hornacek and his team were looking for a 'balloon payment,' a large sum at the end of his contract which would buoy the money and years upfront.

A source indicated that Hornacek is looking for a payment of between $6 and $7 million, and that the Sixers have been dangling the equivalent of a buyout in the area of $2 million.

The source indicated that, if the Sixers did not offer something more, Hornacek would welcome a trade.

"He has a contract, he's supposed to be [with the team]," Katz said. "Can we talk? Yes. We can always talk, but in order for that to happen, the player had to be playing, honoring his contract." (Jasner 1993).

A holdout was inevitable. Both parties were stubborn. Hornacek eventually rejoined the team right before the start of the regular season, under the guise that Katz and his agent would continue discussions. That never really happened though. Jeff suited up, albeit begrudgingly. Conversations never progressed. Hornacek's future was sealed. The prize of the Barkley return was traded in February '94, right before the deadline. In his final game with the Sixers, Jeff scored 25 points and chipped in 6 boards and 4 assists on an efficient 10-17 shooting. Fittingly, the Sixers lost.

Hornacek was a talented player who never really wanted to be here. His play was solid, but his heart was still west of the Rockies. Horny's Philly career will always be tied to that '92 trade. No, he wasn't Charles Barkley. But he wasn't Andrew Lang or Tim Perry either.

The Outcast

Name: Matt Harpring

Height: 6'7"

College: Georgia Tech

Sixers Tenure: 2001-2002

Matt Harpring leaves a complicated legacy. He was pretty decent, but not fondly remembered. There's no Sixers fan with a corner of their basement or study dedicated to Matt Harpring memorabilia. Two friends aren't having a beer somewhere in Delco, fawning over a framed and signed Harpring jersey. That's not an authentic Delco Experience. Those two friends are having a beer, yes, but they're pouring one out for Pelle Lindbergh and ordering a pizza from Pica's.

There are two trains of thought. If you're of the mindset that Harpring was brought in here to be Allen Iverson's wingman, a seemingly impossible role to cast up until AI's eventual trade to Denver, then Matt Harpring was a disappointment. His numbers (just under 12 points per night) and play certainly didn't live up to those lofty expectations. If you feel Harpring was thrusted into a more prominent role as a result of Eric Snow, Allen Iverson, and Derrick Coleman missing a combined 67 games, then Matt was more a victim of circumstance than anything else. The only thing seemingly everyone can agree on was that Matt Harpring struggled to fit in.

He was a standout at Georgia Tech, and the second leading scorer in school history (just ahead of Mark Price and Dennis Scott). Along with Cedric Henderson and Robert Traylor, Cleveland traded Harpring in August of 2001 to Philly for Tyrone Hill and Jumaine Jones. Harpring and a long in the tooth Derrick Coleman were brought in to replace important pieces from the '01 Finals Team. It was a challenging transition for both Harpring and the Sixers. While his durability was an asset - Matt played and started in 81 games - there were often times where Harpring seemed to disappear from the flow of the offense. But that apparently may have been by design.

"When Larry Brown tells you not to shoot, you don't shoot," Harpring said. "He tells me I'm not a shooter, I'm not a scorer. I just wanted to please him. I want to be on the court, and on that team, that's what I needed to do to be on the court.

I honestly tried my best to please him. If he told me not to shoot, I wouldn't shoot. I took away my game to try to please him. It's like they forgot I could score." (Sielski 2003).

Harpring wasn't like the kid on your Little League team who the coach stuck in right field and was told to "not swing until you get two strikes." But he certainly assumed a lesser role in Philly. It was a big adjustment for Matt. The '01 Cavs stunk, but he didn't have to worry about Lamond Murray going 8 for 29 on any given night. Harpring, like most players, was used to a more balanced offense predicated on ball movement, and the early 2000s Sixers were anything but. It's a difficult ask of an established player. Offensively, you're not just taking a backseat. You're locked in the trunk of the car (and hoping that J.J. Redick reports your predicament to the proper authorities). Iverson relentlessly attacked the basket forty plus minutes a night, while four other guys set screens and discussed the most recent episode of *ER*.

The challenges Harpring faced weren't exclusive to Matt, though. It was the same for Van Horn, for Robinson, and for Webber. Iverson's teammates were like wide receivers in a triple-option offense. Their number may occasionally get called, but for the most part, they're just taking up space. But in a strange way, Harpring was the most amicable of Iverson's Robins. The other guys - they couldn't defend. Matt Harpring could. On paper, it seemed like a good fit, and really, it kinda was. Philly didn't implode or self-destruct that year. The Sixers were ravaged by injuries and fell victim to a barrage of three pointers in a 5-game series to Boston.

Despite an uneven playoff series against those Celtics that saw Harpring only reach double figures once, the Sixers expressed interest in bringing him back. They made an initial qualifying offer, but later withdrew it. Harpring - who was looking at a healthy raise - would've put the Sixers, still needing to fill some other holes, over the luxury tax. The money just didn't add up. (Associated Press 2002). He agreed to a deal with the Jazz, and I don't think the Utah nightlife played a large part in his decision. Fit matters and Harpring never seemed comfortable in Philadelphia. The Sixers decided to allocate their resources elsewhere – starting by signing Greg Buckner.

The Hollywood Movie

Name: Raja Bell

Height: 6'5"

College: Boston U.; Florida International

Sixers Tenure: 2000-2002

Never mind the stay in Yakima, Wash., and the aborted stop in Sioux Falls, S.D. Forget the apprenticeships in the alphabet minor leagues, the years playing in near-empty gyms back in college at Boston University and Florida International.

Earlier this year, Raja Bell was playing ball in a YMCA, going against his father and the other 45-year-olds.

"I had to get a run where I could," Bell, a 6-foot-5 guard said last night. "I couldn't take my dad lightly. He's a baller." (Jensen 2001).

Documented ad nauseam during the 2001 Playoffs, Raja Bell's journey was pulled straight from a movie script. Everyone who played pick-up hoops shared that fantasy at one time or another. They're lying if they say otherwise. You, 5'8", but listed as 5'10" on your dating profile, work as an accountant or maybe an elementary school teacher during the day, but an off-guard at night. You're grinding - wind sprints between shooting drills, running the stairs of the high school football field between free throws. You have a ton of critics and naysayers, but you persist. One night, you're at an open run, struggling to find a rhythm. You then think of your grandma, think about how much *your* basketball dreams meant to *her*, and you suddenly start cooking. The jump shot starts falling.

Serendipitously, a rental car lumbers up, hazard lights on. A disheveled man with a loosened tie steps out of the car. He's animated and frazzled, kicking the front tire while on a phone call with a mechanic - complaining about a flat. He needs to be in the big city by morning, he screams. The man suddenly pauses. He tells the mechanic to hold on a second. He's distracted by the pick-up game in the distance. He squints. Who is *that* guy, the man asks himself. What form on his jump shot. Look at that elevation. He must be 5'10". Lord knows this basketball scout could use a hit - funnily enough, he jokingly *prayed* for a new hoops star the night before. The movie? *A Wing and a Prayer*. (Ideally, we cast Steve Guttenberg or Kevin Dunn as the scout, but I'm open to suggestions).

Raja Bell's story does mirror another athlete. Knee-deep in a Goodwill Games medal round run, Team USA sought to fill the roster spot vacated by an injured Adam Banks when captain/assistant coach, Charlie Conway, plucked Russ Tyler and his famed 'knuckle puck' from the Los Angeles street hockey circuit. The risky move paid dividends as Tyler, on Team USA's roster for about twenty minutes, scored the go-ahead goal against Russia.

An injury to Temple legend Pepe Sánchez forced the Sixers hand, but Raja Bell wasn't 'Lil Bow Wow in *Like Mike*. He didn't just find a pair of shoes lying around and *voilá*. Bell wasn't *just* playing YMCA ball. He had originally latched on with the Spurs and later signed with the International Basketball League juggernaut, the Sioux Falls Skyforce, before being picked up by the injury-laden Sixers at the recommendation of Gregg Popovich.

Raja Bell was eating lunch at a Denny's in Sioux Falls, S.D. with some Sioux Falls Skyforce teammates earlier this year when his cell phone rang, and he heard the three letters that Continental Basketball Association veterans wait desperately to hear.

NBA.

He excused himself from the table, went outside and jumped for joy. He never finished the BLT on his plate. And the French fries he loves went untouched.

The Philadelphia 76ers had called. (Povtak 2001).

Signed in April, Bell saw action in just a handful of games before the playoffs. During the early round series against the Pacers and the Raptors, he was an afterthought. This guy was barely playing. No one heard of Raja Bell. The Sixers could've grabbed anyone and announced, '"This is Raja Bell," and the city would have been like, "Cool. I guess that's Raja Bell." In Game 6 of the Milwaukee series, Raja got the call and chipped in eight points in sixteen minutes of action.

Riding the hot hand, Brown called Bell's number again in the 2nd quarter of the deciding Game 7. Raja added ten huge points in the second quarter - two dunks, a triple, and, channeling my inner Zumoff here, the hoop and the harm. Bell had the crowd going bananas. He was such an unknown that when he did anything - and man, did he do a lot in that 2nd quarter - the First Union Center lost their collective minds. As they say, find someone who loves you as much as Philly loves an underdog story.

Game 1 of the Sixers/Lakers Finals is rightfully remembered for the performance of Allen Iverson - AI stepping over Tyronn Lue, pantsing him on national TV, et al. But Lue had given Iverson fits in the second half (not to mention a lot of grabbing). Two and a half minutes into overtime and the Sixers were still scoreless. They trailed by five, desperately needing a hoop. And with the shot clock running down, Raja delivered this left-handed scoop lay-up circus shot in the lane to stop the bleeding. The Sixers don't win the game without that bucket. Iverson's step over of Lue wouldn't have carried nearly the same iconic clout in a loss.

After playing one more season with the Sixers, Bell enjoyed another successful eight years in the league. Raja Bell was an unknown. From a Denny's in South Dakota straight into Sixers lore.

"I had never heard of Raja Bell until Coach brought him to our team," Sixers forward Tyrone Hill said. (Povtak 2001).

We neither, Ty. We neither.

The Other Contract

Name: Kenny Thomas

Height: 6'7"

College: New Mexico

Sixers Tenure: 2002-2005

Overheard at Reading Terminal:

Date: May 22, 2037

Time: Approximately 12:25 PM

"GM TJ McConnell is gonna have some real cap flexibility once Kenny Thomas' contract comes off the books next season."

"Yep, could see TJ kicking the tires on Hollis Thompson. He's shooting 40% from beyond the arc for Panathinaikos in the Greek League."

Kenny Thomas was the other contract. If this was *Family Feud,* and you asked one hundred Sixers fans to name a notoriously long deal in the franchise's history, the #1 answer is either Scott Williams or Kenny Thomas. (Maybe Tobias Harris or Al Horford, too, at this rate). Every list or ranking of bad Sixers contracts doled out always include these two. People may have thought that long contracts went out of style after the Scott Williams Chronicles, but Kenny Thomas proved that lengthy deals, like socks with sandals, are always en vogue. The similarities between the pair end there, though. Health wasn't really an issue with Thomas. Neither was productivity. Kenny wasn't bad here. His contract, however, was a commitment to mediocrity; a white flag to the rest of the Eastern Conference that said, "We can't do any better than this." The Sixers signed the restricted free agent to a seven-year deal. There are third graders who got their driver's license by the time Thomas' contract expired.

Kenny Thomas was the industry standard for early 21st century power forwards. Before there was WAR in baseball nomenclature, there was Wins Above Kenny Thomas.

"Etan Thomas had a pretty good year last year, huh?"

"Eh, measuring by just counting stats, I guess. But he had a -0.6 WAK(t) in only 57 games."

"Damn, that's a rough WAK(t)."

Kenny was the perfectly adequate four in your line-up, an absolutely suitable player to round out your rotation. He had a face-up game at the elbow, and range that flirted with the three-point line but never dared to go all the way. The Sixers acquired Thomas in December of '02, as part of a three-team deal, giving up Art Long, Mark Bryant and a 2005 first round pick. Larry Brown probably knew he wouldn't be coaching the Sixers in '05, so what did he care? Take an '06 and an '07 first rounder while you're at it. Want the Liberty Bell, too? We'll just use the Bell's open roster spot to pick-up Kevin Ollie. Brown and King coveted Kenny Thomas. To management's credit and detriment, if there was a player they desired, they had no problem moving mountains or draft picks, to acquire them.

Thomas had his moments. In a tight win at Orlando at the end of March, Kenny scored 24 points and collected 20 rebounds. He followed that up with a 15-rebound performance, and another 20 boards one game later in a win over Boston. In the postseason, Thomas was decent, mixing in some great performances (15 and 19 against Detroit in Game 2), with some duds (2 points and 4 boards in Game 1). Entering the 2003 offseason, the Sixers had this young power forward that was part of an aging frontcourt. Regardless of their feelings on Thomas - and they were high on him - management was boxed into a corner. King double-downed on Kenny. For better or worse, he was now part of the team's nucleus.

Thomas has no rings to date, but the restricted free agent, whose signing had been described by Sixers president/general manager, Billy King, as his "No. 1 priority," can console himself with the 7-year, nearly $50 million contract. (Fernandez 2003).

I don't remember outrage over the deal at the time. The press conference announcing the contract was July 16th, 2003, the same day when the band Chicago visited the Tweeter Center. Maybe it was the perfect cover for the organization.

"Apparently the Sixers gave Kenny Thomas a seven-year deal. Ashley just texted me."

"Shut up, dude. They're playing 'Saturday in the Park.'"

The majority of fans didn't consider the long-term effects, like the fact that Kenny Thomas' soul, and the Sixers salary cap, now belonged to the devil. Fans didn't have the foresight. It didn't register that Kenny was now the Sixers starting power forward for all of eternity.

In his first year with his newly minted contract, Thomas was really solid. He had his best statistical season of his career, starting over 70 games and averaging a double-double. From about March on he was terrific, helping the Sixers cling to their faint playoff hopes. Six more years of double-double production didn't sound half-bad, and I was one more 20 and 10 away from giving Thomas a key to the city and a twelve-year extension. But the '04 offseason complicated matters. The Sixers acquired Corliss Williamson and signed Brian Skinner to a long-term deal. No longer did Thomas have a monopoly on the power forward slot. He wasn't the only face-up game in town. Now Thomas found himself in a platoon, but not the fun one like Milt Thompson and Pete Incaviglia commandeering left field. This one was messy.

Thomas was the anointed starter, but under new coach, Jim O'Brien, that just made Kenny a figurehead more than a rotation stalwart. In a mid-November home win against Orlando, Thomas was glued to the bench for the second half. O'Brien was playing the hot hand, and on that night, it was Williamson (Juliano 2004). Then undrafted big man and CBA alum, Josh Davis, joined the party. Why not? Put your sleeping bag over there by the ottoman, Josh. It was another cook in the kitchen that only further muddied the waters.

"Right now our starting [power] forward is Josh Davis and our best power forward, I think, is Corliss Williamson," O'Brien said. "It's nothing derogatory to Kenny." (Narducci 2004).

"Jesse, who are your top-10 Sixers power forwards?"

"Probably Barkley, Dolph Schayes ... I thought McGinnis was underrated -"

"No, no. Top-10 on the current roster."

Thomas had excelled the previous season, especially in the latter half playing for interim head coach Chris Ford. O'Brien and Kenny butted heads, though. In a win at Utah in early January, Thomas dropped 18 in the first quarter, and 30 for the game. The next night out, he only played 20 minutes. I suppose there was one way to solve the power forward dilemma. You trade all of them. In February of '05, Thomas, Williamson, and Skinner were all moved to Sacramento to usher in Chris Webber's arrival. It was a feeling of relief for Thomas, who in a twelve-month span, went from building block to sharing minutes with Josh fuckin' Davis.

His relationship with O'Brien?

You [reporters] saw it," Thomas said. "That was crazy. Just being able to get out of there, I'm a little happy, but the organization was good to me. When Billy called and said a trade was going down, I knew it was me. Where was I going?" (Jasner 2005).

Thomas' first game with Sacramento was at the Wachovia Center, as his Kings visited Philadelphia. In a bad omen for the Webber acquisition, the team, and the direction of the franchise in general, the Sixers lost CWebb's debut, 101-99.

Kenny Thomas got a double-double.

The Estranged

Name: Andrės Nocioni

Height: 6'7"

Born: Santa Fe, Argentina

Sixers Tenure: 2010-2012

Andrės Nocioni had an edge to him. Nocioni was one of the few international players who wasn't branded with that stereotypical "soft" stigma. Along with his well-known nickname, "Chapu," Nocioni was also apparently dubbed, "The Wild Bull of the Pampas." That's the nickname of a guy who will give you 14 and 8, and then crash a yacht party. I was intrigued. The Sixers acquired Spencer Hawes and Nocioni from Sacramento for a disgruntled Samuel Dalembert in June of 2010.

Hawes, a young center and former lottery pick, was the prime piece in the return, but Nocioni had the pedigree. He was a fixture of those feisty mid-2000s Bulls teams, along with Ben Gordon, Luol Deng, and Kirk Hinrich. Nocioni was a '3 and D' type - an agitator on the defensive end who shot over 35% from behind the arc. He also had a goatee, like every other guy in the Delaware Valley between the ages of 25-45. He just needed a neckbeard and a baby blue Phillies t-shirt to complete the look.

"I think I saw Nocioni at the Italian Market the other day. He was wearing a Chooch shirsey."

"No shit, really?"

"I think so. Or it was the guy who lives down the street from me. Or actually it might've been Geoff Geary."

Nocioni played early. His jump shot made the flight from Sacramento and he was a staple in Doug Collins' rotation. Between commercials of the 2010 Alamo

Bowl, you may have seen Nocioni Toast-ioni the Suns. In the late December tilt playing without Iguodala, he soaked up over forty minutes for a banged-up Sixers team. Andrés had a big game - registering 22 points and 12 boards in the victory. The game was a reminder of what Chapu had in his arsenal. A dislocated and fractured finger, though, sidelined Andrés for the better part of two months. As the Sixers finished their regular season and prepared for a first-round match-up with LeBron James and the Heat, the casual observer assumed that Nocioni wasn't part of the Sixers' postseason plans.

But let's quickly backtrack. In September, before the start of the regular season, Nocioni was scheduled to play for his native Argentina (along with noted Sixers killer, Luis Scola). Per Andrés:

"Doug Collins lied to my face. Because he told me that I was going to be like Jesus Christ for the Sixers. And that's why they took me out of the World Championship. The one coach who lied to me the most was Collins. He promised me something that later it wasn't true." (HoopsHype 2020).

Good on GM Ed Stefanski for acquiring the Lord and Savior for only Sam Dalembert. That's good value. The relationship between Nocioni and Collins was already strained, going back as far as September before the FIBA World Championships. This meeting, this conversation - per Nocioni anyway - was predicated on a lie. This team was always Iguodala's.

Andrés also referenced a cantankerous relationship with Iguodala himself. Nocioni had a bit of a reputation around the league, earning his fair share of flagrant fouls and fines. Andrés suggested that his blackballing wasn't just a coach's decision. He alluded that the team's best player also had a role.

"Andre did not want me on the team, because I hit him in practice, pushed him, irritated him. He was complaining about it, and instead of having my back, Collins pulled me out of the rotation." (HoopsHype 2020).

Despite the drama, the Sixers qualified for the postseason albeit with a 41-41 record. But we're not done. The alleged lying and deceit continued. According to Nocioni, Collins was prepared to take the tarp off his offseason acquisition just in time for the playoffs.

"Then he lied to me again just before the playoffs. One day he comes and says 'I'm going to rest Iguodala for a few games. I'll give you those games so you are ready for the playoffs. Because this is a big thing, this is not for kids. Be ready'. I played well in the final two games of the regular season, averaging 15 points, and we started the playoffs against LeBron's Miami. I had 10 minutes and never played again." (HoopsHype 2020).

The relationship between the two parties was completely severed at this point. Nocioni wanted out and the Sixers weren't going to play him. Except Andrès still had another year remaining on his deal (and a team option that assuredly was not going to be exercised). Awkwardness abound. Unable to find a willing dance partner and not open to just releasing Nocioni, the Sixers kept him. Chapu was a forgotten man. He appeared in just 11 games during the '11-'12 season. This wasn't a divorce. This was breaking up with your significant other who you share an apartment with. But neither of you can afford a one bedroom on your own, so you're living in awkward silence until the lease ends. It was basically every Dashboard Confessional song ever written. The Sixers finally released Andrès Nocioni in March, and one of the most drama-filled tenures reached its merciful end.

The Rocket Launcher

Name: James Anderson

Height: 6'6"

College: Oklahoma State

Sixers Tenure: 2013-2014

Anderson hit the shot over Lin, who ended the night with nine threes of his own and 34 points. "We went back and forth the whole night," Anderson said of Lin. "It definitely felt good."

"And I was able to get the last laugh." (Perner 2013).

Very few players had their 'career year' in Philly. Dana Barros, Willie Burton, maybe one or two more, but it's a very short list. It seems like every big free agent, every journeyman, every role player who has passed through here has been a letdown or a nonfactor. Outside of Moses and Dr. J, all of the stars are homegrown. Like 31-year-old Calvin Booth didn't come to Philly and suddenly turn into Bob Lanier. The Sixers aren't that lucky. But James Anderson? He was the aberration.

If you look at his career numbers, his one year in Philly jumps off the page. His season wasn't quite Brady Anderson's 50 home runs in 1996, but it was a drastic improvement from past campaigns. Most games played, games started, minutes played, most points, highest FG%, the list goes on. For three years, James Anderson was kept on ice. His legs were fresh, his ankles, feet, his toes, all fresh. Fresh as a daisy. He floated along in obscurity. Anderson was Jigglypuff with a better jump shot.

The Sixers signed the two-guard in July '13, two days after he was waived by the Rockets. James joined a Philly team in transition. Doug Collins was gone, and GM Sam Hinkie had named former Spurs assistant, Brett Brown, as head coach.

After the trading of Jrue Holiday on draft night 2013, the Sixers' rebuilding strategy came into focus. There were still some holdovers from the previous regime - Spencer Hawes, Evan Turner, and Thad Young - but the majority of the roster was either rookies or getting their first legitimate opportunity. Anderson felt much older than he really was, like how Thaddeus Young has been 19 years old for the last decade.

He was just 24 at the time - a toddler by NBA's standards - and now was presented with his first real NBA minutes. Named a starter to begin the season, Anderson lurked in the shadows initially. He bided his time, conceded the spotlight to rookie Michael Carter-Williams, until his former team, the Houston Rockets, came to town.

Then the James Anderson Game happened. Reports say James Harden didn't dress that night, but I think he did. I think he dressed up as James Anderson. Anderson hit triples. He hit floaters. He hung in the air and converted a ridiculous reverse lay-up. With Houston clinging to a three-point lead in the waning moments of regulation, Tony Wroten got caught under the basket and heaved it back towards mid-court - to the waiting arms of our hero, James Anderson. James rose up over Jeremy Lin at the top of the key and buried it. His three tied the game and stirred the Wells Fargo Center crowd into a frenzy. James Harden stood there, stoned-faced, stunned as House of Pain's "Jump Around" blared from the heavens. The arena was rocking. I was amped up. I could've rebuilt the Spectrum brick by brick and finished before sunrise. I was Vai Sikahema punching the goalpost at The Meadowlands. The Rockets ran into a buzz saw that night, and thy saw's name was James Anderson. The Sixers prevailed in overtime, 123-117. Anderson poured in a career-high 36 points, on a crisp 12-16 shooting. He buried six threes, each triple better than the last, none more perfect than his final tally. Nobody in the crowd wanted the night to end.

"Citywides at Bob and Barbara's? Just a quick night cap."

"Definitely. For James Anderson. Just gotta tap the MAC first."

That night was the peak of Anderson's career. The Rocket Killer had some decent games the rest of the way, including another 30-point effort in a loss against Houston in March. Anderson spent 2.43% of his season lighting up the Rockets. It was the other 97.57% we had to fine tune. James was waived after the season. He spent one year in Sacramento, before taking his career overseas. Not many players have *that* game, that one signature outing where people look back and say, "Oh him? Shit, remember that one night he went off?"

That night belonged to James Anderson.

The Lethal Weapon

Name: Brian Oliver

Height: 6'4"

College: Georgia Tech

Sixers Tenure: 1990-1992

In 2018, Wake Forest's Randolph and Brandon Childress eclipsed 2,500 points combined and became the highest scoring father/son duo in ACC history. They surpassed the previous record holders - father/son tandem Brian Oliver and former Sixer, J.P. Tokoto.

Mind. Blown. I just learned that. It's like first hearing the rumor that Marilyn Manson played Paul Pfeiffer in *The Wonder Years*. Next someone is gonna tell me that Lane Johnson is Andy Harmon's kid.

Brian Oliver was good value in the early second round. The 1990 NBA Draft was chock-full of exactly one Hall of Famer (Gary Payton) and bunch of guys who hung around the league without making a huge impact. Taking a proficient scorer from a talented team who reached the Final Four was sound logic. Fans could appreciate the thought-process. Georgia Tech had a dynamic offense centered around the terrifically named trio, "Lethal Weapon 3" (Kenny Anderson, Dennis Scott, and Brian Oliver). In the second round, a team should always gamble on a big scoring talent. The Sixers just got saddled with the worst one of the three. It's like being 11 years old and going trick-or-treating with your two buddies. You all agreed to go as the Legion of Doom line but someone has to be Mikael Renberg.

Post-Georgia Tech Brian Oliver, isolated from Anderson and Scott, is a ghost. The paper trail of his NBA career was seemingly erased during Y2K. Google "Brian Oliver" and the first result is Brian Oliver, Producer of *Black Swan*. I've seen *Black*

Swan. Natalie Portman was great, but I didn't see the connection to ACC Hoops. Almost two hours and not one reference to Bobby Cremins.

Entering the draft, Oliver was considered by many as a mid-to-late first-round talent, but he played the majority of his senior season with a stress fracture in his ankle. He then took time off to recover following the NCAA Tournament. The fracture played a role in his draft stock dip. The Sixers organization was ecstatic that he fell to #32 overall.

In his mock drafts, in his most private of thoughts, in his scribblings on napkins, Bob Weinhauer told himself there was no way.

The kid was too good, too versatile, too appealing to the talent-hungry NBA teams holding the 31 picks ahead of the 76ers in last night's NBA draft.

Brian Oliver, the third partner in "Lethal Weapon 3" from Georgia Tech?

There was no way.

Yes, there was.

The sweet, 6-4 guard whom Weinhauer described as "the closest thing to a young Joe Dumars" in the talent pool became the Sixers' draft gemstone.

"Jimmy (Lynam, Sixers coach) says he resembles (Golden State guard) Mitch Richmond, I say (the Detroit Pistons') Dumars," said Weinhauer, the Sixers' director of player personnel. (Jasner 1990).

Ok, ok, I said Brian Oliver was good value in the second round. No one said anything about Joe Dumars or Mitch Richmond. The team cited his versatility in the backcourt having played both guard positions at Tech. Oliver had played point in school but moved back to his natural shooting guard position with the arrival of Kenny Anderson. He preferred the off-guard position, but point was where the Sixers quickly had a void (Rosenberg 2016).

Point guard Johnny Dawkins tore a ligament in his knee during the fourth game of the season. The unfortunate injury created a huge opportunity for the rookie Oliver, whose only competition at the point suddenly was the 36-year-old Rickey Green. One November game at the Garden the Sixers got blasted by the Knicks,

106-79. A banged-up Green sat out, leaving Oliver as the only healthy, pseudo-point guard on the roster. He logged 45 minutes while Barkley and co. called it a night shortly after halftime. Someone named Jim Farmer suited up for the Sixers. I thought 'Jim Farmer' was one of Ron Anderson's pseudonyms, like how actor Ryan Phillippe checks in at hotels under the name 'Jerome Brown.' But turns out Jim Farmer was a real person. There was no point guard competition though. Green played the majority of the minutes, and with the signing of diminutive guard Andre Turner around Thanksgiving, Oliver was relegated to a spot deep on the bench.

Quick aside: I called Oliver 'Brian Olive' as a kid, which was on brand for me because I thought Mo Cheeks was 'Mo Cheese' and Barkley was 'Charles Broccoli.' I also thought that Hershey Park was where Hersey Hawkins lived, and Ellio's Pizza was named after Mario Elie. I lived a sheltered life.

Oliver never found a role in Philly. Curiously, his shooting touch - he shot over 50% from the field and 38% from behind the arc in school - never followed him to the professional ranks. He was little used his second season and entering his third campaign, Oliver had become more of an inconvenience than a building block.

At the moment, the Sixers have five guards: Hersey Hawkins, Johnny Dawkins, Jeff Hornacek, Greg Grant and Brian Oliver.

Oliver may well be one of the players giving Katz indigestion. Oliver, who will be entering his third season, has received little playing time and is signed to a guaranteed contract for two more seasons. (Ford 1992).

The Sixers cut their losses. Oliver was waived in early November '92 and signed with the Continental Basketball Association (CBA). Outside of a cup of coffee with the Bullets and Hawks later on, that was it. Brian Oliver's NBA career never got off the ground. Draft value doesn't necessarily equate to a guy's success.

It just means that a lot of players were picked ahead of them.

The Sage

Name: Tony Battie

Height: 6'11"

College: Texas Tech

Sixers Tenure: 2010-2012

Tony Battie didn't play in 27 games because of the coach's decision. He missed seven other games with various injuries and another for personal reasons.

Yet 76ers coach Doug Collins said he plans to use Battie, who's in his 13th season, during the final games of the season.

Collins said he didn't play Battie or Andres Nocioni much during most of the regular season because he wanted to keep them fresh for the stretch run and the playoffs. (Frank 2011).

"Hearing Collins wants to unleash Battie for the stretch run and the playoffs."

"Smart. Miami won't ever know what hit 'em."

"Yep. Give Bron, Wade, and Bosh something else to think about."

"And the veteran leadership Tony brings ..."

"Exactly. You can't quantify that."

Tony Battie provided veteran leadership. He stockpiled it, like it was bottled water, flashlights, and batteries tucked away in a bunker. Don't take my word for it. Google "Tony Battie Sixers" and you'll be hit over the head with an article titled, "Sixers' Tony Battie Providing Veteran Leadership" (Leon 2011). It's a cliché as old as time. Finding the best fifteen players to fill out a roster isn't the optimal goal. You need to find fourteen good players and one guy who can help everyone else balance a checkbook. While his on the court contributions for the Sixers were minimal, Battie, oddly enough, is attached peripherally to one of the best Sixers moments of the last twenty years. More on that in a moment.

Battie was the #5 overall pick of the '97 Draft and made his rounds through the league like a college dorm RA. He was part of five separate trades. Additional players involved in these transactions include: Tyronn Lue, Nick Van Exel, Travis Knight, Kedrick Brown, Eric Williams, Ricky Davis, Chris Mihm, Michael Stewart, Drew Gooden, Steven Hunter, Anderson Varejao, Rafer Alston, Courtney Lee, Ryan Anderson, Vince Carter, and Oscar Robertson.

I threw in the "Big O" to see if you were still reading. With nearly half the Eastern Conference on his résumé, Tony Battie got the opportunity to sprinkle his veteran leadership up and down the Atlantic Coast. I actually saw a few specks while passing through Bangor, Maine a few years back.

"Philadelphia 76ers President and General Manager, Ed Stefanski, announced today that the team has signed free agent center Tony Battie. As per team policy, the terms of the deal were not disclosed.

"We see Tony Battie as a player who can come in and give us additional depth in the front court while also providing a valuable veteran presence for our younger players both on and off the court." (NBA 2010).

You're damn right he provides that presence, Ed. Battie played sparingly, but the Sixers saw enough to bring him back the following year. Give the people what they want, Rod Thorn. Don't hold out on us.

The 76ers brought back a veteran presence in the middle, the team announced Monday.

Center Tony Battie, a veteran of 13 NBA seasons, is returning for a second season in Philly.

"We are happy to have Tony back with us," Sixers President of Basketball Operations Rod Thorn said. "He will add depth to our frontcourt and his veteran savvy will be invaluable to our locker room." (NBC 2011).

Veteran savvy. That's the one, Rod.

"You smell great, Randy. New cologne?"

"Thanks, Liz. It's called Veteran Savvy."

In the first round of the postseason, the underdog #8 seed Sixers got a golden opportunity to pull off the upset, playing a Bulls team decimated by injuries. The Sixers held a 3-2 series advantage but trailed in the waning moments of Game 6. Chicago clung to a one-point lead when Omer Asik was fouled underneath the basket. Asik missed both attempts, and Andre Iguodala raced down the court after pulling the defensive rebound. He was fouled attempting the go-ahead lay-up, sending the 62% foul shooter to the line. Iguodala calmly knocked down both free throws to propel the Sixers to the next round.

Following the game, Iguodala said, "On the free throws, Tony Battie gave me some advice. He said, 'Think of something you love when you're shooting free throws,' because I've been struggling all year. I thought of my son, and it was easy after that." (Young 2012).

Doug had Tony Robbins on the bench, yet he tagged Michael Curry as Associate Head Coach? Seems like a waste of resources. Battie didn't see one minute of action in the 2012 playoffs. Why buy a Porsche if you're never gonna take it out of the garage?

He retired after the season.

The Nickname

Name: Henry Sims

Height: 6'10"

College: Georgetown

Sixers Tenure: 2014-2015

Sixers center Henry Sims had a career-high 24 points. "We are on a roll," Brown jokingly said of the Sixers winning two of their last four games. (Pompey 2014).

Here's a definitive list of Sixers players' nicknames, ranked:

10. "The Process" Joel Embiid
9. "Jellybean" Joe Bryant
8. "The Kangaroo Kid" Billy Cunningham
7. "The Sheriff" Rodney Buford
6. "The Answer" Allen Iverson
5. "The Big Dipper" Wilt Chamberlain
4. "The Round Mound of Rebound" Charles Barkley
3. "The Boston Strangler" Andrew Toney
2. "The Doctor/Dr. J" Julius Erving
1. "Chocolate Thunder" Darryl Dawkins

"Murder She Wroten" for Tony Wroten would've cracked the top-10, but that nickname never caught on. Angela Lansbury's star doesn't shine as bright as I had once thought. Rounding out the list of Sixers nicknames at #823 is "The Enormous Mormon," Shawn Bradley, which is just a really poor man's Bryant "Big Country" Reeves. When researching nicknames, I was thrilled to discover that there is a

Wikipedia entry solely dedicated to NBA player nicknames (Wikipedia 2020). Some of the nicknames are obvious. Some are surprisingly morbid. Apparently, Theodore Edwards was dubbed, "Blue," by his sister when he was choking. Fucking ay. I just thought Edwards' favorite color was blue or something else less dire. And then there is "Lick Face" Henry Sims, which I guess is better than Dick Face?

The Lick Face moniker originated from Mike Levin and Spike Eskin's *The Rights to Ricky Sanchez* podcast. I have an idea on the origin story. I think I do anyway, but I'm not *entirely* positive on the Lick Face beginnings - certainly not enough to break Kayfabe anyway. If Sixers fandom was Scientology - bear with me here - knowing Lick Face would be like Level VII of Sixers Operating Thetan. Certainly above knowing where Allen Iverson went to college, but maybe just a level or two below knowing Ivan McFarlin's shoe size.

Sims was a relative unknown at Georgetown his first three seasons. He played sparingly until his senior year, where he, Otto Porter, and Hollis Thompson led the Hoyas to a #3 seed in the NCAA Tournament. They were upset by #11 seed Lorenzo Brown and NC State. Little did anyone know at the time, but that game was the inaugural "Trust the Process" meet-up. Hope they all grabbed a bite at Miller's Ale House afterwards. Henry was brought to Philadelphia in a February '14 deal involving Spencer Hawes. Sims evolved into a Process Era staple. Maybe he wasn't the president of the Hinkie Years, but he certainly ran a strong campaign in the primaries. Sims started 57 of the 99 games he played with the Sixers, an incredible display of longevity during these seasons where change was more frequent than Larry Brown's coaching résumé.

"Let's go to Mitch in the Northeast."

"Hey, Ike. The last caller kinda stole my thunder about Chip Kelly but wanted to get your thoughts on this Sims kid. Think the Sixers have something here? Georgetown is known for its centers – you got Ewing, Mutombo … … … Ewing went there … … Patrick Ewing played at Georgetown under that coach … … They had that famous coach … … Um … Mutumbo went there. He's another one … Imma hang up and listen."

Sims was a placeholder, a guy whose job was to keep the center spot warm for the next interested candidate. Henry was smackdab right in the middle of these growing pains. He was the 'the' in "Trust the Process," a fitting location for a 6'10" center who clogged the middle. He did his best work in the springtime. When the weather got warmer, Sims ran hot. In 2014, his low post play was a nice appetizer before the Flyers battled the Rangers in the first round of the playoffs. Sims, despite his April pedigree, however, couldn't rescue Braydon Coburn on the penalty kill. He was only one man. In a late season game that same year, Henry dropped 24 on the Celtics, shooting a whopping eighteen free throw attempts. Boston, cowardly in defeat, resorted to a Hack-A-Lick Face strategy that produced disastrous results. He converted 14-18 from the charity stripe. Henry Sims was a 76% career free throw shooter. Shaq he was not.

The Marksman

Name: Jodie Meeks

Height: 6'4"

College: Kentucky

Sixers Tenure: 2010-2012

Jodie Meeks holds the University of Kentucky's record for most points in a single game, hanging a 54 spot against Tennessee in 2009. Meeks bested the previous record of 53 by Dan Issel, whose '92-'93 Skybox trading card was wedged into the back seat of my mom's station wagon. We found Cardboard Dan after cleaning out the car before a trade-in at the dealership. I never got to thank Coach Issel publicly, but his presence helped me through a lot of long car rides.

Meeks had a sweet stroke with range as far as the eyes could see. A sharp-shooting off-guard, he carved out a lengthy career in the NBA by stretching defenses and airing it out. He was like Warren Moon in that regard. Meeks' job was to blow the top off the defense, not run between the tackles for three yards and a cloud of dust. Jodie joined the Sixers with Francisco Elson in a 2010 trade from Milwaukee for Primoẑ Brezec and Royal Ivey - two players who will be appearing in the eighth installment of this series. The Sixers won this trade. In just his second career start, Meeks or 'M33ks,' as he was affectionately referred to as on social media, scored 20 points in the first quarter of a game against Larry Brown and the Bobcats. Brown left us at the altar years earlier. Exacting revenge in the form of a meaningless regular season win against the Bobcats six years later wasn't exactly what fans had envisioned, but we can be a spiteful bunch. I basked in any solace I could.

Jodie Meeks had a lot of fun at the Charlotte Bobcats' expense.

Meeks scored a career-high 26 points, 20 in a big first-quarter run, to help the Philadelphia 76ers beat the Bobcats 109-91 on Saturday night.

"He was a like flame thrower out there," 76ers coach Doug Collins said. Meeks' performance left the Bobcats torching each other.

"You can't win in this league if you don't have 15 guys playing hard," Charlotte coach Larry Brown said. "We don't play together, don't move the ball and don't defend." (Associated Press 2010).

I think Greg Buckner could help with that ball movement and team defense, coach. Meeks' insertion into the starting line-up was not without its controversy, however. The Sixers struck some lottery luck earlier that year and landed the #2 overall selection in the NBA draft. Philly then selected all-purpose wing Evan Turner. It was a tough sell for some fans to see the #2 pick relegated to a bench role; a move some fans took as hampering the rookie's development.

"I can't believe Doug is having the #2 overall pick come off the bench."

"He's not ready. And besides, is Turner a two, a three, a small four? No one can tell me."

"Meeks is one-dimensional!"

"Can Turner even shoot?!"

"He was taken #2 overall!"

"It was a weak draft!"

"Your face is weak!"

Meeks held on to the starting spot for over a year, finally relinquishing the position in the second half of the '11-'12 season. With the benefit of hindsight, the starting line-up decision was probably a minor detail, a decision that didn't sway the future of the team one way or the other. But people have argued on the internet over a lot less.

Despite his prowess from beyond the arc, Meeks oddly never earned a spot in the NBA Three-Point Contest. The Three-Point Contest Committee, and in my mind, it's a committee, snubbed Meeks time and time again. If the committee's goal was to preserve Larry Bird and Craig Hodges' three title reign, then mission accomplished. M33ks was a threat. He would've taken Bird down in every NBA arena and even at the French Lick Y with their bullshit double-rims.

Meeks had quiet performances in the team's two playoff appearances - never being that difference maker a player with his skillset offered. After the 2012 season, both parties went their separate ways and Meeks signed with the Lakers. After his time in LA, he bounced around the league, playing with the Pistons, the Magic, Wizards, and the Raptors. There was a rumor that Jodie Meeks won a championship with Toronto in 2019. But I can't confirm. I fell into a coma minutes after Kawhi Leonard's fluke jumper over Embiid in Game 7 and woke up just in time to watch the Eagles tie the Bengals.

The Scapegoat

Name: Brian Skinner

Height: 6'9"

College: Baylor

Sixers Tenure: 2002-2003; 2004-2005

"You like the Skinner move?"

"What's not to like? You lock down that back-up big for five years and the rest of the picture comes into focus."

Time heals. I no longer hold a grudge against Brian Skinner. In fact, I'm not even sure why I was mad at Brian Skinner to begin with. I probably owe him an apology. I placed a lot of blame on the Sixers' struggles at Skinner's feet. He was an easy scapegoat. Skinner was like Eagles kicker Alex Henery. Did we lose the January 2014 Wild Card Game against the Saints solely because of a first half missed field goal? Or because Henery didn't have the leg to boot it through the end zone, giving Darren Sproles a shot at a return? Nah, probably not, but I was depressed and just plowed through an entire bag of Harvest Cheddar Sun Chips. I needed to blame someone to mask my own inadequacies. Skinner, like Henery, was a symptom, not a diagnosis. He played about 15 minutes a night for the Sixers. He only started nine games, but it felt like a gazillion. I swore he played 36 minutes a contest. Every time a bell rings, an angel gets its wings. Every time Brian Skinner missed a baseline jumper, I added five minutes to his perceived playing time.

Skinner played with the Clippers and Cavs before joining the Sixers as a free agent in 2002. He developed a reputation as a banger, a player willing to do the dirty work down low. He was a type of player that Larry Brown hoarded. If Brown had his druthers, he would've eliminated the shot clock and points would've been awarded only through proper execution of screens and box outs. With Derrick Coleman nursing some injuries, Skinner inherited the role as the first big off the bench. He performed admirably, albeit unspectacularly. The Sixers then shortened up their rotation towards the end of the year, with Brown relying on DC to shoulder the load down low. Most Sixers fans probably thought the Brian Skinner Era had reached its unceremonious conclusion, but like *Anchorman 2*, there was a sequel coming that no one asked for.

Skinner left Philly and took a gap year to find himself, or as they call it in the NBA, Milwaukee. We didn't realize we needed Brian Skinner back in our lives, setting hard screens and hedging on pick and rolls. But Billy King did.

Dear Philly:

I hope this letter finds you well. Great news - I brought back Skinner. I gave him five years.

No thanks necessary. Just doing my job.

All the best,

Billy King

Even though Skinner was fresh off a career year in Milwaukee - 10 points and 7 plus boards a game - it was a maddening decision. Skinner had played for three different teams in three years. Were the Sixers bidding against themselves? King was like someone running franchise mode in *Madden*. It seems fun at the time, but then you have to negotiate with third-string offensive linemen and the offseason takes four hours. So you sign everyone to a long-term deal and then you can breeze through to Week 1 in no time. Have we considered that King gave everyone long-term deals to lessen his to-do list? Your job becomes much less stressful when your entire roster is under contract for two decades.

A large and lengthy deal created a whole new set of expectations. Brian Skinner was no longer a scrappy and serviceable front-court player. He was now overpaid and underwhelming. Now, he was fair game for the boo birds. Skinner had five DNPs in his first twelve games. The Sixers rostered Samuel Dalembert, Kenny

Thomas, Corliss Williamson, and Marc Jackson. Unless O'Brien planned on unleashing Brian Skinner, Point God, there weren't nearly enough minutes to justify Skinner's new deal. In the loosest sense, Skinner was a luxury. The contract was a 24-hour QVC bender. You didn't need three different blenders and a weighted blanket, but your credit card was right there.

The big man played just 24 games with Philly before being dealt to Sacramento as part of the Chris Webber acquisition. Skinner's perception among Sixers fans turned quickly in two years. His game never changed. His contract did.

The Independent Thinker

Name: Trevor Ruffin

Height: 6'1"

College: Hawaii

Sixers Tenure: 1995-1996

"When I take the first shot, I try and see what kind of rhythm I have," Ruffin said. "I hit it, felt good. When Scott went down, I didn't wish he went down, but I took advantage of the opportunity."

Opportunity?

"The problem with that team there is, you've got the green light to do anything you want," the Jazz' Karl Malone said after producing 31 points of his own.

"Some of those shots, he wasn't even in an offense. He was just shooting." (Jasner 1995).

There is an old saying about Dominican baseball players: you can't walk off the island. Major League scouts only recognize players who hit and hit aggressively. Trevor Ruffin knew that playing passive would never get him off the Big Island. Ruffin may have gone to Hawaii, but he graduated from the Vernon Maxwell School of Not Giving a Shit. Ruffin was not bashful. He didn't come to Philly to run an offense. He was the offense. His inexplicable rise to prominence and string of monster efforts - that was more shocking than Willie Burton's 53 one year prior. People knew Willie Burton – everyone but my dad anyway.

No one knew Trevor Ruffin. Nobody in the continental United States had access to Rainbow Warrior hoops. University of Hawaii Football occasionally was on The Deuce at midnight, but you only put them on when you were two hundred in the red with your bookie. Always take the over on the Big Island by the way. It's a lock.

But Hawaii Basketball televised? That was a rarity. Your only opportunity to scout Ruffin and his fellow Rainbow Warriors came in the Great Alaska Shootout his senior year, but even those games were on at midnight. How was I supposed to eat a plate full of turkey and yams at Thanksgiving, and then stay up eight more hours for Hawaii/Portland? I barely made it through the second half of the Detroit Lions game. (Former Sixer Glenn Robinson was the MVP of the Great Alaska Shootout that year. The more you know).

Ruffin went undrafted in '94 before latching on with Phoenix. In his first NBA game, he scored 17 points in 14 minutes of action. Those were LSU Pete Maravich type numbers. I would've built my team around Barkley and Ruffin right then and there. Phoenix instead released Pistol Trevor to the '95 Expansion Draft. He was selected #10 overall by Vancouver, but the Grizzlies had no interest in building around a supreme offensive talent who made 23-footers with the regularity of a right-handed lay-up. Canada's loss. The Sixers signed the guard in early December of '95, and the Trevor Ruffin Experience officially began.

In his fourth game in a Sixers uniform, Philly hosted the Utah Jazz. Replacing an injured Scott Skiles, Ruffin decided that passing was only for the weak. He dropped 32 points and went 7-10 from behind the arc. Back then, the three ball wasn't nearly as commonplace as it is today. Today, three fourths of the NBA is jacking up threes. In the 1990s, long-range jumpers were relegated to MTV's *Rock N' Jock Basketball.* Coach Bill Bellamy was ahead of his time. Trevor Ruffin broke all the social norms. Heck, he replaced Scott Skiles, Consummate Point Guard. He was a walking heat check. Trevor said it above: *"When I take the first shot, I try and see what kind of rhythm I have."*

On the annual west coast road trip over the holidays, Ruffin hit double digits in five games, scoring twenty or more in four of them. The Pacific Coast Time Zone was more his speed. He had been playing his home games in Philly at like 7 A.M. Honolulu time. Ruffin was also distributing the ball. He wasn't *only* pulling up from just over midcourt, motion offense be damned. Back-to-back 27-point, 9-assist performances made Sixers fans wonder if they had caught lightning in a bottle.

His offense tapered off a bit in January, but then Ruffin hung 28 at Miami, 32 at Orlando. He attempted nine threes against the Heat, eight against the Magic, eight more against Atlanta. Oh, is that not team basketball? Not enough ball movement for your tastes? What are you gonna do about it, you prude? The game prior to his 32-point outing against the Magic, Ruffin went scoreless in just five minutes against the Cavs. He sought revenge. The Magic was in the direct path of the Ruffin Storm, just a team in the wrong place at the wrong point of the schedule. Sure, Orlando won the game by 19, but this book isn't about the '95-'96 Magic.

"I've been in a slump, so anytime I hit a shot it was a good thing," Ruffin said. "But we still got killed. That's the bottom line."

Ruffin packed 21 of his points into the fourth quarter, when the Sixers rang up 44.

"What do you want me to say?" Lucas said. "The game was [already] over." (Jasner 1996).

In his final game in a Sixers uniform, Ruffin scored 18 off the bench in an overtime win against the Raptors. He went 7-18 from the floor, because why not. Trevor didn't dig out his passport from his sock drawer to put up a couple of shots and fade into the sunset. He averaged just under 13 points per night in his lone season with the club. The drafting of Iverson made Ruffin, another smaller scoring guard, expendable. It's surprising, though, that another NBA team didn't scoop him up. The guy was a dynamo offensively. Surely there was value there. Several years later, I heard the Sixers acquired Ruffin. I perked up. "The ol' gunslinger must still have something left in the holster," I told myself. "Still a lot of jumpers left in that right arm."

But alas, the Sixers had acquired burly power forward Michael Ruffin.

The Distributor

Name: Kendall Marshall

Height: 6'4"

College: North Carolina

Sixers Tenure: 2015-2016

"Pass-first point guard" is one of my favorite basketball descriptors. My 12-and-under travel coach called me a 'pass first point guard,' which was just a fancy euphemism for "don't shoot." Our team only had two plays, and both were for the coach's son, Kyle. "1 for Kyle" and "Motion for Kyle." Everyone in the gym just set a screen for Kyle. Our opponents would quickly catch on. I would then call, "1 for Matt." It would work initially. The other team would run around looking for Matt, who didn't exist. Then I would pass it to Kyle.

Kendall Marshall had one elite skill. He had court vision for days. If Jahil Okafor could theoretically roll out of bed and give you 20 and 10, then Kendall Marshall could brush his teeth and dish out 7.5 assists per night. It's surprising that Kendall didn't stick. If a player is going to be pigeonholed with one skill, passing isn't a bad one to be saddled with. Hell, when Dr. James Naismith invented basketball, dribbling wasn't even allowed. Marshall would've torn up the Springfield YMCA League.

1891-1892 Springfield YMCA League MVP Voting (First Place Votes)

Kendall Marshall ... (8)

Earl ... (1)

Herbert ... (1)

A former Tar Heel, Marshall was drafted 13th overall by the Phoenix Suns in the 2012 Draft. Even with Steve Nash moving on to LA, Kendall saw very little time behind Gorgan Dragic. In his first career start, a meaningless game in late March, he casually dropped 13 assists. Ho hum. Unless it was the same official scorer who generously doled out 23 assists to Nick Van Exel in a '97 game against the Vancouver Grizzlies, this outing highlighted his potential. Passing translates. It was a glimpse of what Kendall offered. But Phoenix made alternate plans that didn't include the point guard, and traded Marshall to Washington in 2013. He was quickly waived by the Wizards and signed with a depleted Lakers squad, where he averaged over 8 assists per night. Following the season, L.A. released Marshall and he once again sought a new home. Why would a young player who averaged close to nine assists a night get released time and time again?

The devil is in the details, or in this case, the defensive side of the ball. Marshall's quickness was a problem at the NBA level. He had trouble staying in front of his man and was often targeted on pick and rolls. His jumper was passable, albeit a slow release (his jump shot was instantly 90% prettier though, since he was left-handed). Kendall Marshall was difficult to project - a terrific passer with flaws seemingly everywhere else. It wasn't so much that Marshall needed to improve, but rather take a time machine to the early 90s where his game would better translate. We would've had hours and hours of footage, crisp entry passes, one after the other, from Marshall to Vin Baker on the low block.

"Remember Kendall Marshall?"

"Of course. Led the league in assists from '92 through '97."

He signed with Philly in September of '15. I understood the negatives, the deficiencies, and the bouncing from team to team. Oh, and the torn ACL. Marshall was rehabbing a torn ACL. Minor detail. But that was all water under a fundamentally-sound chest pass. All I saw was a tall, lefty point-guard with the vision of a city planner. By the time Marshall was healthy and ready to make his Sixers debut on December 11th, Philly had a 1-22 record. 1-22? No, wait, that can't be right. Let me check –

Oh no, that's right. The Sixers were 1-22. They lost that night, a home defeat to Detroit. Philly dropped their next eight contests to make Marshall feel like one of the guys. It was a very inclusive atmosphere. One of those games, a December 23rd loss at Milwaukee saw Marshall hand out 6 assists while compiling 7 turnovers. It was an assist-to-turnover ratio that only a rookie Jerry Stackhouse could love. Kendall was signed to ease Jahil Okafor's transition into the NBA, but that '15-'16 campaign went off the rails by Halloween. Sam Hinkie spoke with ESPN's Zach Lowe about Marshall and his originally planned role with the team.

Marshall could have provided two things the howling critics rightfully suggest the Sixers need: a competent point guard, and some sort of veteran mentor for Jahlil Okafor, their wayward rookie star. "This has been hard," Hinkie says. "We haven't been proud of this kind of start. We had strong desires for a point guard who could help us play at a high tempo and get our best players the ball in positions where they could be successful. We want someone to throw a post entry pass. We thought Kendall was that guy." (Lowe 2015).

Marshall didn't hang around. Fresh off a major injury, Kendall's limited contributions were discouraging, but not surprising. Sporadic playing time coupled with countless DNPs cemented his future in Philly. Before the start of next season, the Sixers moved Marshall to Utah. He never suited up for the Jazz and retired in 2017.

The Catfish

Name: Alan Henderson

Height: 6'9"

College: Indiana

Sixers Tenure: 2006-2007

Overheard on SEPTA – Route 3:

Date: February 23, 2007

Time: Approximately 7:22 AM

"Hear the Sixers traded Alan Henderson to the Jazz?"

"Did they though?"

"Uh – yeah, to the Jazz."

"But DID they though?"

"I mean – that's what I read in the *Daily News*."

Whispers

"Maybe that's what they want you to think. Did you see Alan Henderson board the plane? Is there footage of him touching down in Salt Lake City? I haven't seen anything substantial. I've been reading up on chemtrails. There are a lot of interesting theories out there. It makes you wonder, ya know? What's real and what's not?"

"You know, I think I'm just gonna find another seat."

"Where is Alan Henderson right now? Tell me that. Just tell me that..."

What we have here is a good old-fashioned mystery, a whodunit. There are a lot of GAPS unaccounted for. I checked phone records and bank statements. I penned letters to two different organizations, beat writers, and my local politicians. A Twitter search proved useless. Facebook's a dumpster fire. Basketball-Reference says one thing, ESPN another. Either no one knows anything, or no one is talking. Was this merely an oversight or a giant conspiracy? I'm Charlie Kelly trying to solve the Pepe Silvia puzzle. Alan Henderson is my Pepe Silvia.

What happened to Alan Henderson in the middle of the 2007 season? Where did he go? Or, more specifically, where didn't he go?

After a monster career under Bobby Knight at Indiana, Henderson played eleven years in the NBA - a consummate pro and well-respected teammate by all accounts - before latching on with the Sixers for one final ride. Basketball-Reference says he signed with the Sixers on September 8th, 2006 (Basketball-Reference 2020). ESPN and other platforms confirm that timeline (Associated Press 2006). So far so good, right? If you're playing at home, get your pad of paper, draw your diagrams, get another cup of coffee, do whatever you got to do, because things are about to get weird. In February, the Sixers traded Alan Henderson. I think? From ESPN:

The Utah Jazz acquired veteran forward Alan Henderson from Philadelphia just before the trade deadline Thursday. The Jazz and 76ers exchanged the right to trade second-round picks in the 2007 draft.

Philadelphia also included undisclosed cash considerations in the deal.

"This move gives us increased flexibility and provides us with additional options on draft day," Sixers president Billy King said.

Henderson played sparingly off the bench for the Sixers this season, averaging 3.5 points and 3.1 rebounds in 34 games. (Associated Press/ESPN 2007).

"Undisclosed cash considerations" could not be reached for comment. Here is where things go off the rails. Basketball-Reference doesn't mention *anything* about Alan Henderson and the Utah Jazz. Go to Basketball-Reference, type in 'Greg Ostertag,' and sure, completely different story. The page is all Jazz all the time. But B-R doesn't say that Alan Henderson got traded to the Jazz, played for the Jazz, or even likes jazz music.

Basketball-Reference lists these transactions:

September 8, 2006*: Signed as a free agent with the Philadelphia 76ers.*

April 3, 2007*: Signed as a free agent with the Philadelphia 76ers.* (Basketball Reference 2020).

Where have you gone, Alan Henderson? Our nation turns its lonely eyes to you. What happened in February of '07? Was Henderson traded or not? And if he wasn't traded, then who the hell was Billy King talking to? Or, was this like a Rob Ducey situation where Ducey was traded by the Phillies for a player to be named later, and that player to be named later turned out to be - drum roll please - Rob Fuckin' Ducey. And if that was the case, how am I JUST discovering this now? Ducey is Henderson. Henderson is Ducey. The plot thickened.

I knew my next move. I went back to the ESPN article and clicked on the Alan Henderson hyperlink. ESPN says he was traded to the Jazz. Ok, put your money where your mouth is, Worldwide Leader. Let's see if Alan Henderson actually played for the Jazz.

The hyperlink WAS BROKEN. Or maybe it wasn't broken at all. When I clicked on Henderson's hyperlink in the article, it brought me to the player page of ...

Steve Novak, the sharpshooting Marquette product. Explain that. Unless – wait, was I being catfished by Steve Novak? The hell was going on here. I was flustered. To steal a line from "Rowdy" Roddy Piper, just when I had all the answers, Alan Henderson, and by proxy, Steve Novak, changed the questions. I called my dad. Maybe he knows something.

"This is random, dad, but do you remember if the Sixers traded Alan Henderson to the Jazz in February of '07?"

"The Phils old bullpen coach?"

Dad was a dead end. I regrouped. I revisited the notes on my dry erase board. Got lucky with some new leads. After exhaustive research and reviewing property records in the greater Salt Lake City area (also finding a newspaper article from

2007 helped), I verified that Henderson did not in fact suit up for the Jazz. He was traded, yes, but never played in Utah. He was released shortly after the deal (Moore 2007).

The Sixers re-signed him again in April for the final nine games of the season, because it's not a party or a Fan Appreciation Night without Alan Henderson. He played in four more contests with the Sixers before retiring from the NBA.

Case closed.

The Sixth Best Player

Name: Sharone Wright

Height: 6'11"

College: Clemson

Sixers Tenure: 1994-1996

"Some of the fans come here, I think, just to get drunk anyway," Wright said, after Philadelphia fans booed Wright and most of the other Sixers in a 102-83 loss to the Detroit Pistons on Wednesday night.

"They get out of work, get drunk, sit behind the bench and say things about the team. I don't really worry about that, but it's tough when you're playing at home and all you get is boos." (Bonfatti 1996).

Sharone Wright's own coach called him 'soft.' (Smith 1996). This wasn't some grassroots campaign that started on WIP, or in the concourse center of the Spectrum. I wouldn't visit the Penn State Creamery and find "Sharone Wright's Soft Serve" on the menu. The moniker, "Charmin" or "Sharon," may have spread throughout the arena seats, but it didn't originate there. Wright's brief tenure in Philly - one that lasted just one and a half seasons - was littered with controversy and public spats with his coach. The best thing Wright had going for him was that he wasn't Shawn Bradley.

Setting aside hindsight and Eddie Jones for a moment, Sharone Wright was the sixth best player in a five player '94 Draft. While Wright didn't work out here, he wasn't a reach by any means. There may have been a tinge of jealousy over the players they just missed – Jason Kidd, Grant Hill, and Juwan Howard among others - but the organization certainly didn't show it. In fact, reports from draft headquarters detailed a sense of euphoria. John Lucas went from interview to interview gripping a jersey with "The Wright Stuff" imprinted on it (Jasner 1994). The team was ecstatic. There were some concerns raised about Sharone Wright's weight, but that was quickly put to rest.

TNT last night listed Wright at 279.

"Obviously, Harold wanted me to clear that up right away," Lucas said. "I told Sharone that he just made a friend in me, because I'm a fitness nut. One of my jobs will be to get him in shape.

We now have the twin-tower concept, with Sharone and Shawn Bradley. When you watch Wright play, he reminds you of Moses Malone. We were last in offensive rebounding, 23rd in rebounding overall this season, so we need that. Nobody complained about Shaquille O'Neal weighing 300." (Jasner 1994).

Despite the excitement at headquarters over Wright, that energy didn't trickle down to the rest of the city. I've never seen a Sharone Wright jersey in the wild, at my local Forman Mills, or anywhere else for that matter. He was the #6 pick in the draft, but the powers that be just doubled down on the commercial production of Bradley kits. When you played basketball at the park as a kid, you didn't announce to your buddies, "I'll be Sharone," before clanking a jump hook off the rim. "I'll be Sharone" has never been uttered in the history of mankind. You picked Barros, or you picked Spoon or you just sold out and said you were Jordan or Pippen.

Wright operated exclusively on the block. His low post game was a series of back 'em down dribbles that grinded the shot clock to a nub. He wasn't the outlier in that sense - that was standard fare back in those days - but 46% from the field for a guy predominantly working within an eight-foot radius was discouraging. Sharone also developed a reputation as a bit of a chucker in the low post. He averaged a Yinka Dare-like 0.6 assists per game his rookie campaign. Fans weren't expecting John Stockton on the low block, just a kick out back up top once in a blue moon. Once Wright was fed down low, the ball vanished, reappearing years later as the subject of an *Unsolved Mysteries* episode.

The Sixers at that time had a reputation for a *laissez-faire* approach to defense, ushering opponents into the lane with the resistance of a traffic cone. In January of Sharone's rookie season, Lucas aired out his grievances publicly. Frustrated with his two big men, Wright and Bradley, the coach went on a profanity-laced rant after a January '95 loss in Phoenix.

Most of his shouting was directed at his two biggest players, Shawn Bradley and Sharone Wright.

"Two of the highest-paid assistant coaches in the league," Lucas called them in a snippet of the printable part of his tirade. Bradley and Wright spend a lot of time on the bench, with foul trouble. (Pucin 1995).

In addition to the soft label, Lucas openly questioned and criticized Wright's effort. These accusations were red meat for Philadelphians. Lacking toughness, lacking effort, a sulking attitude - fair or not - made Wright a prime target. Everyone had an opinion.

"Sharone just doesn't seem like a Philly guy, you know? Where's the fire in his belly? Like Moses - he had it. Charles? He had it. Just not sure Wright wants it bad enough."

"Uh, I asked if you knew the bride or the groom."

In his rookie season, Sharone was benched for the entire second half in a loss to the Spurs for walking slowly off the court when subbed out (Jasner 1995). In his second season, not long before he was shipped to Toronto, Lucas wondered aloud if Wright had missed games against San Antonio (left the game two minutes in with a turned ankle) and Orlando (DNP) because of the opposing teams' potent big men, David Robinson and Shaq. It was a damning allegation. Wright and Lucas' relationship grew more and more contentious. Asked about the criticism from his head coach, Wright retorted, *"Nobody listens to Luke."* (Cawthon 1996).

Trade rumors involving the big man seemingly swirled since his arrival. In early '95, Sharone was linked to Chicago along with two first-round picks for Scottie Pippen (Jasner 1995).

"Hearing Sharone and two picks for Pippen."

"Eh, a little too rich for my blood. Sharone is coming around. Think Chicago would take LaSalle Thompson instead?"

Not quite the return of Pippen, Wright was moved a year later to Toronto for Pinckney, Massenburg, and a couple of seconds. The change of scenery was a blessing for Sharone who labeled the Toronto fans as Snow White compared to Godzilla here in Philadelphia (Jasner 1996). Wright's problems here were exacerbated by a coach who had no qualms publicly criticizing the big man. The fans piling on was just icing on the cake. Once Lucas turned on Sharone, his Sixers career was over. The trade to Toronto, and the light return, was just a formality.

The Thanksgiving Eve

Name: Tom Chambers

Height: 6'10"

College: Utah

Sixers Tenure: A couple of weeks in 1997

For all but one minute in the second quarter, the Sixers forgot about their young. They pulled out their Social Security cards and put their fate in the hands of two dinosaurs, Terry Cummings and Tom Chambers.

It almost worked. (Smith 1997).

Writing about a four-time All-Star, who averaged over 27 points a game in the '89-'90 season, doesn't really capture the spirit of this book. Writing about a former Sixer who played exactly one game, however, is EXACTLY in the spirit of this book. Tom Chambers was one of those terrific players from the 1980's who gets lost in the giant shadows of Magic, Bird, and Jordan. His dunk over the Knicks' Mark Jackson in '89 is still a staple on NBA highlight reels even today. Chambers could go. Virtual Tom Chambers could really go. He was a tour de force in *Lakers Versus Celtics* for Sega Genesis. Virtual Tom glided through the air from the elbow with a double pump vicious slam; a signature move that my brother, or any other unsuspecting victim, was powerless to stop. Tom Chambers and the Phoenix Suns were banned from the game, albeit briefly. Virtual Tom was a damn cheat code. My brother and I lifted the ban sometime over the Christmas holidays. Oddjob in *Golden Eye* for Nintendo 64, though, is permanently banned. No exceptions.

His road to the Sixers was certainly less traveled. At the age of 36, Chambers left the NBA to play overseas in Israel. He returned stateside one year later and joined the Charlotte Hornets for a cup of coffee. He latched on with his hometown Phoenix Suns in '97, where most expected he would finish his career - a fitting end for one of the most popular players in Suns history. The Sixers though, and Suns GM Bryan Colangelo, had other ideas. Philly was dealing with some injuries in the frontcourt and had zero players on their roster alive during the Eisenhower presidency - a glaring hole that had to be addressed. Since Robert Parish wasn't available, the Sixers traded their #33 overall pick of that year's draft, Marco Milic, for the veteran Chambers.

Milic was famous for dunking over a car. He instantly became my favorite Sixer and favorite human, and I spent most of that weekend trying to jump over the living room couch since my mom's station wagon was in the shop. NBA trades in the 1990s were like the Wild, Wild, West - a completely lawless world where feedback and criticism was so minimal given the times, that general managers did whatever they wanted with very little repercussions. The Sixers, who were lousy, traded their #33 overall pick for a guy who was basically semi-retired. Larry Brown could've just kept Milic and signed Sugar Ray Leonard at that point.

On paper, it was a dumb trade. In hindsight, it was a really dumb trade. Chambers appeared in only one game for the Sixers.

'Twas the night before Thanksgiving, when all through the bars
No cover band was playing, not even "Whiskey in the Jar"
Beers and shots were drunk quietly, and with great care
In hopes that in the post, Big Tom would be there.
Tom Chambers got some minutes, but the fans watched with dread
As Vitaly Potapenko dunked on their team's head
Our hero scored six, was perfect from the floor
Tom won the battle, but Vitaly won the war.

Chambers went 2-2 from the floor and 2-2 from the foul line. It wasn't quite Babe Ruth mashing three home runs in one of his final games for the Boston Braves, but it was still a half-decent swan song. Tom didn't hang up the jersey after that night. He stuck around for another two weeks – never seeing another minute of action - before announcing his retirement.

Outside of the box score, very little evidence exists of Tom Chambers' stint in Philadelphia. That is except for a pair of game worn Sixers shorts I found on sale for $200. The description says, "only one left in stock." Fitting. If I didn't blow my entire book advance on a Greg Graham jersey, I would've sprung for the shorts. Shorts worn by a 6'10" guy would fit me like a pair of bell bottoms, but still. It's Tom Chambers' Sixers shorts. There's only one left in stock.

The Big Dog

Name: Glenn Robinson

Height: 6'7"

College: Purdue

Sixers Tenure: 2003-2004

The Glenn Robinson situation is getting more and more confusing.

The 76ers forward has been on the injured list all season with left ankle tendonitis, plus we recently learned from Sixers coach Jim O'Brien that Robinson said his ankles are so sore, he can't even walk on a treadmill without experiencing pain.

Also, supposedly he's got a sore elbow. (Whittaker 2004).

If you ranked the sidekicks of Allen Iverson, Glenn "Big Dog" Robinson wouldn't grade favorably. This wasn't a Batman and Robin situation. This was a slightly older Batman, and a thirty-something Robin who was plagued by injuries and a severe allergy to defense. Only some Zyrtec and a time machine could have salvaged this partnership, but Ponce de León never found the Fountain of Youth and neither did the '03-'04 Sixers. Larry Brown left us for dead. Assistant Randy Ayers was now on the bench, and the Sixers were officially a team in transition. I don't think most fans realized it at the time - "Hey, we still have Iverson" wasn't a bad mantra after all - but the door to Eastern Conference contention was unofficially shut.

Dikembe Mutumbo was gone. Snow and McKie were on the wrong side of 30. Derrick Coleman was 36. It was an aging core that Billy King hoped could muster up one more run. There were a lot of similarities to those 2012-2014 Phillies teams. Age wasn't on their side, only nostalgia. Management tried to put a Band-Aid on the many holes of the roster. Glenn Robinson was that bandage - a proven 20 point a game scorer who would help Iverson shoulder the load. That was the intent anyway.

Big Dog pumped in over 30 points per night his junior season and dragged his fellow Boilermakers to the Elite 8 (no disrespect intended for Purdue great, Cuonzo Martin). After a successful run in Milwaukee, he played one season in Atlanta. He then moved to Philly in a massive four-team trade that I think was concocted after a bar crawl. The transaction itself is like six pages, and after re-reading it multiple times, I'm pretty sure Minnesota and Atlanta combined franchises and morphed into the Timberhawks. For the purpose of this chapter, the Sixers sent Keith Van Horn to the Knicks and got back Robinson and Marc Jackson. On the surface, it was an ok deal, but it further accentuated the lack of cohesion on the roster. Iverson now entered the '03-'04 regular season with his third different wingman in three seasons.

On the day Randy Ayers was hired to replace Larry Brown as Philadelphia's new coach, Allen Iverson pleaded with management to get him some scoring help.

"We need another scorer. That's something that needs to be addressed," said Iverson. (Maaddi 2003).

The logic was sound. If Iverson had a bad day, Big Dog would still drop twenty. If Iverson had a good day, Robinson drops his twenty and the Sixers would be nearly impossible to stop. The best-laid plans anyway. Four games into the Big Dog Era, Robinson was sidelined with a left ankle injury (Whittaker 2003). He missed eight games, but the Sixers hovered around the .500 mark when Glenn returned in December. Now healthy, fans expected the team to find their rhythm. Then Iverson got hurt. It took until January for the duo to get on the same court together. *Now* the Sixers can make their run, people thought. Look out Eastern Conference.

Welp. In February, Iverson got hurt again. By March, both players were shut down. Injuries decimated both stars and torpedoed any chance of the team making noise. But the truth was, even when healthy, Iverson and Robinson weren't that good together. In a month's span, from mid-January to mid-February, when both stars were playing, the Sixers managed to win just four games. The losing streak was highlighted by a 30-point loss at home to the Celtics. And this wasn't Bill Russell and John Havlicek taking the Sixers to task. This Celtics team was 23-29. They trotted out a starting line-up of Paul Pierce, Mark Blount, Jiri Welsch, Mike James, and Chris Mihm. I think Pierce picked up those guys from a Blue Coats open try-out.

Glenn Robinson carried the offensive load with 19 points, but he was a defensive liability. At times, it appeared as if the Celtics were running plays for whomever he was guarding, whether it was Paul Pierce or Walter McCarty or Ricky Davis. (Juliano 2004).

Fans hoped for a bounce back year from Robinson, but what they got was a tangled web of confusion. Freshen up your drink.

New Sixers coach Jim O'Brien praised Robinson's effort and conditioning in early October during training camp. He called Iverson and Big Dog the team leaders. O'Brien then did an about face a few weeks later and announced that rookie Andre Iguodala would be starting in place of Robinson. According to O'Brien, Big Dog took the news well. He just wanted to help the team (Whittaker 2004). Shortly before the lineup news broke publicly, Robinson had left due to a family matter. Now, close to a week later, O'Brien suggested that Big Dog may start the year on the injured list due to the time (just a few days) he had missed. It was an odd declaration - a veteran starting the season off on the IL due to missing a few days for personal reasons. Despite the question marks, the coach was adamant that Robinson's departure from the team was not related to his benching. Something was fishy. Then the Sixers put Big Dog on the trading block (Juliano 2004). To recap:

Early October: Robinson was in the best shape of his life

October 27th: But Iguodala is starting

October 27th: Robinson left the team due to a family matter

The next few days: This family matter was in no way related to his benching

November 1st: Placed on injured list due to ankle tendonitis

November 2nd: Sixers put Robinson on the trade block

The '04 Eagles were 7-0 at the time, though, so I'm not sure if people realized or gave a shit. The Robinson drama took a backseat to the Birds' Super Bowl aspirations. Sports talk radio focused on Terrell Owens mocking Ray Lewis with his touchdown celebration, not the whereabouts of our 32-year-old forward. The Big Dog saga was gossip, sure, but news you brought up only when there was a lull in the conversation.

"Looks like rain."

"Yeah."

...

...

...

"Guess there's something going on with Big Dog."

As the calendar rolled into December, more reports came out about Robinson's mounting injuries. Not great developments for a team looking to trade the scoring forward. Then, nothing. Radio silence. Life just moved on. In February, the day before the trade deadline, Billy King and the Sixers garnered national headlines when they landed yet another fading star to complement Iverson. Chris Webber came over and was casted as that next, great supporting actor. Lost in the glow of the Webber acquisition, Glenn Robinson and his expiring contract were finally moved as well. Big Dog was traded to New Orleans, but I'm not sure anyone noticed. C-Webb was our shiny new toy now.

The Hornets waived Robinson a week later.

The Man from Sudan

Name: Manute Bol

Height: 7'7"

College: Bridgeport

Sixers Tenure: 1990-1993; 1994

Another night, after a club-record 13 blocks against New Jersey, Nets coach, Bill Fitch said, "If you get the idea that he's a normal human, you're going to get a lot of shots blocked." (Hofmann 1990).

While playing for the Washington Bullets, Manute Bol fought #33 on the Chicago Bulls. He was raining down haymakers on a guy half his size. Countless players and staff were trying to break up the melee. When I first saw the clip a few years back, I remember thinking, "Wow, I had no idea Bol and Pippen fought. How was I just seeing this for the first time?" Turned out it wasn't Scottie Pippen. It was Bulls center Jawann Oldham. Oldham was seven feet tall.

"Yo, you see what happened last night? Apparently Nute got into a fight with some little French guy in South Philly. Roughed him up pretty bad. It's all over the news. It was crazy, dude."

"That French guy was Andre the Giant."

Manute Bol was a presence. He owned the room. He commanded your attention. When I went to the Spectrum as a kid, I couldn't help it. I just stared at Nute. My eyes followed him all over the court. I wanted to cheer a block, a made basket, a three – oh my god I wanted to cheer a Manute three pointer. I tugged at my dad's coat.

"Think he'll shoot one? Think he'll shoot one tonight?"

Bol was this massive athlete. This massive man who transcended sports. From his huge smile, big personality, and relentless humanitarian efforts in his native Sudan, everything about Bol was larger than life. There are so many stories about Manute that fact and fiction blend together. Bol killed a lion. Bol finished 7th in the 1991 Philadelphia Mayoral race. Bol's dick was so big it had its own locker. He even coined the phrase, "My bad." What's true, what's not? Bol was Paul Bunyan and Davy Crockett. He was also Nick Foles. Even his height was in question. Was Manute 7'6"? Was he 7'7"? Should we just round up and say he's 8'0", maybe 9'0"? Years after Bol's passing, there was a report from former Cleveland State coach, Kevin Mackey, who said that Manute didn't even know his own age when he recruited him back in 1984.

"I gave him his birthday because they didn't know how old he was," Mackey told Zagoria. "[Bol] had no idea of his age and the kid who came over with him didn't know how old he was. No one knew how old he was."

Mackey went on to explain that he made Bol 23 years old at the time but thinks the player might have already been in his 40s in 1984. (Gaines 2017).

Is that true? Who knows? Was Bol Drew Barrymore in *Never Been Kissed*? Did he have a reoccurring role in *21 Jump Street?* All we know for certain was that when Manute was drafted, he was either 23 or 50, or somewhere in between. Bol averaged 6.4 blocks per 36 minutes for his career, but if he did that at age, 45, 50, as it was suggested, what could've Manute done as a spry 25-year-old? He would've changed the game. We all would be shooting on eleven-foot rims because this 7'7" behemoth rendered ten-foot baskets obsolete. Manute was arguably the best ever at blocking shots. While the rest of his game was severely limited, it didn't matter to fans. Nute was above criticism.

Teammates loved Manute. Charles Barkley and Rick Mahorn famously played a prank on Bol, where Barkley led Nute to a buffet spread. There was a hole cut out in the table, where Rick Mahorn's head popped through. Mahorn's head was covered by a serving tin. Manute lifted the serving tin, and there was Rick to scare the shit out of Nute. Manute busted out into laughter and said, "That was Rick

Mahorn, man!"

Bol had two separate stints with the Sixers, and let's be clear here, the fans never booed him. Ever. They were screaming, "Nuuuute," like when Birds fans called for "Duuuuce" (Staley). No Sixers fan complained about Bol's playing time, or style of play, or trouble on the glass, or lack of strength, or anything else. Winning was secondary when Bol was out there. The pageantry trumped the results. Bol was a career 21% three-point shooter, yet when he got the ball beyond the arc, The Spectrum crowd bellowed the same instruction in unison.

"Shoooooooot!"

While playing for Golden State, Don Nelson concocted a strategy to take advantage of the NBA's illegal defense rules. He pulled his 7'7" center beyond the three-point line, which in turn, pulled Bol's defender outside the lane. This tactic created more freedom for Nute's teammates and removed a shot blocker from the equation. Since Bol was already standing out there, Nelson gave him the freedom to hoist. In 1988, Manute Bol, three-point specialist, was born. Bol's jumper was a spectacle. His delivery was slow. He cocked the ball behind his head like a throw-in in soccer. There was the moment a teammate – let's say Ron Anderson for this exercise – passed him the ball from the wing. This pass was a surrender in and of itself. A punt and a Hail Mary rolled up into one slow and deliberate jump shot. Bol would catch and pause. "Should I really be doing this? Isn't anyone going to stop me?" Fans, of course, weren't helping. It was peer pressure at its finest. Go on, Nute. Do it. Everyone's doing it, Nute. The defense stopped. Time seemed to stop. Manute's shot, his release, it moved at the speed and efficiency of firing and reloading a musket.

"Shoooooooot!"

"Shoooooooot!"

In a game at Phoenix in '93, Bol obliged. Nute buried six threes on twelve attempts, dropping a career-high 18 points. It was the greatest two-hour plus block of entertainment to ever air on Prism, and I'm including the repeated showings of

The Hunt for Red October and *Patriot Games*. The Suns home crowd loved it. New Phoenix Sun Charles Barkley was slapping Bol high-five down the court. The Sixers lost by double-digits, but no one seemed to care. It was a high point in a lost season. While offensively Bol was considered a sideshow, defensively he was a legitimate problem. He averaged five blocks a game his rookie campaign. He finished second in voting for Defensive Player of the year, losing out to Alvin Robertson.

Bol was officially drafted by the Bullets in the 2nd round of the 1985 NBA Draft, but only after he was ruled ineligible on a technicality two years prior. San Diego Clippers coach Jim Lynam, on a tip he received from a coaching friend, selected the mysterious Sudanese big man in the 5th round of the '83 Draft. Bol though didn't register for the draft within the necessary timeframe and was deemed ineligible. So Nute played a year at Division-II University of Bridgeport in Connecticut.

"Here's the thing," Lynam says. "Listen to this. He really should have been with the Clippers. They should have kept his draft rights. It all got very confusing.

One of the things everyone was looking at was his passport. His passport said he was 19 years old. His passport also said he was five feet two."

Lynam asked Manute about the discrepancy. Manute said he had been sitting down when Sudan officials measured him. (Montville 1990).

Lynam eventually reunited with Bol in 1990, when the Sixers acquired Manute from Golden State for a first-round pick. It was a gamble, albeit - per Sixers management - a calculated one.

Good move? Bad move?

How could a guy who's 7-7 inspire so much indecision?

"When Jack McMahon was my chief scout, he hated Manute," said Harold Katz, the Sixers owner. "He thought he was the worst player he ever saw. Then Jack went to work for Golden State, and he told me that Manute was the greatest defensive player he ever saw." (Hofmann 1990).

As for the acquisition itself, Manute Bol did Manute Bol things. He blocked a boatload of shots and provided next to nothing offensively. Did I mention he blocked a ton of shots? In his first season with the Sixers, Bol averaged 1.9 points per night. He also did this: 6 block efforts against Atlanta and Washington, 6 against New Jersey, 6 against Orlando and Denver, 8 against Minnesota, 10 swats against Sacramento on Valentine's Day, 7 against Utah, 9 against Boston, the list goes on and on and on.

The franchise stumbled into anonymity after that '91 season, but the blocks kept piling up. Two nights after his 18-point effort against Phoenix in '93, the Sixers traveled to Los Angeles to meet the Lakers. Bol swatted away 9 shots. Vlade Divac and Benoit Benjamin shot a combined 12-38 from the floor. The lasting memory Sixers fans have of Bol was that spectacle against Phoenix and the unexpected barrage of threes, but that's only because the swats were so commonplace. When you record 580 blocks in a Sixers uniform, it's difficult to discern one from the other 579.

After bouncing around with Miami and Washington in the '93-'94 season, Manute signed a ten-day contract with the Sixers that March. Towards the end of that contract, Bol skipped a home game against the Timberwolves. It was considered an unexcused absence by the team. He wasn't sick. He didn't have car trouble. Bol told the Sixers he left Philly that day to speak to the United Nations on behalf of his war-torn Sudan (Cobourn 1994). Manute Bol remains one of the most beloved figures in NBA History. He was way more than just a basketball player. Manute was Manute.

The Offensive Rebounder

Name: Furkan Aldemir

Height: 6'10"

Born: Konak, Turkey

Sixers Tenure: 2014-2015

When asked to describe Aldemir's style of play, Brown chose one word: "Rebounder." (Cooney 2014).

Rebounding translates. It's the universal language. If you can rebound in the Belarusian Premier League, you can rebound in the Guam Basketball Association (GBA), then you can rebound in the NBA. Furkan Aldemir developed a reputation as THEE premier international rebounder. Loosely translated, 'Furkan Aldemir' means 'Wes Unseld' in Turkish. Reggie Evans made a career of pounding the glass, and so did Aldemir. There were limitations elsewhere with Furkan, but when you lead the galaxy in rebounding, no one pays much mind. Aldemir wasn't mistaken for an offensive savant. The Sixers weren't drawing up plays for the big man, isolating him on the low block. But when things went to shit, and a contested Michael Carter-Williams jumper was the best the Sixers could muster, Furkan was there, offensive rebounder extraordinaire. Aldemir was like an attentive father rebounding for their young son or daughter. "Keep shooting, sport. You'll get it. Bend those knees."

Furkan was a second-round pick of the Clippers in the 2012 Draft, a 'draft and stash' player which has become commonplace in today's NBA. Teams without the roster space will draft an international player and bring them to the States years later on a rainy day. Arvydas Sabonis was a first-round pick of the Trailblazers in 1986 but didn't join the NBA until 1995. It can be a crapshoot. The Sixers acquired

Aldemir and Royce White in 2013. White was a former first round pick from Iowa State. Aldemir was probably considered the less heralded player of the two, but that's only because Furkan was a mystery. I called my local cable provider, trying to get a head start on my scouting.

"Good afternoon, I'm looking to expand my cable sports package. Do you know which channel airs the Turkish Basketball Super League?"

"For $149.99 plus tax we can bundle your cable and internet, and also provide you with a landline, sir."

"Ok ... thanks. That's good to know. But I'm mostly concerned about the Turkish Basketball Super League and what channel carries the action."

"I can sweeten the deal with three free months of Showtime, sir."

Fans were in the dark. I still knew nothing about Aldemir, so I just binge watched *Dexter* until his arrival. Philly embraced the Turkish big man immediately; if for no other reason than to create a pun from his first name. You're Furkan right they did. There was always this cloudy forecast on these 'draft and stashes.' Will they ever join the NBA ranks? The Sixers acquired Croatian Dario Šarić in 2014. He's been in the NBA for six seasons, and I'm still not sure he's ever coming over.

In November of 2014, reports came from overseas that Aldemir asked for his Euro contract to be terminated (Pompey 2014). The next month, Furkan was a Sixer. He started slow, like a Mike McMahon-led offense. But then in an early January win against Cleveland, Aldemir displayed his singular elite skill in all its glory. He grabbed ten boards in 19 minutes. He didn't attempt a shot. Didn't need to. I'll have to watch the film again, but I'm not even sure Furkan ever got into the triple-threat position. In a road tilt at Cleveland in March, Aldemir registered his only career double-double. A noted Cavs killer like Michael Jordan, Furkan poured in 11 points and collected 10 boards, 7 on the offensive glass. Aldemir boxed out the entire arena, pushing those in attendance to the Ohio/Michigan border.

Outside of the destruction of the Cavs though, Aldemir wandered through his only season in Philly. Brett Brown said Aldemir had a "C- Body" (Gonzalez 2015). Hey, that's right in the meat of the curve. It's basically knocking on the door of the honor roll.

Aldemir's lack of a second skill destroyed his chances at a successful NBA career. Offensive deficiencies aside - and that's a big aside - Furkan wasn't a shot blocker or a strong defender. See rebound. Get rebound. He was a caveman in that regard. All other matters were irrelevant.

The Footnote

Name: Vonteego Cummings

Height: 6'3"

College: Pittsburgh

Sixers Tenure: 2001-2002

I'm surprised there isn't an indie band out there called, Vonteego Cummings. Just seems so obvious. Heck, Pearl Jam used to be named Mookie Blaylock so there's clearly a precedent here. You're telling me you can't see Vonteego Cummings, the band, with its deliberate tempo and cutting lyrics opening up for The War on Drugs at The Fillmore? A couple of Philly kids jamming one night with the '01-'02 Sixers on in the background trying to come up with a clever name when Vonteego's stat line suddenly flashes on the screen? Just saying.

Vonteego Cummings was a throw-in, a footnote in the Derrick Coleman deal that brought the big man back to Philadelphia in '01. Every article about the acquisition ended along these lines:

The Warriors got forward Cedric Henderson and a conditional first-round draft pick in 2005 from the Sixers, as well as cash from Charlotte. Philadelphia also received guard Vonteego Cummings and forward Corie Blount from Golden State. (Associated Press 2001).

No player description, no additional details, no nothing. Vonteego got lumped in with the movie's extras, Corie Blount and "cash from Charlotte." You may as well have just changed Vonteego's name to "And Considerations." The former University of Pittsburgh star deserved better. There was a charm, a star quality about Cummings. Perhaps it was his first name. Vonteego's mom named him after her two favorite cars, a Volkswagen and the Mercury Montego (Taylor 2017).

'Vonteego Cummings' rolls off the tongue. He stuck out. Heck, you don't see former Sixer Terry Cummings in this book, do you?

Drafted in the late first round of the '99 NBA Draft by the Pacers and quickly moved to Golden State, Cummings was a shoot first, shoot second, and shoot third type guard. There were similarities to Trevor Ruffin, a guy who could ignite an offense for spurts. Cummings wasn't a player you'd want starting 82 games, but with the shot clock winding down? Yeah, why not. Let it rip, Vonteego.

The '01-'02 Sixers entered the regular season decimated by injuries. Half the roster required surgery in the offseason. Usually it's a post-finals hangover for the losing team, not a post-finals torn rotator cuff, but such was life for the Black Shirts. Iverson and Aaron McKie missed the entire preseason. Eric Snow broke his thumb and the Sixers limped in with a 1-6 preseason record. (Maaddi 2001). And while preseason results carry little weight, it's a bit more predictive than the NFL preseason where fans watch Matt McGloin underthrow swing passes for four weeks. In an opening night loss at Minnesota, the Sixers labored their way to 74 points. Coleman and Harpring went a combined 9-30 from the floor, and without the heroics of Speedy Claxton (20 points), Philly would've flirted with some unwanted history post-shot clock era. Despite the injuries, Larry Brown didn't call Cummings' number often. He appeared in every game, but not long enough to make an impact or, at the very least, hoist up twelve to fifteen contested jumpers.

Then Memphis happened. The Sixers were on the road for a December 8th tilt against the Grizzlies. Amy Grant was playing at the First Union Center that night, and South Philly wasn't big enough for both the Black Shirts and the contemporary pop icon. Iverson, McKie, Snow, and now Derrick Coleman were sidelined. The Sixers had Kevin Ollie and Joe Smith on standby. Larry Brown needed a spark, no, a fire. He needed a scoring punch.

He needed Vonteego. Cummings played 43 minutes and pumped in 28 points on a crisp 12-16 shooting. The 28 points may seem rather pedestrian, but that's before you consider the snail's pace these teams employed. It was the slowest game outside of two-player Risk. There was a better chance of fortifying the borders of Europe and Asia than the Sixers breaking 90. The fact that any one player cracked double digits was a minor miracle. That night in Memphis, however, was Vonteego's lone big moment. His playing time dropped drastically. As the team got healthy, Cummings racked up DNPs.

He appeared in only one game in the Boston playoff series, where he played all of one second. A career 38% shooter from the field, Cummings wasn't efficient enough to stick in the league. While his NBA career ended after the '01-'02 season, his name lives on in bars, water coolers, and whenever someone is asked to name a random Sixer.

"What about Vonteego Cummings?"

"That's a good one. Damn, that's a good one. Vonteego, shit. I haven't heard that name in forever."

The Redemption Story

Name: Derrick Coleman

Height: 6'10"

College: Syracuse

Sixers Tenure: 1995-1998; 2001-2004

Derrick Coleman's story really was a tale of two tenures. The first act, a mailed-in performance of epic proportions, left many fans pining for a return to the Golden Age of the Shawn Bradley Era.

"Bradley wasn't that bad."

"Yep, agreed. And he was making strides with that sky hook."

Coleman's second act, his reacquisition a surprise in its own right, was more fruitful, an olive branch of sorts to Philadelphians who still held a grudge from the disastrous first stint. Derrick Coleman's mood and effort changed with the weather. Combine those ingredients with a career full of nagging injuries and you have an enigma - albeit a talented one - a frustrating lump of clay that you hoped could be molded into any semblance of consistency. The many controversies of DC didn't begin in '95 when he arrived in Philly. None of his actions, his tendencies, should've been a surprise to the Sixers brass. Coleman came with a warning label. It was understood. You knew the risk when he arrived on your doorstep, but hey, 20 and 10 is 20 and 10.

After four years at Syracuse, Coleman was the consensus top pick in the 1990 Draft. The Nets selected him #1 overall, and coupled with Kenny Anderson and Dražen Petrović, Coleman spearheaded a New Jersey team that NBA Twitter would've salivated over. From '92 through '94, the Nets reached the postseason as a lower seed but fell in the first round all three years. The sudden passing of

Petrović certainly stunted their growth, and the Nets fell back to the dregs of society (right in the gutter with the Sixers). DC then asked management for a trade. The losing season may have been the final straw for Coleman, but the problems had been bubbling beneath the surface for years. His apathy towards practice and issues with the coaches - and, boy, were there issues with the coaches - created a laundry list of controversies involving the big man. Let's go to the videotape:

April 1992

Last week, forwards Chris Morris and Derrick Coleman refused to go back into a game - during crunch time of the playoff drive. Coleman reportedly told Fitch, "Get out of my face, you pig-headed (bleep)." (Pluto 1992).

I'm sure there's a logical explanation here.

November 1994

Beard, who coached at Howard University last season, already has been undermined. He implemented a dress code for the team when it travels but Coleman, who prefers the casual look, instead gave Beard a blank check to take care of his fines. (Bembry 1994).

Disney's *Blank Check* - a classic - came out in February of 1994. Have we considered that Coleman and Coach Butch Beard we're just working on some sort of roleplay, or maybe brainstorming sequel ideas? I acted out the final scene of *Home Alone* all the time, setting booby traps all over my house waiting for a sibling to slip on some Micro Machines. Just saying. Let's not jump to any conclusions.

December 1994

"Everybody misses practice. I miss practice, the coach misses practice. Where were all you guys when Dwayne [Schintzius] missed practice, or when Jayson [Williams] missed practice?" asked Coleman, who will not play tonight against the Pacers because of his injured left hand.

When it was pointed out that Anderson is an All-Star and supposed team leader,

Coleman replied, "Well whoop-de-damn-do. This is all blown out of proportion." (Brennan 1994).

Ok, that's pretty funny. Coleman wanted to go to a winner so the Nets organization, at wits end, obliged and traded him to the worst team in the league. Katz and Lucas punted on Bradley - unhappy with the lack of development in year three. It was trading a problem for a problem. I mentioned that Coleman wanted to go to a winner, right?

"He didn't want to be a Sixer, no," Williams said. "He was so upset, if he plays there, he might wear no. 666." (Cawthon 1995).

Dogged by an ankle injury, Coleman played just 11 games for the Sixers that first season. Philly plummeted in the standings clinging to their only life raft, "When Derrick Coleman comes back..." Coleman played in 57 games his second year, and strictly from a number's vantage point, DC was pretty good. He averaged 18 and 10. You just had to turn a blind eye to everything else.

Derrick never improved his conditioning. It had to drive Sixers' owner Pat Croce crazy. Here was a guy (Croce) who probably started every morning with a smoothie and 200 burpees – maybe flipped over a giant tire up and down his street just for kicks. Then there was DC. Conditioning and practice, which he often boycotted, was an inconvenience for Coleman, like realizing the state inspection on your car is due. During timeouts, DC wouldn't join the team. He'd hang out by the scorer's table, like a parent taking a cigarette break during a PTA meeting. Coleman then asked to be traded again. When he remained a Sixer after the trade deadline, he sulked (Cawthon 1997).

I watched a bunch of Sixers games from that season on YouTube, because, you know, research. Just to make sure my personal memories coincided with actual events. They lost every game I watched. They lost one contest to the Raptors at the cavernous SkyDome. (I was expecting the starting line-ups to enter the court on a wrestling cart ala Wrestlemania VI, but it was a vanilla entrance). My memories held up though. Coleman was the guy playing pick-up who always trailed the action, pointing to an opposing player in the distance. The "get my man" guy. Everyone played with the "get my man" guy at one time or another. The half-hearted jog back on defense, one finger in the air, motioning into the distance.

"Get my man!" they would say, before crossing half-court a minute later.

During the Sixers/Mavericks game from December of '96 (the Sixers coughed up a late lead), Philly defended the Mavs one possession 5-on-4, and to their credit, they got a stop. Iverson then found a wide open, cherry-picking Coleman for the slam. Coleman had 21, 11, and 5 assists that game, and I'm not sure he was even trying.

(The telecast flashed scores from other sports, and the Birds played a Thursday night game in Indianapolis. They got blasted. Ty Detmer got benched for the ageless Mark Rypien. It wasn't a great night for Philly sports. I think even the KiXX lost).

Coleman played one more season in Philly, this time under Larry Brown. Brown told reporters he wanted to bring DC back, but that wasn't a realistic option. Pat Croce did not like DC. Apparently, Coleman had flaked out on a team function at a children's hospital, and that was it for Croce. He vowed never to bring Coleman back as long as he was owner. (Associated Press 2001).

But now Croce was gone. There was obviously a good bit of trepidation from fans about DC's return in 2002. Coleman wasn't in great shape in his 20s, and now he was 34. The only people who get in better shape as they got older are the CrossFit folks, and I know that because they never shut up about it. Coleman extended his range the second time around. He only shot around 33% from behind the arc in his second stint, but it felt much higher than that. A healthy 33%. Every attempt was from the top of the key, and whether it was the camera angle or the Milwaukee's Best at college, I felt a calmness wash over me. An unabashed confidence, like any shot Nick Young ever took.

"That's good," I said after every DC release.

Coleman never played a full season with the Sixers - that ship had sailed - but he was a gamer. At that stage, he was more suited for a role as a complementary piece. He came up large in the Hornets series in '03 and played really well against Detroit in the next round. Derrick evolved from embattled, underachieving superstar to grizzled veteran. DC was no longer the focal point. He was just another contributor. Nobody seemed to stress about the number of games he missed, or his energy at practice.

"Oh, that's just DC," fans reasoned, like how Chris Wheeler labeled every left-handed reliever as 'quirky.'

Derrick Coleman left Philadelphia on much better terms. DC didn't completely salvage his legacy here in this city, but he certainly improved it.

The Next Barkley

Name: Clarence Weatherspoon

Height: 6'6"

College: Southern Mississippi

Sixers Tenure: 1992-1998

Here we are. We've made it. Let's all put our hands together for the man of the hour, the reason we're all here, the legend, the incomparable, the unparalleled Clarence Weatherspoon. If you're a child of the 90s, Spoon was your guy, the bridge from Barkley to Iverson, the Antonio Bastardo connecting Roy Halladay to Ryan Madson. Clarence Weatherspoon WAS my guy. I have his Wikipedia page saved to My Favorites. I search his name on Twitter a few times a week just to see what the world is saying about him. I'm his staunchest defender and his biggest supporter. If someone mentions Weatherspoon on Twitter, I invade their replies like a lantern fly. No one speaks about Clarence Weatherspoon, good or bad, without me knowing about it. I loved Spoon.

In fact, everyone loved Spoon. His teams had a lower winning percentage than Michael Martinez' batting average, but Clarence is still fondly remembered. Spoon was a beacon of light in a world of despair. His teams were terrible. The mid-90s Sixers were the NBA's graveyard shift, yet Weatherspoon clocked in every night without complaint. He was undersized, undervalued, and underappreciated. Those Philly teams were wretched, but not because of Spoon, but in spite of him.

In 2013, I was a "celebrity" judge for the amateur dunk contest, the Sprite Slam Dunk Showdown. My only dunking credential consisted of owning the '87 Dunk Contest on VHS, but alas, there I was, lending my expertise. There were two other judges – some rando and then Darryl Dawkins (R.I.P.). (Chocolate Thunder was such a nice guy, the salt of the earth).

I told myself going in that I wasn't going to be a pushover. These dunkers had to earn my 10s. I was taken my duties very seriously. Sprite Slam Dunk Showdown attendees would label me the hard ass judge, and I was fine with that. I was there to critique dunks, not make friends. But that didn't last. I was in way over my head. I caught myself peeking at Dawkins' scorecard most of the time, like this was the SATs and Chocolate Thunder was the captain of the Mathletes.

"You thinking a '9' here, Thunder? Yeah, same."

Air Kodiak (great name) snuck past Frequent Flier (great name!) in controversial fashion. Fortunately, the fans voted in the finals so I was off the hook. I snuck away from the judges' table with my reputation intact.

As a rookie, Weatherspoon competed in the '93 Slam Dunk Contest. He finished second to Harold Miner ("Baby Jordan"). Spoon battled, unleashing a series of ferocious power dunks that were scored critically by the judges. Clarence wasn't graded on a curve by any means. I think dunk contest judges should be subject to promotion and relegation like the English Premier League. Clearly, the moment was too big for Judge M.L. Carr. Maybe M.L. needed to drop down to the Sprite Slam Dunk Showdown to work on his craft. Cameras flashed to Weatherspoon's disgust after hearing his scores. Like Spoon, every guest at little Brian's birthday party felt he deserved better.

"Spoon was robbed!" I screamed at the TV.

Little Brian agreed, nodding between pieces of chocolate cake. Miner was better (debatable) on this night, but Spoon's obscurity cost him. He lacked name recognition. "That was a great dunk," said analyst, Doug Collins, at one point. "I just don't think the people know who Clarence Weatherspoon is."

Clarence had the best pump fake in the business. Listed generously at 6'6", Spoon made a living getting his defender off their feet. He was persistent. If one pump fake didn't work, he'd try another, and another, and another. I bit. I bit every time from my living room. If I was covering Spoon, I'd have fouled out before *Wheel of Fortune* rolled its closing credits. It was an exercise in patience. He trademarked that move. Kids emulated it. According to a 1994 study by M.I.T., free throws attempted increased 675% in youth leagues across the Delaware Valley after Spoon was drafted.

"I drew six fouls, mom" was the new, "I got fifteen points."

Clarence Weatherspoon was the greatest athlete to ever come out of Southern Miss. Brett Favre threw into double coverage. Weatherspoon *drew* double coverage. Try averaging 18 a game while Shawn Bradley's man doubles you in the post. Antonio Freeman won't be able to bail you out then, Brett. Spoon won the Metro Conference Player of the Year so many times (three) that Florida State high-tailed it to the ACC. They were tired of living in Spoon's shadow. The entire league soon disbanded after Spoon's reign of terror left the conference in ruins. Clarence was a natural fit for the Sixers. Dubbed "Baby Barkley" due to his stature and style of play, the Sixers suddenly had an opening at the power forward position after trading Charles days prior to the '92 NBA Draft. Philly selected him #9 overall, and he quickly adjusted to the rigors of the league. He averaged over 15 a game and captured Second Team All-Rookie Team.

In his second campaign, Iron Spoon again played in all 82 games and averaged a double-double. There was certainly a push to get Weatherspoon All-Star recognition around these parts. Without the benefit of social media or a winning team though, Weatherspoon faced an uphill climb. But I did my part. Change starts at the local level and I felt an obligation to help. My mom mailed the "Got Spoon?" stickers I created to all Eastern Conference coaches and league officials. Twelve of fourteen coaches wrote me back, thanking me for my support of the young upstart power forward. They also told me to do all my homework and help out around the house. Weatherspoon was unfortunately snubbed, but I did learn that all NBA coaches have very similar handwriting.

Despite Clarence's success and consistency, he was never considered 'the guy.' 'The guy' was Stackhouse, and then it was Coleman, followed by Iverson.

Weatherspoon was reliable and durable, but always considered a secondary piece. As his Sixers tenure progressed, he fell further down the pecking order. His role diminished. Spoon was moved to the small forward spot when Sharone Wright arrived. He didn't complain. He took three fewer shots a game when Stackhouse was drafted. Spoon took it in stride. His usage decreased even more after Iverson took over. Spoon still competed.

By the time Larry Brown seized the franchise, it was clear Weatherspoon was not part of the team's future. He was part of the failed Dino Radja trade in June of '97. The whole experience left a sour taste in Spoon's mouth. Management never allegedly told Clarence, a guy who had been a dependable stalwart the past few years about the trade. Spoon felt he deserved better.

"I've been here for five years. I should have gotten a courtesy call to tell me something," lamented Weatherspoon. "But they just figured, 'Good ol' 'Spoon is gonna come back and work his butt off so we can take him for granted.'

"I wasn't looking for an apology. A trade is part of the business. But it's about respect. I've been overlooked and underappreciated for five years. Every year we start new and I stay solid. Some nights it's like I'm isolated on an island and don't even see the ball. But I stay solid." (Long 1997).

Despite the mistrust and disappointment with management, Weatherspoon soldiered on for the '97-'98 campaign. He was relegated to a fourth or fifth option, but he still put up numbers. He recorded double-doubles against Atlanta, Seattle, Indiana, and Miami before the calendar turned. Weatherspoon was no longer a focal point, but he wasn't forgotten. That was until a December 19th loss at home to the Heat.

Spoon played just 15 plus minutes that night - certainly lower than his season's average, but not completely an aberration. It was Larry Brown's postgame comments, however, that raised eyebrows and cemented the schism between Weatherspoon and the organization. Spoon inexplicably didn't play at all the entire first half.

"Brian damage," Brown said, when asked about Weatherspoon's absence. "I was diagramming plays at halftime and looked at him and said, 'oh, no.'"

"I was teasing him, telling him I thought he was already in Toronto," Brown continued, commenting on the trade rumors that have Weatherspoon going to the Raptors. (Associated Press 1997).

That's bullshit. Spoon was pissed and rightfully so.

"It shows the respect and attitude they have for me," said Weatherspoon, who had eight points and three rebounds in 16 minutes. "That about sums it up," he added as he left the locker room, unwilling to answer any more questions. (Associated Press 1997).

Two months later, Weatherspoon was traded to Golden State along with Jim Jackson (the shooting guard, not the Flyers play-by-play announcer) for Brian Shaw and Joe Smith. It was a sad end for a fan favorite. It was a sad end for my favorite player. Spoon outlasted countless coaches and roster turnover, but the latest regime just cast him aside. Larry Brown attempted to trade him every chance he had.

The postgame quotes after the Heat game were embarrassing. Brown forgot Spoon was still on the team? Fuck that. Weatherspoon deserved a better fate. He deserved transparency from a team that failed him every step of the way since his draft selection. Those Sixers teams were some of the worst in organization history, but Spoon's legacy has remained above the muck, above the suck. Clarence Weatherspoon gave a shit. When you're a kid, you just want a player to care as much as you do. That's all.

Larry Brown may have forgotten about Spoon, but I didn't.

Bibliography

"All-Star Voting." *Philadelphia Daily News*. January 24, 1990.

"Basketball," *Philadelphia Daily News*, April 21, 1990.

"Charles Barkley Trade Wins Approval – People Poll." *Intelligencer Journal*. June 20, 1992.

"Tonight: Heat at 76ers," *Miami Herald*, November 17, 1999.

Abrams, Jonathan. "Boys Among Men: When Kwame Brown Made a Bold Promise to MJ." *ESPN*. March 15, 2016. Accessed August 18, 2020. https://www.espn.com/nba/story/_/id/14929620/kwame-brown-decided-go-pro

Associated Press. "Jazz Acquire Veteran Forward Henderson." *ESPN*. February 22, 2007. Accessed May 27, 2020. https://www.espn.com/nba/news/story?id=2775504

Associated Press. "76ers Sign Veteran Forward Henderson." *ESPN*. September 8, 2006. Accessed May 27, 2020. https://www.espn.com/nba/news/story?id=2579441

Associated Press. "76ers Tell Massenburg Thanks." *The Morning Call*. July 23, 1996.

Associated Press. "76ers' Willie Green Rebounds After Knee Injury." *DAOnline*. April 23, 2008. Accessed May 25, 2020. https://www.thedaonline.com/76ers-willie-green-rebounds-after-knee-injury/article_5fa7a336-2941-5464-981c-d6e4952d7eb1.html

Associated Press. "Coleman Returns to Sixes; Hornets Get Lynch." *ESPN*. October 26, 2001. Accessed July 18, 2020. http://www.espn.com/nba/news/2001/1025/1268822.html#:~:text=In%20exchange%20for%20Coleman%2C%20the,was%20waived%20by%20the%20Hornets

Associated Press. “Ex-N.C. State Basketball Star Charles Shackleford Found Dead.” *The Times and Democrat*. January 28, 2017.

Associated Press. “I’ve Been Clean Since I’ve Been In…” *Los Angeles Times*. December 12, 2005.

Associated Press. “Iverson Keys 17-Point Comeback.” *ESPN*. December 15, 1999. Accessed July 9, 2020. https://www.espn.com/nba/2000/991215/recap/torphi.html

Associated Press. “Jodie Meeks Scores 20 of His 26 Points in First Quarter for Philadelphia.” *ESPN*. December 4, 2010. Accessed May 1, 2020. https://www.espn.com/nba/recap?gameId=301204020

Associated Press. “Maybe Rockne Can Coach Sixers.” *Miami Herald*. May 29, 1992.

Associated Press. “New Lineup, Same Result for Sixers.” *Intelligencer Journal*. December 20, 1997.

Associated Press. “Plus: Pro Basketball; 76ers Withdraw Offer to Harpring.” *New York Times*. July 25, 2002.

Associated Press. “Rockets Waive Vernon Maxwell.” *Great Falls Tribune*. July 13, 1995.

Associated Press. “Sixers Deal Hill to Cavs,” *The Times Leader*, August 4, 2001.

Associated Press. “Sixers Rally for Rare Win on the Road,” *The Daily News*, February 14, 1996.

Associated Press. “Sixers-Hornets Trade Rescinded.” *ESPN*. February 8, 2006. Accessed July 17, 2020. https://www.espn.com/nba/news/story?id=2323730

Associated Press. “Wolves’ Mahorn Threatening to Retire.” *St. Cloud Times*. September 27, 1989.

Baker, Chris. “Growing Pains: A Failure at 22, Benoit Benjamin Vows Clippers Will See a Change in Their Center of Controversy.” *Los Angeles Times*. September 16, 1987.

Bembry, Jerry. “Honeymoon Ends Quickly in Nets-Beard Marriage.” *Baltimore*

Sun. November 15, 1994.

Benjamin, Amalie. "Allen Stops Garnett." *The Boston Globe*. May 19, 2012.

Bonfatti, John. "Pistons Paste Sixers." *The Danville News*. February 15, 1996.

Bostrom, Don. "Sixers Select Payne with 19th Pick in Draft." *The Morning Call*. June 28, 1989.

Bracy, Aaron. "James Becomes No. 10 Career Scorer," *Courier-Post*. November 6, 2016.

Brennan, John. "Nets Attract Notice." *The Record*. December 30, 1994.

Brown, Curt. "Only the Bad Boy Cries Wolf." *Star Tribune.* June 16, 1989.

Bruton, Mike. "Trade Was Made As Teams Played." *Philadelphia Inquirer*. January 18, 1988.

Buckley, Tim. "Marvin Williams Looks Ready to Soar with Hawks." *ESPN*. July 21, 2006. Accessed June 29, 2020. https://www.espn.com/nba/news/story?id=2526765

Buschel, Bruce. "In Search of Raymond Lewis." *Philly Sport*. November 1989.

Carchidi, Sam. "Myers, Bats Lead Them Into First." *The Philadelphia Inquirer.* May 31, 2008.

Cawthon, Raad. "76ers Give Up Lead Late, Fall to Denver." *Philadelphia Inquirer*. December 31, 1995.

Cawthon, Raad. "Determined to Do What It Takes." *Philadelphia Inquirer*. June 28, 1996.

Cawthon, Raad. "MacLean Finds the Going Tough. *Philadelphia Inquirer*. November 8, 1996.

Cawthon, Raad. "NBA Iron Man Plans to Test Sixers' Mettle." *Philadelphia Inquirer*. October 6, 1996.

Cawthon, Raad. "Nets Are Shocked by Sixers." *Lancaster New Era*. January 13, 1996.

Cawthon, Raad. "Potshot at 'Little Man' Lucas. *Philadelphia Inquirer*. December 10, 1995.

Cawthon, Raad. "Sixers' Bradtke Ready to Suit Up," *Philadelphia Inquirer*, November 9, 1996.

Cawthon, Raad." Sixers' Streak Ended by Pistons." *Philadelphia Inquirer.* February 25, 1996.

Chandler, Charles and O'Brien, Kevin. "4 Ex-N.C. State Players Linked to Point-Shaving." *Orlando Sentinel*. March 1, 1990. Accessed May 18, 2020. https://www.orlandosentinel.com/news/os-xpm-1990-03-01-9003012932-story.html

Chandler, Charles. "Hornets Get Their Man in Graham." *The Charlotte Observer*. July 1, 1993.

CNN. "CNN: BYU Official: 'Dumping Brandon Davies Wasn't Hard.'" *YouTube*. March 4, 2011. Accessed September 1, 2020. https://www.youtube.com/watch?v=CfAq9_B68IM

Cobourn, Tom. "Bol Pulls Vanishing Act." *The News Journal*. March 19, 1994.

Colgan, Greg. "Sheriff Does Nickname Justice – Like the Legendary Lawmen of the Old West, Rodney Buford Is a Straight-Shooter and a Natural Leader." *The London Free Press*. January 26, 2012.

Cooney, Bob. "Brown Puts Roberts in Talented Company." *Philadelphia Daily News*. October 2, 2014.

Cooney, Bob. "Keeping Tabs on Forward in Turkey." *Philadelphia Daily News*. November 25, 2014.

Daily News Wire Services. "Former NBA Center Amaechi Revealing He's Gay in Book." *Philadelphia Daily News*. February 8, 2007.

Daily News Wire Services. "Ruland's At a Loss in Lawsuit," *Philadelphia Daily News*, May 26, 1995.

Deitch, Dennis. "International Center Coming to Philly," *Delaware County Daily Times*, October 18, 1996.

Deitsch, Richard. "A Chat with Charles Barkley About Analytics and Beyond." *Sports Illustrated*. February 15, 2015. Accessed July 7, 2020.

https://www.si.com/more-sports/2015/02/15/charles-barkley-analytics-interview-nba-all-star-weekend

Downey, Mike. "The Hammer Can Deliver a Pounding." *Los Angeles Times*. March 28, 1987.

Eskin, Spike and Levin, Mike. "Joel Embiid Finally Comes on the Ricky and Sixers Bubble Predictions." Spike Eskin and Mike Levin. July 29, 2020. https://rightstorickysanchez.com

ESPN. "#NBArank 1: LeBron James." *ESPN*. October 17, 2001. Accessed June 2, 2020. https://www.espn.com/nba/story/_/id/7116977/nba-player-rankings-1

ESPN. "76ers Win Despite Missing Injured Iverson." *ESPN*. March 8, 2004. https://www.espn.in/nba/recap?gameId=240308020

ESPN. "Sixers F Randolph out indefinitely with broken ankle." *ESPN*. November 30, 2006. Accessed by June 25, 2020. http://www.espn.com/espn/wire/_/section/nba/id/2681666

ESPN. "Toronto Forward Ties NBA Record With 12 3-pointers." *ESPN*. March 13, 2005. accessed May 17, 2020. https://www.espn.com/nba/recap?gameId=250313028

ESPN.com "Sorry Lavoy." *ESPN*. October 17, 2001. Accessed June 2, 2020. https://www.espn.com/blog/truehoop/post/_/id/43732/sorry-lavoy

Fagan, Kate. "Inside the 76ers: Damage Assessment," *Philadelphia Inquirer*, April 11, 2010.

Fernandez, Bernard. "Shackleford One Moe Dissenter." *Philadelphia Daily News*. February 17, 1993.

Fernandez, Bernard. "Thomas Wants to Have a Ball." *Philadelphia Daily News*. July 17, 2003.

Finocchiaro, Ray. "NBA and 76ers Hope Fans Will Let the Healing Begin." *The News Journal*. February 7, 1999.

Fleischman, Bill. "Round Mound of Sound: Bigger Barkley Full of Opinions in TNT Studio Job." *Philadelphia Daily News*. February 9, 2001.

Ford, Bob. "76ers Trade Barkley for Three Players." *Philadelphia Inquirer*. June 18, 1992.

Ford, Bob. "Anderson and Sixers Rip Bullets." *Philadelphia Inquirer*. November 23, 1988.

Ford, Bob. "Daunting Mission for Rookie Bradley." *Philadelphia Inquirer*. October 31, 1993.

Ford, Bob. "First Lesson for Sixers: Chemistry." *Philadelphia Inquirer*. October 9, 1991.

Ford, Bob. "For the Sixers, a New Season, Many Questions." *Philadelphia Inquirer*. November 1, 1991.

Ford, Bob. "Gilliam Shoots Back at Barkley with Some Tough Talk of His Own." *Lancaster New Era*. December 18, 1991.

Ford, Bob. "Season of Decision Ahead for Sixers' Kenny Payne." *Philadelphia Inquirer*. August 1, 1991.

Ford, Bob. "Sixers Close Out Exhibition Season with Loss to Bulls." *Philadelphia Inquirer*. October 30, 1993.

Ford, Bob. "Sixers Turn to Addition By Subtraction, But Plenty of Problem Solving Remains." *Philadelphia Inquirer*. June 21, 1992.

Ford, Bob. "Sixers Turn to Addition by Subtraction, But Plenty of Problem Solving Remains." *Philadelphia Inquirer*. June 21, 1992.

Ford, Bob. "Sources: Hinkie Reneged on Kirilenko Agreement." *Philadelphia Inquirer*. January 9, 2015.

Ford, Bob. "Weatherspoon 2d in Dunk Contest." *Philadelphia Inquirer*. February 21, 1993.

Frank, Martin. "Collins Likes Battie's Brawn, Playoff Experience." *The News Journal*. March 24, 2011.

Frank, Martin. "Hawes the Odd Man Out for Sixers." *Courier-Post*. May 22, 2012.

Frank, Martin. "Smith, McFarlin Earn Roster Spots." *The News Journal*. October 31, 2006.

Gaines, Cork. "7-Foot-7 Basketballer Might Have Been 50 Years Old When He Played in the NBA." *Business Insider*. November 23, 2017. Accessed July 1, 2020.

Goldaper, Sam. "Basketball; 76ers Did Work on Shackleford." *New York Times*. July 18, 1991.

Goldstein, Alan. "Barkley, Worthy Rumored Part of Blockbuster Trade." *Baltimore Sun*. February 12, 1992.

Gonzalez, John. "Sixers Player Evaluation: Furkan Aldemir." *NBC Sports Philadelphia*. April 20, 2015. Accessed September 11, 2020. https://www.nbcsports.com/philadelphia/philadelphia-sixers/sixers-player-evaluation-furkan-aldemir

Groller, Keith. "'Free Willie' Scores 53; Burns Heat." *The Morning Call*. December 14, 1994.

Groller, Keith. "76ers Reach Eastern Semifinals." *The Morning Call*. May 6, 1990.

Groller, Keith. "Barkley Buries 76ers, But Only During Game." *The Morning Call*. March 29, 1993.

Groller, Keith. "Ron Anderson Real Catalyst For the 76ers." *The Morning Call*. January 29, 1989.

Groller, Keith. "Ruland Deal Comes with Limitations." *The Morning Call*. January 8, 1992.

Gscottdesign. "Greg Grant NBA Highlight Reel." *YouTube*. April 24, 2014. Accessed May 12, 2020. https://www.youtube.com/watch?v=aVKdpqPg8fg

Gun, Milt. "Jeff Ruland's Lawsuit Against Celtics Opens." *Philadelphia Inquirer*. May 17, 1995.

Hayes, Marcus. "Marshall's Act Never Grows Old for Sixers." *Philadelphia Daily News*. April 20, 2009.

Heisel, Andrew. "Throwback Thursday: Willie Burton's 53-Point NBA Game and the Likeliness of Unlikely Greatness." *Vice*. December 10, 2015. Accessed May 13, 2020. https://www.vice.com/en_us/article/kbdep3/throwback-thursday-willie-burtons-53-point-nba-game-and-the-likeliness-of-unlikely-greatness

Hilt, Ed. "Sixers Make Louisville Forward Top Selection." *Press of Atlantic City*. June 28, 1989.

Hofmann, Rich. "Height of Stupidity." *Philadelphia Daily News*. August 2, 1990.

Hofmann, Rich. "Height of Stupidity." *Philadelphia Daily News*. August 2, 1990.

HoopsHD, "Happy Draft-iversary!: HoopsHD Interviews Former NBA Rebounding Champ Michael Cage." HoopsHD. https://hoopshd.com/2019/06/15/happy-draft-iversary-hoopshd-interviews-former-nba-rebounding-champ-michael-cage/. June 5, 2019. Accessed July 1, 2020.

HoopsHype. "Doug Collins Lied to My Face." *HoopsHype*. May 1, 2020. Accessed by May 21, 2020. https://hoopshype.com/rumor/1340386/

Hudrick, Paul. "Why Charles Barkley Is as Philly As It Gets." *NBC Sports Philadelphia*. August 30, 2019. Accessed May 18, 2020. https://www.nbcsports.com/philadelphia/76ers/why-charles-barkley-philly-it-gets

IFPA. "Todd MacCulloch [TOD]." IFPA: International Flipper Pinball Association." https://www.ifpapinball.com/player.php?p=442 (accessed May 8, 2020).

IMDb. "Eric Leckner." *IMDb*. Accessed May 27, 2020. https://www.imdb.com/name/nm4834782/

James, Michael. "Sixers in Ruins, But Nets Worse," *New York Daily News*, April 9, 1996.

Jasner, Phil. "76ers Get J. Malone, No. 1 for Hornacek." *Philadelphia Daily News*. February 25, 1994.

Jasner, Phil. "Backup Big Helps as Sixers Skid Ends." *Philadelphia Daily News*. November 15, 1993.

Jasner, Phil. "Bradley Talking Real Tests Now." *Philadelphia Daily News*. August 26, 1993.

Jasner, Phil. "Coleman, McCaskill to Piston for Williamson." *Philadelphia Daily News*. August 5, 2004.

Jasner, Phil. "Croce: Expect Allen to Be Here." *Philadelphia Daily News*. August 14, 2000.

Jasner, Phil. "Deal Lets Sixers Look to Future." *Philadelphia Daily News*. September 4, 1993.

Jasner, Phil. "For Night, Burton Joins Sixers' Elite." *Philadelphia Daily News*. December 14, 1994.

Jasner, Phil. "Freeze Already on for Barros." *Philadelphia Daily News*. November 2, 1994.

Jasner, Phil. "GM Nixes Barkley Trade Talk." *Philadelphia Daily News*. June 10, 1992.

Jasner, Phil. "Gminski Traded to Hornets." *Philadelphia Daily News*. January 5, 1991.

Jasner, Phil. "Hunter Fails Physical, So That Trade's on Hold." *Philadelphia Daily News*. February 4, 2006.

Jasner, Phil. "It Could Be That Radja Is Just Another Rumor." *Philadelphia Daily News*. June 24, 1997.

Jasner, Phil. "Losing Rubs Wright Wrong." *Philadelphia Daily News*. March 20, 1995.

Jasner, Phil. "Lucas Doesn't Hide Delight." *Philadelphia Daily News*. June 30, 1994.

Jasner, Phil. "McKie Keeps a Cool Head." *Philadelphia Daily News*. December 21, 1999.

Jasner, Phil. "No Trail Is Blazing for Barkley." *Philadelphia Daily News*. January 14, 1992.

Jasner, Phil. "Now, Hornacek Talking and Playing." *Philadelphia Daily News*. October 26, 1993.

Jasner, Phil. "Ruffin Ready When Needed." *Philadelphia Daily News*. December 21, 1995.

Jasner, Phil. "Ruland: Mixed Medical Review." *Philadelphia Daily News*. May 12, 1992.

Jasner, Phil. “Shackleford Meets Sixers’ Brass Again.” *Philadelphia Daily News*. July 11, 1991.

Jasner, Phil. “Shackleford Won’t Be Charged in Scandal.” *Philadelphia Daily News*. September 20, 1993.

Jasner, Phil. “Shackleford Won’t Be Charged in Scandal.” *Philadelphia Daily News*. September 20, 1993.

Jasner, Phil. “Sharone’s in Wright Place.” *Philadelphia Daily News*. March 1, 1995.

Jasner, Phil. “Sixers Give Williams What He Wants.” *Philadelphia Daily News*. July 29, 1994.

Jasner, Phil. “Sixers Sign Grant Agent Says Guard Deserved Better.” *Philadelphia Daily News*. October 2, 1992.

Jasner, Phil. “Sixers Sign Leckner; Renounce Lang’s Rights.” *Philadelphia Daily News*. August 28, 1993.

Jasner, Phil. “Sixers Slip Into History.” *Philadelphia Daily News*. February 21, 1996.

Jasner, Phil. “Steven Smith Keeps Sixers Commitment After Warriors.” *Philadelphia Daily News*. July 13, 2006.

Jasner, Phil. “The Sixers Draw a Lethal Weapon.” *Philadelphia Daily News*. June 28, 1990.

Jasner, Phil. “Thomas Has No Hard Feelings...Well, Maybe a Few.” *Philadelphia Daily News.* February 28, 2005.

Jasner, Phil. “Wright’s Image of Philly Fans Monstrous.” *Philadelphia Daily News*. March 12, 1996.

Jasner, Phil. “Without Iverson, Sixers No Match for Shaq, Heat.” *Lancaster New Era*. November 22, 2004.

Jauss, Bill. “He’s Off the Shelf and Checking Out Just Fine.” *Chicago Tribune*. July 29, 1985.

Jensen, Mike. “From Zero to Hero: It’s the Unlikely Story of Raja Bell.” *Philadelphia Inquirer*. June 4, 2001.

Jerardi, Dick. “Glad Max is Lucas’ Point Man,” *Philadelphia Daily News*,

September 27, 1995.

Jones, Jason. "Rookie Robinson Gets Thrown Out." *Sacramento Bee*. November 8, 2012.

Juliano, Joe. "76ers Go Backward, Get Routed by Celtics." *Philadelphia Inquirer*. February 8, 2004.

Juliano, Joe. "Feeling Good About Hanging On." *Philadelphia Inquirer*. April 14, 2007.

Juliano, Joe. "Nelson Gets a Warm Welcome Home." *Philadelphia Inquirer*. November 15, 2004.

Juliano, Joe. "Sixers Seek to Deal Robinson." *Philadelphia Inquirer*. November 2, 2004.

Juliano, Joe. "Sixers Trade Hunter and Sign Hamilton." *Lancaster New Era*. February 2, 2006.

Juliano, Joe. "Williamson May Get Rare Start in Opener." *Philadelphia Inquirer*. October 31, 2004.

Kaskey-Blomain, Michael. "Eric Bledsoe Thinks Kentucky Could Beat 76ers in Seven-Game Series." *Philadelphia Inquirer*. November 19, 2014. Accessed April 28, 2020. https://www.inquirer.com/philly/blogs/sports/sixers/Eric-Bledsoe-thinks-that-Kentucky-could-beat-the-Sixers-in-a-seven-game-series.html

Kelly, Matt. "Ruland Blames Injury on Boston." *The Boston Globe*. February 2, 1992.

Kilinski, Fran. "Kwame Brown Says Sixers' Medical Staff Misdiagnosed Career-Ending Injury." *New York Daily News*. July 19, 2017.

Lawlor, Frank. "Kidd Shows He's the Pick of Rookies." *Philadelphia Inquirer*. November 6, 1993.

Laye, Leonard. "Hornets Make Draft Deal with Lakers." *The Charlotte Observer*. June 23, 1988.

Leon, Matt. "Sixers' Tony Battie Providing Veteran Leadership." *CBS Sports*.

March 14, 2011. Accessed June 23, 2020. https://philadelphia.cbslocal.com/2011/03/14/sixers-tony-battie-providing-veteran-leadership/

Levick, Noah. "'Excruciating Pain,' Hobbled Heroics and Stories from 2000-01 Sixers' Supporting Cast." *NBC Sports Philadelphia.* April 20, 2020. Accessed May 14, 2020, https://www.nbcsports.com/philadelphia/76ers/sixers-2000-01-sixers-allen-iverson-eric-snow-george-lynch-interview-jumaine-jones

Levin, Mike. "You Know Nothing, Lavoy Allen." *Liberty Ballers*. April 12, 2013. Accessed August 24, 2020. https://www.libertyballers.com/2013/4/12/4216840/you-know-nothing-lavoy-allen-sixers-nikola-vucevic

Long, Ernie. "Don't Break a Young Stallion's Spirit: Let Allen Be Allen." *The Morning Call.* December 5, 1996.

Long, Ernie. "Hail, Hail, the Gang's All Here – Physically, at Least." *The Morning Call.* October 3, 1997.

Long, Ernie. "Sixers Go From Charmed to Harmed." *The Morning Call*. November 25, 1999.

Long, Ernie. "Sixers Hope the Wright Deal Made with Raptors." *The Morning Call.* February 23, 1996.

Longer01. "Kareem Rush Mix by Longer." *YouTube*. April 21, 2008. Accessed June 5, 2020. https://www.youtube.com/watch?v=xhJWb2OHh2g

Lowe, Zach. "The Hinkie Chronicles' Latest Chapter." *ESPN*. December 11, 2015. Accessed June 25, 2020. https://www.espn.com/nba/story/_/id/14344789/sam-hinkie-stands-as-philly-looks-jump-start-future

Lynam, Dei. "Brett Brown Upset by Sixers' Trade of Brandon Davies." *NBC Sports Philadelphia*. December 11, 2014. Accessed May 23, 2020. https://www.nbcsports.com/philadelphia/philadelphia-sixers/brett-brown-upset-sixers-trade-brandon-davies

Lyon, Bill. "Heart Is Not Sixers Problem; Scoring Is." *Philadelphia Inquirer*. May 27, 2001.

Maaddi, Rob. "Feuding Philly Falls to New York." *The Daily News*. December 23, 2000.

Maaddi, Rob. "Injuries, Trade Remake the Sixers Into a New Team." *Washington Post*. October 28, 2001.

Maaddi, Rob. "Iverson Finally Gets Scoring Help As League Approves Four-Team Trade." *The Danville News*. July 24, 2003.

McGeachy, Ashley. "76ers, Foes Rip Suspensions." *Philadelphia Inquirer*. May 15, 2000.

Missanelli, M. G. "Sixers' Braintrust Feels Ex-Suns Will Help Philly Shine." *Lancaster New Era*. June 18, 1992.

Mitchell, John N. "The 76ers: What Went Wrong." *Philadelphia Inquirer*. June 29, 2013.

Mitchell, John N. "Maybe Bynum Should Stay Around." *Philadelphia Inquirer*. April 23, 2013.

Montville, Leigh. "A Tall Story." *SI Vault*. December 17, 1990. Accessed July 1, 2020. https://vault.si.com/vault/1990/12/17/a-tall-story-manute-bol-the-sixers-7-ft7-in-center-views-life-from-a-unique-perspective

Moore, Tom. "Sixers Re-Sign Henderson." *The Daily Intelligencer*. April 4, 2007.

Moser, Paul. "Buckner, Williams Added for Depth," *The Reporter,* July 26, 2002. https://www.thereporteronline.com/sports/buckner-williams-added-for-depth/article_05bf0dc6-cd64-5663-b7d9-eeca3c51482f.html

Murrow, John. "BYU's Davies Joins Sixers." *Philadelphia Daily News*. October 29, 2013.

Narducci, Marc. "East Is Back on the NBA Map." *Philadelphia Inquirer*. November 1, 2005.

Narducci, Marc. "Korver Has Taken to Being a Starter, Not Just a Shooter." *Philadelphia Inquirer*. November 27, 2004.

NBA. "Sixers Sign Free Agent Tony Battie." *NBA*. July 21, 2010. Accessed June 23, 2020. https://www.nba.com/sixers/news/100721_battie.html

NBA. "TOM's Talks: Todd MacCulloch." *NBA*. April 10, 2020. Accessed September 9, 2020. https://www.nba.com/sixers/news/toms-talks-todd-macculloch

NBC Sports. "Battie Back With Sixers." *NBC Sports Philadelphia*. December 12, 2011. Accessed June 23, 2020. https://www.nbcphiladelphia.com/news/sports/tony-battie-sixers/1918187/

NBC Sports. "Why In the World is Jason Kapono Wearing Number 72?," *NBC Sports Philadelphia,* December 6, 2008, accessed May 9, 2020, https://www.nbcsports.com/philadelphia/why-world-jason-kapono-wearing-number-72.

News Service Reports. "Sixers' MacCulloch Facing End of the Line." *The Record*. October 2, 2003.

Obert, Richard. "Perry, Lang Set to Be Sixers, Hornacek Not So Sure." *Arizona Republic*. June 20, 1992.

Pavorsky, Jake. "Larry Brown: Sixers Rated Pierce Higher, but "Promised" to Select Hughes." *Liberty Ballers*. May 6, 2015. Accessed June 19, 2020. https://www.libertyballers.com/2015/5/6/8560821/larry-brown-sixers-rated-pierce-higher-but-promised-to-select-hughes

Perner, Mark. "Sixers Prevent Rocket Launch." *Philadelphia Daily News*. November 14, 2013.

Pompey, Keith. "Injuries Hurting Sixers," *Republican and Herald*," October 7, 2015.

Pompey, Keith. "It Was Best of Times, Not Worst," *Philadelphia Daily News*, April 6, 2016.

Pompey, Keith. "MCW Feels Right at Home As 76ers Win." *Philadelphia Inquirer*. April 5, 2014.

Pompey, Keith. "Raving About Moultrie." *Philadelphia Inquirer. November 19, 2013.*

Pompey, Keith. "Sixers Add Forward, Annoy Nets." *Philadelphia Inquirer.* February 25, 2015.

Pompey, Keith. "Sixers Talking Turkey." *Philadelphia Inquirer*. November 25, 2014.

Povtak, Tim. "Bell Making the Right Noise in His Chance With Philadelphia." *Orlando Sentinel*. June 10, 2001.

Pucin, Diane. "Lucas All Smiles a Day After Blistering Tirade." *Philadelphia Inquirer* January 6, 1995.

Pulto, Terry. "Nets Survive Infighting in Fitch's Toughest Year." *The Sacramento Bee*. April 22, 1992.

Rosenberg, I.J. "Whatever Happened to: Brian Oliver." *Atlanta Journal-Constitution*. September 4, 2016.

Schuler, Jeff. "Ollie Gives the Sixers Exactly What They Need." *The Morning Call.* November 2, 2006.

Sefko, Eddie. "It's Report Card Time – Bulls Top the Class; Clippers Keep Improving." *Houston Chronicle*. June 28, 1989.

Shappell, Lee. "2nd Round Not Always 2nd Rate." *Arizona Republic*. August 4, 1989.

Sharp, Drew. "Palace Free-For-All." *Detroit Free Press.* April 20, 1990.

SI Vault. "He Shoot. He Scores. He Packs." *Sports Illustrated*. March 28, 2005. Accessed May 11, 2020. https://vault.si.com/vault/2005/03/28/he-shoots-he-scores-he-packs

Sielski, Mike. "Harpring Not Fond of His Sixer Days." *The Morning Call.* January 1, 2003.

Smith, Sam. "Verdicts Are In: Dual Roles Aren't Working." *Chicago Tribune*. January 28, 1996.

Smith, Stephen A. "Brown Is Calm Despite Growing Pile of Sixers Bodies." *Philadelphia Inquirer*. December 24, 2000.

Smith, Stephen A. "Lucky Rex Walters, Now with the Heat, Comes Back to Philly." *Philadelphia Inquirer*. February 4, 1998.

Smith, Stephen A. "MacLean Becomes a Sixer." *Philadelphia Inquirer*. July 17, 1996.

Smith, Stephen A. "MacLean Becomes a Sixer." *Philadelphia Inquirer*. July 17, 1996.

Smith, Stephen A. "On Eve of All-Star Festivities, Hughes Talks of Being Traded." *Philadelphia Inquirer*. February 12, 2000.

Smith, Stephen A. "Sixers Hold Off Hornets for 30th Win of the Season." *Philadelphia Inquirer*. April 9, 1988.

Smith, Stephen A. "Sixers Rally Late But Fall Short." *Philadelphia Inquirer*. November 27, 1997.

Sports Reference LLC. "Alan Henderson." Basketball-Reference.com – Basketball Statistics and History. https://www.basketball-reference.com/players/h/hendeal01.html. Accessed May 27, 2020.

Sports Reference LLC. "Greg Graham." Basketball-Reference.com – Basketball Statistics and History. https://www.basketball-reference.com/players/g/grahagr01.html. Accessed June 6, 2020.

Sports Reference LLC. "Michel Cage." Basketball-Reference.com – Basketball Statistics and History. https://www.basketball-reference.com/players/c/cagemi01.html (accessed July 1, 2020).

Stein, Marc. "Geiger Really Kept Iverson a Sixer." *ESPN*. March 6, 2001. Accessed July 20, 2020. https://www.espn.com/nba/columns/story?columnist=stein_marc&id=1132286

Taylor, Phil. "Vonteego Cummings Remains a Symbole of Those Dark Warriors Year, But One That Always Brings a Smile." *The Athletic*. November 16, 2017. Accessed July 15, 2020. https://theathletic.com/156816/2017/11/16/taylor-vonteego-cummings-remains-a-symbol-of-those-dark-warriors-years-but-one-that-always-brings-a-smile/

Van Dusen, Ryan. "Two times Grant Hill Abused Don MacLean and Dunked on

Two of the NBA's Biggest Dudes." *YouTube*. December 31, 2019. Accessed June 22, 2020. https://www.youtube.com/watch?v=yRGY2xXlcRM

Weiss, Dick. "Inept? You Can Say That Again." *Philadelphia Daily News*. February 11, 1993.

Weiss, Dick. "Sixers Dressed for Success: Gminski, Mahorn Now Have Earrings." *Philadelphia Daily News.* February 14, 1990.

White, George. "It Plays in Peoria Hersey Hawkins Can Turn Any Defense Into a Basket Case." *Sun Sentinel*. January 24, 1988, https://www.sun-sentinel.com/news/fl-xpm-1988-01-24-8801050855-story.html

Whittaker, Celeste E. "Iverson Will Rest Swollen Knee, Sit Out Tonight." *Courier-Post*. November 19, 2003.

Whittaker, Celeste E. "MacCulloch Back from Sydney, Doing As He Pleases for Sixers." October 5, 2000.

Whittaker, Celeste E. "Robinson Mess Getting Murkier As Time Goes On." *Courier-Post*. December 12, 2004.

Whittaker, Celeste E. "Robinson Not Among 76ers' Starting Five." *Courier-Post*. October 27, 2004.

Whittaker, Celeste E. "Sixers Will Be Trying to Find Center Help." *Courier-Post*. October 15, 1999.

Whittaker, Celeste E. "Sixers' McKie, Jones Pick Up the Slack." *Courier-Post*. May 21, 2001.

Wikipedia. "List of Nicknames Used in Basketball." *Wikipedia*. 2020. Accessed June 30, 2020. https://en.wikipedia.org/wiki/List_of_nicknames_used_in_basketball

Wojnarowski, Adrian. "Sources: 76ers Claim Thomas Robinson Off Waivers to Meet NBA's Salary Minimum." *Yahoo Sports*. February 24, 2015. Accessed June 21, 2020. https://www.yahoo.com/?err=404&err_url=https%3A%2F%2Fsports.yahoo.com%2Fnews%2Fsources--76ers-claim-thomas-robinson-off-waivers-to-meet-

nba-s-salary-minimum-220713319.html

Yagoda, Ben. “Stand and Deliver.” *Philly Sport*. November 1989.

Young, Royce. “Sixers Knock Out Bulls With Improbable Finish.” *CBS Sports*. May 10, 2012. Accessed June 23, 2020. https://www.cbssports.com/nba/news/sixers-knock-out-bulls-with-improbable-finish/

Zumoff, Marc (@marczumoff). 2020. “https://t.co/95WC3wG9PS?amp=1”. August 21, 2020. https://twitter.com/marczumoff/status/1296807693919883264

1677091 Productions. “K.J. McDaniels 76ers 2015 Season Highlights.” *YouTube*. March 7, 2015. Accessed August 29, 2020. https://www.youtube.com/watch?v=5w8wAtjgxT0

Made in the USA
Monee, IL
13 November 2020

47501830R00173